The Simple Art of
Vegetarian Cooking

To Kelly
with best wishes
ENJOY

Martha Rose Shulman

TEMPLATES AND LESSONS FOR MAKING DELICIOUS
MEATLESS MEALS EVERY DAY

The Simple Art of
Vegetarian Cooking

MARTHA ROSE SHULMAN

RODALE.

Rodale books may be purchased for business or promotional use or for special sales. For information, please write to: Special Markets Department, Rodale Inc., 733 Third Avenue, New York, NY 10017.

Printed in the United States of America
Rodale Inc. makes every effort to use acid-free ⊗, recycled paper ♲.

Book design by Laura Palese
Art direction by Amy C. King

Food styling by Chris Lanier and Mariana Velasquez
Prop styling by Paige Hicks

Photographs by Tom MacDonald/Rodale Images and Mitch Mandel/Rodale Images

Library of Congress Cataloging-in-Publication Data is on file with the publisher.
ISBN-13: 978-1-62336-129-7 hardcover

Distributed to the trade by Macmillan
2 4 6 8 10 9 7 5 3 1 hardcover

We inspire and enable people to improve their lives and the world around them.
rodalebooks.com

To my beloved stepmother,

Mary Gordon Shulman,

Who taught me to cook and always supported me as I, in her words,

"took a frying pan and a piece of paper and forged a career."

Contents

Introduction

"WHAT'S FOR DINNER?" Growing up in my family, the answer to that question was always the name of the meat we were having—"Steak." "Chicken." "Lamb chops." That was good enough, as it is in most meat-eating households. But if you're a vegetarian or a carnivore who doesn't eat meat every night, the answer to "What's for dinner?" can be wordy.

But not in my house. When my son asks what we're having, I can always give a one-word answer, the name of a generic dish: "Gratin." "Risotto." "Frittata." "Stir-fry." "Lasagna." "Tacos." The sound of these words is reassuring. He knows what a risotto and a stir-fry is and if he wants to know more he just asks, "With . . . ?" The response will be the name of the vegetable that's going to go into the dish—"Chard." "Mushrooms." "Roasted squash." "Asparagus." Any of the foods that are at the heart of my cooking.

TEMPLATE COOKING

I CALL MY MASTER RECIPES for these vegetarian main dishes *templates*. A template is a formula for a generic dish such as a risotto or a frittata. I realized after decades of creating, adapting, and writing recipes that I always use the same formulas—essential ingredients plus method—for certain types of dishes. For example, when I make risotto, I always use ½ cup of minced onion, about 7 cups of stock, and 1½ cups of Arborio rice. No matter what type of risotto I'm making, I always use the same basic ingredients in the same proportion as a jumping off point to which I then add whatever vegetables I've brought home from the farmers' market, or what I have in my refrigerator. Once I realized this, I began writing down these templates, and this streamlined my cooking and writing process and also became a great tool for teaching.

In this book, the template recipes will give you the framework for making a main dish, using whatever produce you want to cook based on availability or seasonality. What defines a *specific* vegetarian risotto or a frittata, a lasagna or a gratin, is the produce that goes into it, and that produce usually requires its own sub-recipe before it can be plugged into the template. For example, the variation recipe on page 76 for a frittata with chard or greens and green garlic includes a list of ingredients with instructions for cooking the wilted greens, green garlic, and seasonings together in olive oil. Once this step is completed, you can proceed with the template recipe for a frittata, stirring the chard into the beaten eggs and making the frittata.

HOW TO USE THIS BOOK

WITH THE EXCEPTION OF THE FIRST chapter, The Building Blocks, on page 1, where you'll find some fundamental vegetable, tomato sauce, egg, and tofu preparations that are called for throughout the book, each chapter in *The Simple Art of Vegetarian Cooking* presents basic templates followed by specific recipes labeled *Variation* or *Filling* that call for additional ingredients. These represent the "vegetable filling of your choice" or "prepared vegetables of your choice" that you see in the template ingredient lists. Steps are provided so you'll know how to prepare the additional ingredients and when to introduce them into the template. Some templates include lists of suggestions for additional fillings and variations whose recipes are in the Building Blocks chapter or that don't require a separate set of ingredients and steps. Some variations on a theme, such as the Big Bowl meals in Chapter 7, make the most sense if all the ingredients and procedure steps are spelled out, so these are not presented as Variations, but as stand-alone recipes.

Many of the chapters in this book have more than one template. Soup, for example, is an excellent one-word answer to "What's for dinner?" but there are many different types of soup. So in the soup chapter (page 35) you'll find templates for two different types of minestrone, two types of Asian noodle soup, a pureed vegetable soup, and a garlic soup. The recipes that follow the templates call for specific vegetables, seasonings, and other ingredients (for example, Minestrone with Cabbage and Winter Squash, Japanese-Californian Meal in a Bowl with Spinach, Mushrooms, and Tofu). The pasta chapter (page 97) includes a template for pasta and vegetables with a tomato sauce, a template for pasta and vegetables without a tomato sauce, and two templates for lasagna.

All of these recipes are designed to work as main dishes. My goal is to provide you with a language for cooking delicious vegetarian meals every day and to help you to become a confident cook. Master all of the templates (or just the ones you and your family like the best) and pretty soon you'll have amassed a repertoire that will empower you to impulse-buy at the market or simply use up whatever may be lingering in your refrigerator; to give a spontaneous dinner party for six; or get a dinner for two or four on the table in 20 minutes after a long day of work, school, sports, and music lessons. With the templates under your belt, you'll be equally at home with the Tuscan kale, winter squash, or tomatoes you bought at the farmers' market as you are with the broccoli on offer at the supermarket and the huge box of summer squash or lowly turnips that arrived in your weekly CSA allotment. You'll know how to give the produce a home in a lentil minestrone (page 45) or an omelet (pages 82–83), a Mediterranean pie (pages 228 and 230) or a quiche (pages 224–227), a couscous (pages 253–259) or a simple pasta (pages 98–105). You'll also know how to be a frugal cook who can use template recipes for garlic soup (page 65) or fried rice (page 175), how to turn an almost-bare cupboard into a luscious meal with just a few cloves of garlic, some rice or stale bread, and the last two eggs in your refrigerator.

The templates and recipes in this book reflect a range of flavors and cuisines. They represent the types of dishes that I cook the most often and that I feel will be easiest for you. Mediterranean cuisines are the most widely represented, as these are the cuisines I'm most passionate and knowledgeable about. But I also love simple French food, tacos and stir-fries, Vietnamese *phô* and noodle bowls. You'll find that there are certain types of dishes that you'll return to again and again. Some families prefer stir-fries, some could eat tacos or quesadillas a few times a week, some love soup, others never get tired of pasta. Having a fundamental understanding of the templates will allow you to vary the dishes—while still being able to give one-word answers to "What's for dinner?"—by plugging in whatever produce inspires you at the market or that you have on hand.

COOKING AHEAD

ONE OF THE ADVANTAGES OF TEMPLATE cooking is that it lends itself to cooking ahead. When I go to my Thursday farmers' market I'm bound to come home with a bunch of beets with the greens attached, some Swiss chard, tomatoes and peppers if they're in season. Over the weekend, I'll roast the beets, blanch all the greens, make some tomato sauce for the freezer, and cook up some of the peppers. All of these preparations will keep for at least 3 days in the refrigerator and I can use them as I please for frittatas or gratins, risottos or tacos, pasta or polenta through the week. You'll get the recipes for some basic vegetable preparations in Chapter 1 so that, if you choose to cook like this, you can have some elements of your vegetarian main dishes prepared in advance.

I'm a big fan of using the freezer for cooked grains and beans. Although there are many grain choices that require no more simmering time than it takes to prepare their companion vegetables, sometimes it really helps to have some farro a microwave-zap away from serving. You can always cook twice as many grains or beans as you need and freeze what you don't use. It's also great to have wilted greens on hand, and every year I make as much tomato sauce as I can for the freezer so that I can make simple pasta dinners or more complex lasagnas on a whim.

I also love to recycle leftovers. You never have to throw out food if you know how to cook. With the templates it's fun to turn certain leftovers into other dishes altogether. Last night's risotto, for example, can be stirred into beaten eggs for a wonderful frittata. The remains of your simmered or baked beans can be tossed with pasta or used to fill a taco or enrich a quesadilla. Leftover grains can be stir-fried or added to a gratin, and that last scrumptious spoonful of sautéed mushrooms can be added to a quiche.

THE WAY I COOK AND EAT

THERE ARE MANY WAYS TO ENJOY a diet that does not revolve around meat. I have always cooked to please palates rather than to satisfy ideologies, but as it turns out, all kinds of ideological eaters can find something they like in my broad repertoire.

My own everyday diet is an eclectic one that revolves around produce and includes dairy products and eggs, but *many* of the recipes you'll find in this book, particularly in Chapters 2 (Soups), 7 (Big Bowls), 9 (Stir-Fries), 10 (Beans and Lentils), and 13 (Couscous) are vegan. I've marked those recipes to make it easier for you to identify them. They're not vegan because I set out to make them that way or manipulated foods to mimic animal products; they just don't happen to call for animal products.

Although my expertise is in vegetarian cooking and I'm most inspired by produce, I appreciate all foods. So, much as I don't like definitions, if pressed I would define myself not as a vegetarian but as a *flexitarian*, which Merriam-Webster defines as "one whose normally meatless diet occasionally includes meat or fish." But that is neither here nor there; because being a vegetarian is not a requirement for being a good vegetarian cook. And that is what I hope to help you to become with this book.

THE VEGETARIAN PANTRY

THE PANTRY—WHICH ENCOMPASSES MY FREEZER and my refrigerator as well as the shelves where I store dry goods—is crucial to good cooking of all kinds; keep it well stocked and you never have to be stressed about what you're going to cook for dinner. You may not have had time to go to the farmers' market or the supermarket to buy vegetables, but if you have rice, whole grains like farro or bulgur, canned tomatoes, and pasta on the shelves, Parmesan and eggs in the refrigerator, and frozen peas and edamame in the freezer, you can always rest assured that a great dinner of pasta or soup, risotto or frittata, is just a recipe away.

You can't really get started with these recipes without a few fundamental items in the cupboard and refrigerator. Sea salt and pepper; olive oil and vinegar; a cooking oil that has a neutral flavor (sunflower or grapeseed, for example); spices; onions and garlic; Parmesan, eggs, and milk if these products are part of your diet. These are some of the foods that will come up often in the recipes. Here's a bit of general information about some of these essential ingredients:

EXTRA VIRGIN OLIVE OIL: Be sure to buy oil that is labeled, at minimum, "extra virgin." The oil will be of lesser quality if you don't see those words. Even so, there is a lot of adulterated olive oil being sold on supermarket shelves, so if you can, seek out a reputable purveyor. For an excellent guide to buying olive oil, see the website truthinoliveoil.com (from the author of the excellent book *Extra Virginity*, Tom Mueller). I prefer milder-tasting olive oils to the dark, peppery oils that make my throat tingle. My "work-horse" olive oil is a Greek oil I buy for $8.99 a quart. I love the golden-green oils I've tasted that come from Spain, and some oils (but not all) from Provence. I've also been very impressed with the olive oils now being produced in California. Taste and choose. For cooking, you shouldn't spend an arm and a leg. For drizzling and finishing a dish, you can spend a bit more.

NEUTRAL COOKING OIL: These oils are usually extracted from seeds or nuts. When I'm not making Mediterranean food, I need an oil other than olive oil. For example, when stir-frying over high heat, I cook with either sunflower oil, canola oil, or grapeseed oil. Lately I've been using mostly sunflower oil. Peanut oil is also good for stir-fries because it has a very high smoke point.

BUTTER: While I don't use a lot of butter in my cooking, you'll find it in some recipes like the whole wheat *pâte brisée* on page 223. I use exclusively unsalted butter. For baking, look for French-style butter, such as Plugrà, which is 82 percent fat.

MILK: I use whole milk for baking, and either whole or 2 percent for cooking. Milk with a lower fat content is too watery. In this book, the one exception is my béchamel (used in the lasagna recipes on pages 110–115), for which you can also use 1 percent milk if you prefer, as the finished sauce will still be creamy enough.

YOGURT: I prefer organic, low-fat or full-fat yogurt. Like lower-fat milk, nonfat yogurt is too watery. Seek out yogurt that does not have thickeners and stabilizers added to it. Ideally it should just contain milk, milk solids perhaps, and the bacilli that make it yogurt.

EGGS: I use large or extra-large eggs, and seek out organic free-range eggs from small farmers at the farmers' market. The next best choice is cage-free eggs.

SPICES: With the exception of cinnamon and cayenne, I use whole spices and grind them in a spice mill when I need them. I usually toast cumin seeds, coriander seeds, and caraway seeds very lightly in a small, dry skillet first, just to bring out their aroma, which only takes a few minutes. Keep spices in the freezer if you can; they'll last for a long time there.

SALT: I use fine sea salt, coarser *fleur de sel* for sprinkling onto some dishes, and kosher salt. Some cooks only use sea salt and can taste the difference. I'm not sure if I can, quite honestly.

Making Food Taste Good

WHATEVER TYPE OF SALT YOU DO use, use enough of it. If you're not under doctor's orders to reduce your salt intake, then you should not eschew this important seasoning. Taste the food you make, and if it doesn't make you want to take another bite immediately, if it tastes like there's something lacking, chances are it needs more salt. Salt has a way of finishing a dish; taste a poached egg with and without salt (and you need very little in this case) and you'll see what I mean. In my recipes I indicate "salt to taste" most of the time, but I also give some ballpark ranges, and in some recipe steps I call for specific amounts. Salt to taste assumes that you will *taste the food*; you're the final judge. Vegetarian food sometimes has a reputation for being bland: If it's undersalted, it *is* bland.

Undersalting can also result in an imbalance with the other seasonings in a dish. If, for example, you've undersalted a dish containing hot spices and/or chiles, you *will* feel the heat but you won't necessarily experience the full round warmth of the hot ingredient, and heat alone is not necessarily pleasant. In an undersalted dish, garlic can taste merely sharp instead of flavorful. If there are lots of pungent, vivid herbs in, say, an undersalted Greek pie, they'll dominate rather than finish or accent the flavors. Salt has a tempering effect that's important in cooking.

Fresh Herbs

If you have access to sun and a space for a few simple pots, I urge you to grow some of your own herbs, such as thyme, mint, sage, and tarragon. You rarely need all the thyme and sage that comes in the expensive packages available at the supermarket (on the other hand, you may need more mint than comes in the packages); it's far easier to grow them whether you live in the country or the city. When I lived in Paris I grew thyme, sage, basil, mint, chives, and tarragon in pots on my balcony. In California they're still in pots (except the tarragon and thyme, which thrive in my small garden) outside by my garden. Sage, thyme, and rosemary require very little water (that's why they're so popular in the Mediterranean, where the climate can be very hot and dry). Rosemary is a little trickier to grow because it's easy to kill it by overwatering, but once you have a bush you'll never need to buy it again (assuming you don't live in a cold area, like New England).

PANTRY CHECKLIST

THESE ARE THE FOODS I TRY to always keep in stock. They will allow you to make any of the template recipes in this book. Keep grains, beans, and flours double-sealed in plastic bags, or in plastic storage containers or jars.

Dry goods to keep on shelves, preferably away from light

Rice, including Arborio rice

Other grains (see Chapter 7 for specific grains)

Dried beans (such as black beans, white beans, lima beans, borlottis, pintos, chickpeas, black-eyed peas, and heirlooms like scarlet runners or Christmas limas; see Chapters 2, 10, and 13)

Canned beans (I recommend chickpeas and white beans)

Lentils

Dried pasta, including soup pasta and no-boil lasagna noodles

Couscous

Canned tomatoes (both 14.5-ounce and 28-ounce)

Tomato paste (tubes are convenient; refrigerate after opening; if you buy cans, once open, spoon out what you don't use by the tablespoon, wrap in plastic, and freeze)

Buckwheat noodles (soba)

Rice noodles (sometimes called rice sticks)

Soy sauce (can also keep in the refrigerator)

Dried shiitake and/or porcini mushrooms

Kombu seaweed

Salt

Polenta

Whole wheat flour

Unbleached all-purpose flour

Cornstarch or arrowroot (for stir-fries)

Canned chipotles (transfer to a jar and refrigerate once opened)

Red wine vinegar or sherry vinegar (sherry vinegar is my go-to vinegar)

Balsamic vinegar

Seasoned rice vinegar

Sugar

Honey

OILS

Extra virgin olive oil (store in a cool, dark place but not in the refrigerator)

Sunflower or grapeseed oil (refrigerate once opened)

Peanut oil (refrigerate once opened; optional)

Dark sesame oil (refrigerate once opened)

Walnut oil (refrigerate once opened)

DRIED HERBS (I use fresh more often but these are the ones you should keep in the cupboard)

Bay leaves

Oregano

Thyme

SPICES (can be stored in the pantry, but I keep mine in the freezer; they stay fresh much longer that way)

Allspice

Black pepper

Caraway seeds

Cayenne

Chili powder

Cinnamon and cinnamon sticks

Cloves

Coriander seeds

Cumin seeds

Curry powder

Ground ginger

Ground sumac

Nigella seeds

Paprika

Red pepper flakes

Saffron

Star anise

Vegetable bins (not refrigerated)

Onions

Garlic

Shallots

Refrigerator

Parmesan rinds (for flavoring soups and beans; can also keep in freezer)

Parmesan (block, not grated; preferably Parmigiano Reggiano)

Firm tofu

Eggs

Gruyère

Feta

Goat cheese

A melting cheese such as Monterey Jack or cheddar

Butter

Yogurt

Shao-hsing rice wine or dry sherry (for stir-fries)

Dry white wine such as pinot grigio or sauvignon blanc

Bottled salsa or homemade salsa (pages 205 to 208)

Harissa (page 255)

Aromatics and produce used regularly and that keep well: ginger, carrots, celery, lemons, limes

Freezer

Breadcrumbs

Vegetable stock (page 149)

Cooked grains

Corn tortillas

Marinara sauce (pages 24, 26, or 27)

Wilted greens (page 2)

Peas

Edamame

Walnuts

Herbs to grow in pots or in your garden if you can

Thyme

Tarragon

Chives

Mint

Rosemary

Sage

CHAPTER ONE

The Building Blocks: Basic Recipes

T HESE ARE THE BASIC, mostly vegetable preparations that I use most often as building blocks for main dishes. Rather than repeat the instructions for preparing the vegetables every time they're used, I've grouped them as recipes here. My frittatas and gratins, for example are often filled with seasoned wilted greens (page 3)—kale or chard, beet greens, broccoli raab, or spinach. Those same greens, in turn, could easily top a big bowl of grains or make up part of a taco filling. I'll use the pan-cooked mushrooms on page 11 or the wild mushroom ragout on page 12 in a risotto, and the same mushrooms in a taco; the Mediterranean stewed peppers (page 6) or roasted winter squash (page 15) that I stir into a risotto on page 158 can also be spooned over polenta, top a big bowl of grains, or fill a frittata.

Some of these recipes can also stand alone, to be enjoyed as a side dish or a small plate. But in this book they're the vegetarian building blocks that make up bigger, more substantial dishes. If you are relatively new to cooking, this is the place where you can begin to walk before you run with the main body of recipes in this book.

WILTED GREENS

THIS IS MY METHOD FOR DEALING with most dark, leafy greens—kale, chard, turnip greens, spinach, or beet greens. It's the first step I take with them before I use them in most recipes, such as gratins and pastas, frittatas and tacos, quesadillas and pizzas. Sometimes, if I'm really organized, I'll blanch (*blanching* means cooking for a short time in boiling water) or steam my greens as soon as I get them home from the market, before I even know what I'm going to do with them. I refresh the wilted greens with cold water, drain, and squeeze out the excess water, then store them in a covered bowl in the refrigerator (they keep better in a covered bowl than they do in a plastic bag) for about 3 days.

If I find that I'm not going to be able to use the greens because I'm going out of town, or I bought too much at the market, I double wrap the blanched or steamed greens in plastic, bag them, and freeze. It's always great to have them on hand, ready to transform into a delicious dinner.

Each green is a little different in terms of the toughness of the leaf and the amount of time it takes for the leaf to wilt. Collards are toughest and require the most time in boiling salted water or steam before the leaves soften. Some types of kale are relatively tough as well. Spinach is much more delicate and requires hardly any cooking at all, only about 20 seconds. Beet greens and chard are somewhere in between. The sturdier greens lose less volume when you wilt them. Spinach, no matter how lush the bunch is when you begin, cooks down to a mere handful.

After I wilt the greens, I usually season them with olive oil, garlic, salt, and pepper, sometimes red pepper flakes, and herbs—thyme and/or rosemary. I don't proceed with this step until close to the time that I'm ready to make the dish, as the flavors won't be as fresh if the seasoned greens sit in the refrigerator.

Kale, Beet Greens, Chard, Turnip Greens, Spinach, Collards

VEGAN /// **SEE NOTE ON YIELD ON PAGE 4**

Whether blanched or steamed, once your greens are drained, you must squeeze excess water out of the leaves. The most efficient way to do this is to take up one handful at a time and squeeze. Once all of the greens have been squeezed, place the clumps on your cutting board and chop coarsely or fine, depending on the recipe.

¾ to 1 pound greens, stemmed, leaves washed in 2 changes of water

Salt

TO BLANCH

1. Bring a large pot of water to a boil over high heat and fill a bowl with cold water or ice water.

2. When the water in the pot comes to a boil, salt it generously (see "How Much Salt is Enough . . . ?" on page 4), then add the greens. Blanch mature spinach for 20 seconds only (baby spinach needs only 5 seconds); chard, beet greens, and turnip greens for about 1 minute; kale for 2 to 3 minutes; collards for 3 to 4.

3. Using a Chinese mesh skimmer if you have one, or a slotted spoon or spider, lift the blanched greens from the water and transfer directly to the bowl of cold water. Let sit for about half a minute, then drain.

TO STEAM

1. Heat 1 inch of water in a steamer; I prefer to use a pasta pot with an insert, as the insert can accommodate a large volume of greens. Fill a bowl with cold water or ice water.

2. When the water in the pot comes to a boil, place the greens in the insert. Cover and steam until they collapse, 1 to 2 minutes for spinach (less than a minute for baby spinach); about 2 minutes for chard, beet greens, and turnip greens; 3 to 4 minutes for kale; and 4 to 5 minutes for collards. To allow the greens to steam evenly, uncover halfway through the steaming time and turn them using long-handled tongs.

3. Remove the greens from the steamer and transfer to the bowl of cold water. Let sit for about half a minute, then drain.

NOTE: Different types of greens yield different amounts. On average, with the exception of spinach, 1 pound of greens (about 8 cups tightly packed leaves) will yield about 1 cup of chopped wilted greens. Spinach yields only $\frac{1}{2}$ cup and will serve 1 or at most 2. However, when the greens are building blocks for other dishes, they'll serve on average 4 to 6.

ADVANCE PREPARATION: Wilted greens will keep for 3 days in the refrigerator in a covered bowl and freeze well for a month or two.

How Much Salt Is Enough for Blanching Vegetables?

A cooking teacher at the CIA Boot Camp (at the Culinary Institute of America) in Hyde Park, New York, taught me that the water for blanching vegetables should "taste like the ocean" (he said the Atlantic, but any ocean will do), and I think that's about right. How much salt you need to get it to that point depends upon the size of your pot and the amount of water in it. Tasting the water is the best way to ascertain whether or not you've added enough. It should taste like seawater. If you're using a big pasta pot full of water, begin with 1 heaping tablespoon; taste, and you'll probably add another.

Broccoli Raab (Rapini)

VEGAN /// **MAKES ABOUT 2¼ TO 3 CUPS CHOPPED, SERVING 4 TO 6**

I always blanch broccoli raab; I find it more efficient than steaming and like the flavor better. Because the greens and flowers cook more quickly than the thick stems, I add them separately to the boiling water.

1 bunch broccoli raab (¾ to 1 pound)

Salt

1. Bring a large pot of water to a boil and fill a bowl with cold water or ice water. To prepare the broccoli raab, first trim away the thick ends and cut the stems where they taper, so that the thinner, leafier ends with the flowers are separated from the thicker ends.

2. When the water in the pot comes to a boil, salt it generously. Add the thick ends of the broccoli raab and set the timer for 5 minutes. After 2 minutes, add the thinner, leafier pieces so that they boil for 3 minutes.

3. When the raab is tender and wilted, transfer with a slotted spoon to the bowl of cold water and let cool for half a minute. Drain and squeeze to expel excess water. Chop medium-fine or fine, depending on the recipe. Most will instruct you to toss it in a pan with garlic, olive oil, and red pepper flakes as well, which broccoli raab adores.

ADVANCE PREPARATION: Wilted broccoli raab will keep for 3 days in the refrigerator in a covered bowl and freezes well for a month or two.

PEPPERS

I PICK UP A FEW RED peppers every week, even if I don't have a plan for them. They keep well in the refrigerator; they're always welcome in a salad; and stewed or roasted they are endlessly useful as fillings (for frittatas, omelets, gratins, and risottos), toppings for pizzas, and, accompaniments to pasta. Once roasted or stewed, even relatively dull-tasting hothouse peppers pick up plenty of flavor. But nothing compares to the peppers you buy from your local farmer.

Mediterranean Stewed Peppers: Peperonata, Pipérade, and Chakchouka

VEGAN /// **MAKES 2½ TO 3 CUPS, SERVING 4 TO 6**

There are variations on the stewed pepper theme throughout the Mediterranean. Italian *peperonata* is a sweet mixture of onions, tomatoes, bell peppers, and garlic. Basque *pipérade* has more spice because of their slender piquant peppers called *piments d'espelette*. The Tunisian version, *chakchouka*, is even spicier still, seasoned with the red pepper paste, harissa, and *tabil*, a spice mix that includes caraway, coriander, cayenne, and garlic.

There are so many ways you can use this preparation, no matter how you choose to season it. Use it the way the Basques do, as an addition to scrambled eggs, or the way Tunisians do, with eggs poached on top (the words *pipérade* and *chakchouka* are also the names for the egg and pepper dishes). Stir it into a frittata or a risotto, toss it with pasta, spread it on pizza, serve it with grains for a beautiful Big Bowl dinner, or use it for tacos or quesadillas, a gratin, or a quiche.

2 tablespoons extra virgin olive oil

1 medium onion, chopped

Salt

2 large garlic cloves, minced

3 large red bell peppers, or a combination of red and yellow bell peppers, seeded and thinly sliced or chopped

1 (14.5-ounce) can chopped tomatoes

1 teaspoon fresh thyme leaves or ½ teaspoon dried

Freshly ground black pepper

ITALIAN PEPERONATA

1. Heat the oil over medium heat in a large heavy skillet or Dutch oven and add the onion. Cook, stirring, until tender, about 5 minutes. Add a generous pinch of salt, the garlic, and bell peppers. Cook, stirring often, until the peppers are tender 5 to 10 minutes.

2. Add the tomatoes, thyme, more salt to taste (½ teaspoon or more), and black pepper and bring to a simmer. Cook, stirring from time to time, until the tomatoes have cooked down somewhat, about 10 minutes. Cover, reduce the heat, and simmer over low heat for another 15 to 20 minutes, stirring from time to time, until the mixture is thick and fragrant. Taste and adjust seasonings.

Substitute 1 or 2 green bell peppers for 1 or 2 of the red bell peppers. Add 1 Anaheim pepper, seeded and thinly sliced, and 1 minced jalapeño or serrano chile along with the bell peppers.

NORTH AFRICAN CHAKCHOUKA

Use 2 green bell peppers, 2 red bell peppers, 2 Anaheim peppers, and a chile pepper if desired. Along with the tomatoes, stir in 1 teaspoon harissa (page 254) or more to taste, $\frac{1}{2}$ teaspoon ground coriander seeds, $\frac{1}{4}$ teaspoon ground caraway seeds, and $\frac{1}{8}$ teaspoon cayenne. When the stew has cooked down to a thick, fragrant mixture, stir in 2 tablespoons chopped flat-leaf parsley. Top with poached eggs (page 32) (dish will no longer be vegan).

ADVANCE PREPARATION: The stewed peppers will keep for about 5 days in the refrigerator.

Roasted Peppers

VEGAN /// **MAKES 4 ROASTED PEPPERS (ABOUT 2 CUPS DICED)**

Roasting or grilling peppers is one way to preserve peppers for a few weeks if you have a lot in your CSA box. Once roasted or grilled, cover them with olive oil and keep in the refrigerator. Bell peppers will become incredibly sweet once roasted; if they're grilled, the resulting sweetness contrasts in a mouthwatering way with the bitter edge of the char created by the grill or the broiler. You can grill them under a broiler, over a burner flame (right over the flame or in a perforated grill pan), or over coals. If I want really sweet peppers with lots of juice, and especially if I've got several to roast, I'll roast them in a 425°F oven. You don't get the layer of charcoal flavor this way but it's easy (and it won't set off the smoke alarm, which sometimes goes off in my apartment when I grill a lot of peppers).

4 medium or large red, green, or yellow bell peppers

Sea salt (fine or coarse) or kosher salt and freshly ground pepper

OPTIONAL

2 to 4 tablespoons extra virgin olive oil (more to cover and preserve)

1 or 2 garlic cloves, minced or pureed

OVEN-ROASTED PEPPERS

1. Heat the oven to 425°F. Line a baking sheet with foil. Place the peppers on the foil and bake in the oven for 30 to 40 minutes, using tongs to turn the peppers every 10 minutes. The peppers are done when their skins are browned and puffed. They won't be black and flaky the way they are when you grill them.

2. Transfer the peppers to a bowl. Cover the bowl with a plate or with plastic, and let sit for 30 minutes, until cool.

Slivered fresh basil leaves or chopped fresh tarragon, thyme, chervil, or marjoram

1 teaspoon balsamic or sherry vinegar

3. Carefully remove the skins, holding the peppers over the bowl so that no juice escapes. The peppers will be very soft. Separate into halves or quarters and remove the stems, seeds, and membranes; cut into strips if desired. Place the peppers in another bowl and strain the juices into the bowl. Season to taste. If storing for more than a day, toss with 2 to 4 tablespoons extra virgin olive oil. If storing for a week or two, submerge the peppers in olive oil. Refrigerate until ready to use but remove from the refrigerator in time for the olive oil to liquefy before using. If you wish, toss with the optional ingredients shortly before serving.

BURNER-ROASTED PEPPERS

Turn on your exhaust fan. Light a gas burner and place a pepper directly over the flame. As soon as one section has blackened, turn the pepper, using tongs, to expose another section to the flame. Continue to turn until the entire pepper has blackened. Place in a plastic bag and seal, or place in a bowl and cover tightly. Allow to sit until cool, then remove the charred skin. You may need to run the pepper briefly under the faucet to rinse off the final bits of charred skin. If so, pat dry with paper towels. Cut the pepper in half, holding it over a bowl, remove the stems, seeds, and membranes. Season and store as instructed above.

NOTE: Sometimes, depending on the gnarliness of my peppers, I find it's easier to roast them over the burner in a perforated grill pan, rather than setting the peppers directly over (or in) the flame. It's a little neater too; not as much ash gets in my stove.

BROILED PEPPERS

Heat the broiler. Cover a baking sheet with foil and place the peppers on top. Place the baking sheet under the broiler at the highest setting. Broil, checking the peppers every 2 to 3 minutes and turning regularly as they char, until uniformly blackened. Place in a plastic bag and seal, or place in a bowl and cover tightly. Proceed as in burner-roasted peppers above.

NOTE: You can also use these methods to roast poblano peppers for Mexican dishes.

ADVANCE PREPARATION: Roasted peppers keep for a few days in the refrigerator and for a few weeks if you submerge them in olive oil.

ONIONS

MANY, IF NOT MOST, OF MY recipes begin by cooking onions in a small amount of oil until soft and translucent. This only takes about 5 minutes, but you want to be careful that you use medium and not high heat, because you don't want the onions to stick to the pan and brown or they will become bitter. One way to prevent this is to add a pinch of salt, which draws out some of their water and lubricates the onions. I use brown onions (sometimes called yellow onions) for almost all of my recipes, unless otherwise specified. I look for onions of medium size, weighing about 6 ounces.

Softened Onions and Melted Onions (Onion Marmalade)

VEGAN /// MAKES 1 TO 2 CUPS

If you want the onions to reduce down to a sweet, spreadable mixture that I call *onion marmalade*, once the onions have wilted, continue cooking over low heat for a long time. In Provence the cooked-down onions find their home most often atop a pizza crust (*pissaladière*), and that's a wonderful place for them. But melted-down onions are also welcome in a frittata or a risotto, a quesadilla or a taco, on top of grains in a big bowl, or spread on a bruschetta or sandwich.

1 to 2 tablespoons extra virgin olive oil (2 tablespoons for melted onions)

Up to 2 pounds onions, either chopped, or quartered lengthwise and thinly sliced across the grain

Salt

2 tablespoons capers, rinsed and coarsely chopped (optional)

2 teaspoons fresh thyme leaves (optional)

2 garlic cloves, minced (optional)

Freshly ground pepper

1. Heat the olive oil over medium heat in a large, heavy lidded skillet (I like a heavy nonstick skillet for this). Add the onions and cook, stirring, until they soften and appear translucent, about 5 minutes. Add a generous pinch of salt if the onions appear to be sticking to the pan or browning. Remove the softened onions from the heat and use as called for in recipes.

2. To continue cooking to make onion marmalade, add about $1/2$ teaspoon salt, capers (if using), the thyme, and garlic. Turn the heat to low, cover, and simmer gently, stirring often, until the onions have cooked down and are very soft and lightly colored but not browned, 30 to 40 minutes. They should taste sweet. Season to taste with salt and pepper and remove from the heat.

ADVANCE PREPARATION: The melted onions will keep for at least 4 days in the refrigerator.

MUSHROOMS

LIKE PEPPERS, I BUY MUSHROOMS AS a matter of course when I go to the supermarket, even if I don't have anything specific in mind for them. I slice them up for salads, or pan-cook and add to frittatas and omelets, pasta and pizza, risottos and big bowls of grains. When I can get hold of wild mushrooms, I make more complex ragouts, which can also be used as a component of another dish—a sauce for pasta, the vegetable element of a risotto, a filling for a taco or a tart.

Pan-Cooked Mushrooms

VEGAN /// **MAKES ABOUT 2 CUPS, SERVING 4 TO 6**

This is a simple, delicious way to prepare mushrooms. You can toss them with pasta (along with other vegetables or on their own), use them as an omelet filling, line a tart shell with them, or pile them onto bruschetta or onto grains for a big bowl. I've used this recipe for cooking up mushrooms I just bought, as well as for mushrooms that were beginning to dry out in my refrigerator. (It's a way to save older mushrooms before they've shriveled to the point of no return. The older mushrooms don't yield as luscious a preparation as fresh ones, but I've saved them from oblivion and enjoyed many a mushroom frittata!)

1 pound white or cremini mushrooms, wiped if gritty

2 tablespoons extra virgin olive oil

2 shallots, minced (optional)

2 garlic cloves, minced

2 teaspoons chopped fresh thyme, rosemary, or sage (or a combination), or ½ teaspoon dried, or 1 to 2 tablespoons chopped fresh parsley

Salt and freshly ground pepper

¼ cup dry white wine, such as sauvignon blanc

1. Trim off the very ends of the mushroom stems and cut into thick slices. Heat a large, heavy skillet over medium-high heat and add 1 tablespoon of the olive oil. When the oil is hot (you can feel the heat when you hold your hand above the pan), add the mushrooms. Don't stir for 30 seconds to 1 minute so that the mushrooms will sear, then cook, stirring or tossing in the pan, for a few minutes, until they begin to soften and sweat.

2. Add the remaining 1 tablespoon oil, turn the heat to medium, and add the shallots (if using), garlic, and thyme, rosemary, or sage. (If using parsley, wait until you add the wine.) Stir together, add salt (about ½ teaspoon) and pepper to taste, and cook, stirring often, until the shallots and garlic have softened and the mixture is fragrant, another 1 to 2 minutes.

3. Add the wine and parsley (if using) and cook, stirring often and scraping the bottom of the pan, until the wine has evaporated. Taste and adjust seasonings. Remove from the heat.

ADVANCE PREPARATION: Pan-cooked mushrooms will keep for a day or two in the refrigerator.

Mushroom Ragout

VEGAN /// **MAKES ABOUT 4 CUPS, SERVING 6**

This mushroom preparation is more complex than the previous recipe for simple pan-cooked mushrooms. I begin the recipe by reconstituting dried mushrooms—porcinis are my favorite—in boiling water. The rich infusion from soaking goes into the ragout and helps to create a great depth of flavor, which is even more nuanced if I can include fresh (not dried) wild mushrooms in the mix. For their meaty texture, I try to include oyster mushrooms, which are cultivated and not difficult to find even at my local grocery store. The ragout is wonderful on its own; tossed with pasta; used as the basis for a risotto or the filling for an omelet, frittata, tart, or taco; or spooned over polenta or on top of a big bowl of grains. If you like "meaty" vegetarian dishes, this is your dish, whether you use cultivated mushrooms, wild mushrooms, or a combination.

1 ounce (about 1 cup) dried porcini mushrooms

2 cups boiling water

2 tablespoons extra virgin olive oil

2 shallots, finely chopped

2 garlic cloves (or more to taste), minced

1 pound cremini (preferably) or white mushrooms, cleaned, trimmed, and sliced ½ inch thick

1 pound wild mushrooms, trimmed and brushed clean, or oyster mushrooms, trimmed and torn into pieces if very large*

2 teaspoons chopped fresh rosemary or 1 teaspoon crumbled dried

2 teaspoons chopped fresh thyme or 1 teaspoon dried

Salt

2 teaspoons all-purpose flour (optional; it helps to create a thicker mixture, but if you're gluten intolerant just leave it out)

½ cup either fruity red wine, such as a Côtes du Rhône, or dry white wine such as sauvignon blanc or pinot grigio (see Note)

Freshly ground pepper

2 to 4 tablespoons finely chopped fresh flat-leaf parsley

1. Place the dried mushrooms in a measuring cup or a bowl and cover with the boiling water. Soak for 30 minutes while you prepare the other ingredients. Place a strainer over a bowl, line the strainer with cheesecloth or paper towels, and drain the mushrooms, reserving the soaking liquid. Squeeze the mushrooms over the strainer to extract all the flavorful broth. Then rinse the mushrooms, away from the bowl with the soaking liquid, until they are free of sand. Squeeze dry over the strainer. If very large, chop coarsely. Set aside. Measure out 1½ cups of the mushroom broth and set aside.

2. Heat the olive oil over medium heat in a large, heavy, skillet or a wide saucepan and add the shallots. Cook, stirring often, until tender, 3 to 5 minutes. Add the garlic, stir together for about 30 seconds, until fragrant, then add the fresh mushrooms, rosemary, and thyme and turn up the heat slightly. Cook until the mushrooms begin to sweat, then add ½ teaspoon salt, or more to taste. Stir for about 5 minutes over medium-high heat as the mushrooms continue to soften and sweat. Add the flour (if using) and continue to cook the mushrooms, stirring, until they have softened a little more and you can no longer see the flour, about 2 minutes.

3. Add the reconstituted dried mushrooms and the wine and turn the heat to high. Cook, stirring, until the liquid boils down and glazes the mushrooms, about 5 minutes.

4. Stir in the mushroom soaking liquid, bring to a simmer, add salt to taste, and cook over medium-high heat, stirring often, until

the mushrooms are thoroughly tender and fragrant and the surrounding broth is thick and gravy-like, 10 to 15 minutes. Remove from the heat, stir in some pepper and the parsley, taste, and adjust the salt.

If you can't find wild mushrooms or oyster mushrooms, use 2 pounds white or cremini mushrooms.

NOTE: Either red or white wine, or a dry rosé for that matter, will work here. Red wine has a richer, more tannic flavor, but mushrooms are big drinkers—they like any kind of wine. If you don't use wine in your cooking, just leave it out; the ragout will still taste delicious.

ADVANCE PREPARATION: The ragout can be made up to 3 or 4 days before you wish to serve it. Keep in the refrigerator. Reheat gently on top of the stove.

ROASTED VEGETABLES

ROASTING ADDS A CARAMELIZED DIMENSION TO vegetables. Some, like winter squash and root vegetables, already have a lot of sweetness going for them and roasting intensifies it.

Roasted Winter Squash

VEGAN /// **MAKES 2 TO 2½ CUPS, SERVING 4 TO 6**

If you're going to use the squash in a soup or puree, just cut it into big chunks. If you'll need small dice for a risotto (page 158), a gratin or taco, a Big Bowl, or another dish, you should dice before roasting. Then you'll have lots of caramelized edges contributing to the overall flavor of the dish. I'm giving directions for diced squash here, as you can use this basic preparation in many recipes in this book.

1 to 2 pounds winter squash (½ to 1 good-size butternut, for example), peeled, seeds and membranes scraped away, and cut into ½-inch dice

1 to 2 tablespoons extra virgin olive oil

Salt and freshly ground pepper

Heat the oven to 425°F. Line a baking sheet with parchment or foil. Toss the squash with the olive oil and season with salt and pepper. Spread on the baking sheet in an even layer. Place in the oven and roast until tender and caramelized, 20 to 30 minutes, stirring every 10 minutes.

NOTE: To roast big chunks of squash, do not bother to peel. Brush or toss with olive oil and place on the baking sheet. Roast until tender, 30 to 40 minutes, turning the squash every 10 minutes. When the squash is cool enough to handle, cut or scoop away from the peels.

ADVANCE PREPARATION: Roasted squash will keep for 3 or 4 days in the refrigerator.

SUBSTITUTIONS AND ADDITIONS: Roast root vegetables and bulbs in place of the winter squash; combine these vegetables or just choose one or two: Peel 1 to 2 pounds carrots, parsnips, turnips, and/or onions and cut into 1-inch chunks. Toss with the olive oil and proceed as directed above, but after the first 20 minutes reduce the heat to 375°F. Roast until the vegetables are soft and the edges caramelized, 20 to 25 minutes. (Roasted root vegetables will keep for a day or two in the refrigerator but they will dry out more than winter squash, so it's best to roast them when you need them.)

Choosing Winter Squash

Farmers' markets, and more and more regular supermarkets, offer an array of winter squash. It can be difficult to know which one to choose, so we usually just go with butternut. Which is fine with me, as I find this to be one of the best all-around winter squashes and one of the few that's easy to peel before you roast it. The flesh is moist and sweet.

The variations from one variety of winter squash to the next are the sweetness and texture. Some squash, like acorn (one of my least favorites) is dryer, drabber, and earthier in flavor than others. I found a good guide to winter squash by Molly Watson at about.com/LocalFoods. Her list includes 14 varieties. I then found more varieties on another site called A Cook's Thesaurus, and even more in Deborah Madison's excellent *Vegetable Literacy*. No doubt I've missed a few, but you get the idea. One thing to note is that if you buy a hard, knobbly, thick-skinned squash like a kabocha on impulse and don't get around to doing anything with it for a while, have no fear. They keep for months as long as the stem is intact.

Winter Squash Chart

SQUASH	SHAPE & COLOR (COLOR OF FLESH)	FLAVOR	TEXTURE
Acorn squash	Acorn shaped, dark green skin, sometimes mottled with orange (yellowish orange flesh)	Nutty, earthy, a bit drab	On the dry side; somewhat starchy
Banana squash	Light orange skin, found cut up in supermarkets (golden flesh)	Mild, nutty	Moist
Blue Hokkaido pumpkin	Round with gray-blue skin (bright orange flesh)	Deep, rich, sweet, and nutty	Somewhat starchy but moist
Buttercup squash	Squat, not too big, with dark green striated skin (orange flesh)	Sweet	Dense, fine texture
Butternut squash	Smooth, beige, elongated with bulbous end; easy to peel (bright orange flesh)	Sweet	Very moist and smooth, not many seeds and fibers
Cheese pumpkins (also known as Long Island Cheese)	Squat beige/orange (bright orange flesh)	Sweet; good for pies	Firm, moist, somewhat fibrous
Delicata squash	Elongated light green with dark green, orange, and bright yellow stripes; easy to peel (orange-yellow flesh)	Sweet, nutty	Somewhat dry according to some descriptions, creamy according to others; has been described as tasting like sweet potatoes
Hubbard squash	Very large, tear-shaped dark green and knobbly; hard to cut through the skin but often sold cut into pieces (dark orange flesh)	Sweet, rich	Fine textured

SQUASH	SHAPE & COLOR (COLOR OF FLESH)	FLAVOR	TEXTURE
Kabocha squash	Round, squat dark green skin with pale green stripes, difficult to cut through (dark orange flesh)	Sweet, nutty	Dense, smooth, can be on the dry side; good for soups
Marina de Chioggia	Ribbed, warty blue-green skin, turban shape (deep orange flesh)	Sweet	Creamy
Queensland Blue	Blue-green skin with deep grooves (deep orange flesh)	Sweet	Dense
Red Kuri pumpkin	Small orange-red pumpkin without ridges (bright orange flesh)	Mellow, nutty, sometimes sweet	Good for baked goods and in soups
Rouge Vif d'Etampes pumpkins (Cinderella)	Bright red-orange squat pumpkin with deep ridges (bright red-orange flesh)	Sweet	Moist, dense; good for roasting
Spaghetti squash	Pale yellow or beige, oval shape, thin skin (yellow-orange flesh)	Somewhat bland	Fibrous; separates into spaghetti-like strands when cooked
Sugar Pie pumpkin	Small version of classic jack-o-lantern pumpkin (orange flesh)	Much sweeter than regular field pumpkins	Somewhat starchy and fibrous
Sweet Dumpling squash	Small ridged pumpkin-shaped squash with yellow skin and dark green or bright orange stripes (deep yellow flesh)	Mild, slightly sweet flavor	Starchy
Turban squash	Turban shaped, mottled dark green, orange or yellow, knobbly, varying sizes (yellow-orange flesh)	Mild (some say dull) flavor	Floury
White pumpkin	Squat ridged field pumpkin, though some are heirloom varieties and good for eating (yellow to light orange flesh)	Some are dull, others are sweet	Somewhat starchy

Roasted Broccoli

VEGAN /// **MAKES 2 TO 2½ CUPS, SERVING 4 TO 6**

When you roast broccoli, the tiny flowers become a little bit charred, resulting in a bitter edge that contrasts with the sweet tasting broccoli.

1 bunch broccoli

1 to 2 tablespoons extra virgin olive oil

Salt and freshly ground pepper

1. Heat the oven to 450°F. Line a baking sheet with parchment or foil. Cut the broccoli crowns away from the stems. Peel and slice the stems. Slice crowns ⅓ inch thick, letting the florets on the edges fall off. Peel any large pieces of stem still attached to the florets by gently pulling away the thick skin.

2. Toss everything—stem and floret slices and the unattached florets—with the olive oil and salt and pepper to taste. Place on the baking sheet in an even layer.

3. Roast for 8 minutes, then stir and flip the large slices over with tongs. Continue to roast until the stems are tender when pierced with a knife and the tops are nicely browned, usually another 7 to 8 minutes (15 to 16 minutes total).

ADVANCE PREPARATION: Roasted broccoli will keep for a day or two in the refrigerator.

Roasted Cauliflower

VEGAN /// MAKES 2 TO 2½ CUPS, SERVING 4 TO 6

This is one of my favorite ways to prepare cauliflower. The edges of the florets caramelize slightly and acquire a toasty flavor. If you find cauliflower bland, prepare it this way and you'll change your mind.

1 head cauliflower

1 to 2 tablespoons extra virgin olive oil

Salt and freshly ground pepper

1. Heat the oven to 450°F. Line a baking sheet with parchment or foil. Cut away the bottom of the cauliflower stem and trim off the leaves. Cut the cauliflower into ⅓-inch-thick slices, letting the florets on the edges fall off. Toss all of it, including the bits that have fallen away, with the olive oil and salt and pepper to taste. Place on the baking sheet in an even layer.

2. Roast for 15 to 20 minutes, stirring and flipping over the big slices after 8 minutes, until the slices are tender when pierced with a paring knife and the small florets are nicely browned. Remove from the oven and cut the large slices into smaller pieces.

ADVANCE PREPARATION: Roasted cauliflower will keep for a day or two in the refrigerator.

Roasted Beets

VEGAN /// **SERVES 2 TO 4 (DEPENDING ON THE SIZE OF THE BEETS)**

I've been roasting beets like this for decades. I put a small amount of water in the bottom of the roasting dish with the beets so they steam and roast at the same time. This method loosens the skins slightly so that they're very easy to slip off. The beets have the depth of flavor that roasted beets always have, and they're moist too. And because of the water, they won't burn if you leave them in a little too long.

1 bunch beets (usually about 4 beets)

1. Heat the oven to 425°F. Cut the greens away from the beets, leaving about 1/4 inch of stems. Scrub the beets and place in a baking dish or lidded ovenproof casserole. Add 1/4 to 1/2 inch of water to the dish. Cover tightly. Place in the oven and roast until easily penetrated with the tip of a knife: small beets (3 ounces or less) 30 to 40 minutes, medium beets (4 to 6 ounces) 40 to 45 minutes, and large beets (8 ounces) 50 to 60 minutes.

2. Remove from the oven and allow to cool in the covered baking dish. Cut away the ends and slip off the skins when ready to use.

ADVANCE PREPARATION: Unpeeled roasted beets keep well in the refrigerator for up to 5 days, even a week. Remove them from the baking dish and place in a bowl. Cover the bowl if desired—it isn't necessary—and refrigerate. Once peeled the beets deteriorate more quickly but they'll keep for 2 to 3 days. You can toss them with a little vinegar or salad dressing to preserve them for longer.

Roasted Eggplant

VEGAN /// **MAKES ABOUT 1½ CUPS DICED OR PUREED EGGPLANT, SERVING 4**

A long time ago (and I mean *really* long ago, before I wrote my first book), I sought to find a way to cook eggplant for various Mediterranean dishes without using a cup of oil, which is what an eggplant will drink if you let it. If you simply slice up eggplant and sauté it, you'll end up with a heavy, greasy dish. But if you roast it at high heat first, it will soften and you won't need to use all of that oil. If you need neat slices or diced eggplant for your dish, you slice or dice it, and then roast it until it's almost soft all the way through, and then you let it steam in its own heat until it's soft. If you're not going to need neat pieces, you can cut it in half and roast it cut side down on a baking sheet until it's soft all the way through and has collapsed slightly, and you won't need to wrap it in the foil afterwards to steam. Here are both methods.

1 medium eggplant cut into ½-inch dice or sliced about ⅓ inch thick

Salt

1 tablespoon extra virgin olive oil, plus additional oil for the baking sheet

SLICED OR DICED EGGPLANT

1. Heat the oven to 450°F. Slice the eggplant or dice as directed in your recipe, and toss with salt to taste and the olive oil. Line 1 to 2 baking sheets (as needed) with foil and oil with olive oil.

2. Lay the eggplant on the foil in one layer. Place in the hot oven and roast until the pieces are soft when pierced with a knife and browned in spots, 15 to 20 minutes. They'll look dry on the surface but when you pierce them with a knife you should be able to see that the flesh is soft.

3. Remove from the oven and carefully fold the foil up over the eggplant (be careful not to burn yourself!). Crimp the edges of the foil so that the eggplant is hermetically sealed in a big foil packet. Allow the eggplant to cool inside the foil packet, outside of the oven, for 15 to 20 minutes. The hot eggplant will continue to steam inside the packet and will moisten up and be soft all the way through by the time it has cooled. Carefully remove from the foil and proceed with your recipe.

1 medium eggplant, halved lengthwise

Extra virgin olive oil for the baking sheet

HALVED EGGPLANT

1. Heat the oven to 450°F. Line a baking sheet with foil and oil with olive oil. With the tip of a paring knife or a chef's knife, score each eggplant half down the middle of the cut side, cutting down to but not through the skin. Lay the eggplant cut side down on the oiled foil and place in the oven. Roast until you see that the skin is shriveled and the edges of the cut side are beginning to brown, about 20 minutes.

2. Using a spatula, transfer the eggplant halves to a colander, placing them cut side down. Place the colander in the sink and allow the eggplant to cool and drain. Cut into pieces or puree as directed.

NOTE: Small eggplants and long Asian eggplants are roasted using the same method as bulbous Mediterranean eggplants. But check the eggplants after 15 minutes, as they won't take as long to soften.

ADVANCE PREPARATION: You can roast eggplant up to a day ahead of proceeding with your eggplant recipe. Keep in a covered bowl in the refrigerator.

Salting Eggplant (or Not)

When I was learning to cook, virtually every eggplant recipe I came across had you salting the eggplant and allowing it to sit and sweat before proceeding with the recipe. That is the custom around the world, because ancient varieties of eggplant were quite bitter. Today's eggplant is not so bitter, especially if it's locally grown and freshly picked. Deborah Madison points out in her book *Vegetable Literacy* that eggplants, being a tropical plant, do not like the cold, and that when you buy eggplants that have been in cold storage they will be bitter and should be salted. She doesn't salt when she cooks freshly picked or farmers' market eggplant, as long as she uses it within a few days of harvesting. But she always salts supermarket eggplant. I think that sounds like a good rule of thumb.

I sometimes salt just for flavor. If you do salt your eggplant, toss diced eggplant with salt or sprinkle salt onto rounds or halved eggplant and let sit for 30 minutes. Blot the dark beads that form on the surface with paper towels and proceed with the recipe.

TOMATO SAUCE

WHEN TOMATOES ARE IN SEASON, THEY dominate my cooking. I spend time each week in late summer and early fall making marinara and freezing it in ¼-cup and ½-cup portions. I pull it from the freezer whenever we decide on pasta. I use a scant ¼ cup for each 3- to 4-ounce (dry weight) serving of pasta. If you're a family of two, you can freeze it in ½-cup portions, and on up. While I'm waiting for the water to boil for the pasta, I thaw the sauce in the microwave in a large Pyrex bowl, then toss the sauce with the pasta in the same bowl.

If you buy your tomatoes at the farmers' market you may find that certain farmers sell their bruised or overripe tomatoes "for sauce" at a much lower price. These are the tomatoes to buy. But be sure that you examine them well to make sure that none of the tomatoes have begun to rot. They're easy to detect: They will smell bad and have very soft spots. One rotten tomato can ruin the flavor of a sauce. So inspect when you buy and inspect again when you get home.

Only a good tomato can make a good sauce, so there's no reason to make a marinara sauce with fresh tomatoes if they aren't sweet, local, and vine-ripened. Excellent tomato sauce can also be made with canned tomatoes (see page 26).

Uncooked Tomato Sauce

VEGAN /// **MAKES 2 CUPS**

In summer I make a lot of sauce to put away, but I always save some of the sweetest and juiciest tomatoes for quick pasta dinners—I can't get enough of my homegrown tomatoes.

1 pound sweet, ripe tomatoes, peeled, seeded, and finely chopped or grated (see Note)

½ to 1 teaspoon balsamic vinegar (optional)

1 to 2 garlic cloves (to taste), minced or pureed

2 tablespoons extra virgin olive oil

2 tablespoons slivered or snipped fresh basil

Salt and freshly ground pepper to taste

Combine all of the ingredients. Let sit for about 15 minutes or longer to allow the flavors to emerge. Taste and adjust seasoning. Serve with pasta or as a topping for bruschetta.

NOTE: Grating is an easy and efficient way to prepare tomatoes. Cut the tomato in half along the equator. Squeeze the seeds out into a strainer set over a wide bowl, and rub the seed pods against the strainer to catch the sweet pulp that surrounds the seeds. Set a box grater in the bowl. Cup a half tomato in your hand and rub the flat side of the tomato against the large holes of your grater until it flattens out with the skin pressed against your hand. The skin will protect your hand against the grater holes.

ADVANCE PREPARATION: This can be made several hours ahead of serving.

Fresh-Tomato Marinara Sauce

VEGAN /// **MAKES 2 TO 2½ CUPS, SERVING 8 TO 10**

Marinara is tomato sauce, and having a good one under your belt will contribute to your confidence as a cook. This one is so good (yet so simple) that your friends will wonder why you don't market it.

The type of tomatoes you use will determine the cooking time for your sauce. I prefer dense, sweet tomatoes like Romas or San Marzanos, which don't give off a lot of juice when they cook so will cook down more quickly than round, juicy tomatoes. But I'll take whatever tomatoes are on offer at the farmers' market (or in my garden), as long as they're delicious.

I highly recommend that you invest in a food mill if you make a lot of tomato sauce. Then you won't have to go through the step of peeling, coring, seeding, and chopping the tomatoes before you begin. All you have to do is quickly cut the tomatoes into wedges—quarters or sixths, depending on their size—and cook them down. When the sauce is thick, fragrant, and clinging to the pan, you put it through the food mill and the skin, core, and bitter seeds stay behind.

3 pounds tomatoes

1 to 2 tablespoons extra virgin olive oil

3 large garlic cloves, minced

⅛ to ¼ teaspoon sugar (to taste)

½ teaspoon salt (or more to taste)

2 sprigs fresh basil

2 tablespoons slivered fresh basil (optional)

1. If you have a food mill, cut the tomatoes into wedges—quarters for small or medium tomatoes, sixths or eighths for large tomatoes. If you don't have a food mill, peel, core, and seed the tomatoes following the directions on the opposite page. Make sure to retain the delicious gelatinous pulp surrounding the seeds as it's very flavorful and contributes great texture to your sauce. Cut peeled, cored tomatoes into small dice.

2. Heat the oil over medium heat in a large, wide, preferably nonstick skillet or a shallow 3-quart saucepan. Add the garlic and cook until the garlic begins to sizzle and starts to smell fragrant and look translucent, about 30 seconds.

3. Add the tomatoes, sugar, salt, and basil sprigs and stir and turn up the heat. When the tomatoes begin to bubble briskly, turn the heat to medium and cook, stirring often, until thick and fragrant, 15 to 30 minutes, depending on the type of tomato and the amount of water they throw off. I like to use a heavy nonstick pan because the sauce can cook down until a thin layer adheres to the pan (it's my indication that the sauce is just about done), but it won't burn and you can stir the sticky layer back into the sauce, contributing a sweet, caramelized flavor. Remove from the heat, taste, and adjust seasoning. Pull out the basil sprigs and discard.

4. If you used unpeeled tomatoes, set a food mill fitted with the fine disk over a bowl and strain the sauce through. If you used peeled diced tomatoes and want a smoother texture, pulse in a food processor. Stir in the slivered basil if using.

INCREASING OR DECREASING THE RECIPE: You can use this recipe for any quantity of tomatoes. For each pound of tomatoes use 1 clove of garlic. One tablespoon of olive oil is plenty if you're only cooking 1 pound of tomatoes, and after that 2 tablespoons will work for a range of weights; you don't have to increase the amount exponentially. Use a pinch of sugar for 1 pound, $\frac{1}{4}$ teaspoon for 2 to about 4 pounds. Then you can go up to $\frac{1}{2}$ teaspoon. Use your taste buds and your judgment to decide how much more to use after that, as well as how much salt the sauce requires. A great tomato sauce has a perfect balance of sweet and savory. Too much salt will destroy that balance but not enough and you'll miss out on some flavor potential. ALWAYS TASTE.

ADVANCE PREPARATION: Tomato sauce keeps well. You can hold it in the refrigerator for about 5 days, and freeze it for a few months—or until it runs out. To freeze: Line a cup or a glass with a piece of plastic or a small freezer bag and measure out $\frac{1}{4}$-cup portions, $\frac{1}{2}$-cup portions, or whatever works best for you and your family, figuring on $\frac{1}{4}$ cup per serving. If you're using a sheet of plastic, make sure it's large enough so that you can envelop your portion; place each wrapped portion on a baking sheet, then place in the freezer until solid. Double wrap once frozen in a freezer bag and freeze for up to 6 months.

Seeding Tomatoes

Place a strainer over a bowl. Cut tomatoes in half along the equator. Squeeze seed pods into the strainer, then rub them against the sides so you don't lose the sweet pulpy juice that surrounds the seeds. Discard the seeds and add the juice to the chopped tomato pulp.

Canned-Tomato Marinara Sauce

VEGAN /// MAKES 2¾ CUPS

Invariably, you'll run out of your stash of frozen marinara sauce before the year is out unless you have a huge tomato garden. No worries; you can make a delicious sauce with canned tomatoes using the same recipe.

I like organic Muir Glen tomatoes, but there are also delicious Italian brands, and frankly, I've got no qualms with my supermarket's special when they're selling ten cans for $10. Sometimes these need a little more sugar, but you can still coax them into a delicious sauce. Buy them diced or whole in juice (not in puree, which tastes too much like tomato paste to my palate), boxed or canned.

I use the same ratio of garlic to tomato that I use with fresh—1 clove per can—which is actually a little less than a pound, as a small can has a net weight of 14.5 ounces. Canned tomatoes will yield a little more sauce per pound. One 28-ounce can yields a little under 2 cups sauce.

Make the *Fresh-Tomato Marinara Sauce* (page 24) with the following substitution:

1 (28-ounce) can diced or whole tomatoes in juice

1 (14.5-ounce) can diced or whole tomatoes in juice

Pulse the canned tomatoes in a food processor or mini-chop. (No need for a food mill unless you want an extremely smooth sauce.) Proceed with the recipe at Step 2.

Marinara Sauce with Aromatics

VEGAN /// **MAKES 2½ TO 3 CUPS**

Aromatics—onion, carrots, celery—will add different dimensions of flavor and texture to a sauce, more savory than sweet. I am so focused on the sweetness of my tomatoes that I don't usually bother with onions, though this wasn't always the case. Up until fairly recently I always began my marinara sauce by sweating an onion. Gradually I added finely diced carrot and celery to the mix. But in recent years I've simplified my tomato sauce, preferring the pure flavor of the tomatoes seasoned with garlic, basil, and salt. But play around and see what you like.

Make the *Fresh-Tomato Marinara Sauce* (page 24) or the *Canned-Tomato Marinara Sauce* (opposite page), with the following additional ingredients and specifications:

Additional 1 tablespoon extra virgin olive oil

½ medium onion, finely chopped

1 small carrot, finely chopped

½ celery stalk, finely chopped

1 tablespoon finely chopped fresh parsley (optional)

1. Heat 2 to 3 tablespoons olive oil over medium heat in the skillet or saucepan and add the onion. Cook, stirring, until it begins to soften, 2 to 3 minutes. Add the carrot, celery, and a pinch of salt and cook, stirring often, until the vegetables are tender and fragrant, about 8 more minutes. Add the garlic (from the template recipe) and parsley (if using), and stir until the garlic is fragrant, about 30 seconds.

2. Proceed with Step 3 of the recipe, using the fresh tomato wedges or dice, or the canned tomatoes.

PESTO AND PISTOU

STORE-BOUGHT PESTO DOES NOT COMPARE WITH pesto you make yourself. Freshly made pesto has a luscious flavor—with the herbs, garlic, and Parmesan in perfect balance. You want to eat it with a spoon. But once pesto is made, the garlic begins to deteriorate and over time it becomes acrid, which is the lingering flavor that commercial pestos always seem to leave behind. So when basil is abundant, make your own. Blend the basil and olive oil to a puree, and store in the freezer without the garlic and cheese, adding those ingredients when you thaw it.

Serious cooks use a mortar and pestle to make pesto, which does yield the most intensely flavored and smoothest pesto, as the herby oils are coaxed from the basil leaves when you grind them down with the pestle. I have a high-speed hand (immersion) blender, and that's become my favorite tool for the job; it's certainly faster than the mortar and pestle. I put the basil, garlic, nuts, and olive oil in a jar, insert the hand blender and in seconds have a smooth puree. But a hand blender that doesn't have a super-strong motor won't work so well. Most of you will likely use a food processor, which chops rather than grinds the leaves. If you're making a big batch of pesto, this is an efficient tool, and your pesto will still taste pretty darn good.

Pistou is the Provençal cousin of pesto, from the south of France. Unlike its Italian counterpart, it doesn't contain nuts and sometimes includes a tomato. The flavor of the two is very similar, but Italian pesto has a more substantial, meaty texture because of the ground nuts. In Provence, particularly in Nice and its environs, where basil itself is often called *pistou,* the condiment is used most often to enhance the iconic summer vegetable minestrone, *soupe au pistou.*

As for what nuts to use in pesto, the classic pesto Genovese calls for pine nuts, or *pignoli.* But Mediterranean pignoli are becoming harder and harder to find, and some people suffer a reaction to the Asian pine nuts that are replacing them. I am one of those people; when I eat a certain variety of pine nuts I sometimes get what is known as "pine nut mouth," which means that everything I eat for the next week or two has a bitter aftertaste. It's most unpleasant, and I'm consequently very careful about where my pine nuts come from. If I can't be sure, I substitute unsalted, raw pumpkin seeds, pistachios, or chopped walnuts.

Pistou

To make French pistou, use the same process as you would for pesto (opposite page), using the same amounts of ingredients, but omit the nuts. If desired, after you've broken down the garlic, basil, and nuts, add a small peeled, seeded tomato. Blend in the food processor or jar using a powerful immersion blender or grind in the mortar and pestle, to make a paste, then add the olive oil and cheese as directed. The color will not be the same vivid green, but this version makes a nice condiment for minestrones.

Basil Pesto Genovese

MAKES ½ TO ⅔ CUP

1 or 2 garlic cloves (to taste), halved, green shoots removed

2 cups tightly packed fresh basil leaves (2 ounces)

2 tablespoons Mediterranean pine nuts, pumpkin seeds, unsalted pistachios, or chopped walnuts

Salt (I use ½ teaspoon) and freshly ground pepper

⅓ cup extra virgin olive oil

1½ ounces freshly grated Parmesan (⅓ cup), or a mixture of Pecorino Romano and Parmesan (or more to taste)

USING AN IMMERSION BLENDER

1. Place the garlic, basil, nuts, salt, pepper to taste, and olive oil in a straight-sided 1-pint container. Stick a high-powered immersion blender right down into the mixture and turn on. Blend until smooth. At the beginning, you may have to stop a few times and scrape down the sides of the container.

2. Add the cheese and stir or blend together.

USING A FOOD PROCESSOR

1. Turn on a food processor and drop in the garlic. When the garlic is chopped and adhering to the side of the bowl, stop the machine and scrape down the sides with a spatula.

2. Add the basil, nuts, salt, and pepper to taste and process until the basil is finely chopped and much of it is adhering to the sides of the bowl. Stop the machine and scrape down the sides of the bowl.

3. Turn on the processor and, with the machine running, slowly add the olive oil and process until smooth and creamy. Add the Parmesan and pulse until well combined.

USING A MORTAR AND PESTLE

1. Allow the basil leaves to dry out for a few hours or for up to a day at room temperature.

2. Grind the garlic with the salt to a paste. Add the nuts and mash with the garlic to a paste. Remove from the bowl and set aside.

3. Add the basil leaves to the bowl a handful at a time and mash with the pestle. When all of the leaves have been reduced to a puree, return the nut and garlic paste to the bowl and mash together with the basil. Little by little, work in the olive oil and the Parmesan.

NOTE: The reason I remove the garlic and nut paste from the mortar before I grind the basil is that if I keep pounding and grinding the garlic it will become too pungent. When you pound garlic, the volatile compounds that give garlic its pungency are released as the garlic breaks down; the more you pound, the stronger it will become.

ADVANCE PREPARATION: You can freeze pesto or pistou for several months, and it will keep in the refrigerator for a few days. If you are making this for the freezer, you'll get the best results if you puree the basil with the olive oil and salt only. When ready to use, thaw the basil puree and mash the garlic and pine nuts. Combine the garlic and nuts with the puree and blend together, then blend in the cheese.

Parsley Pesto

MAKES ABOUT ½ CUP

Parsley pesto has a fresh, grassy taste without the hints of anise and sweetness of basil pesto. It does have the same herbal/garlicky/Parmesan depth of flavor, and a pleasant, slightly bitter edge. I make it more often than I make basil pesto. For one thing I have a garden full of flat-leaf parsley that provides me with more parsley than I know what to do with. But it's also because parsley pesto keeps in the refrigerator better than basil pesto; it retains its shimmering bright green color and its fresh flavor, and I find that it's more versatile. In addition to stirring it into minestrones, I like to stir it into cooked grains (it's especially good with quinoa because of its complementary grassy flavor) and pasta dishes, and I use it as a garnish for soups.

Follow the *Basil Pesto Genovese* recipe (page 29), using the following ingredients:

2 garlic cloves, halved, green shoot removed, roughly chopped

Salt

⅓ cup extra virgin olive oil, as needed

2 cups tightly packed flat-leaf parsley leaves (2 ounces), coarsely chopped

1 tablespoon tightly packed mint leaves, coarsely chopped (optional)

1½ ounces freshly grated Parmesan (⅓ cup)

Freshly ground pepper (optional)

Follow the directions for any of the methods.

ADVANCE PREPARATION: Parsley pesto keeps well in the refrigerator for about a week. It freezes well, like basil pesto (see "Advance Preparation," above).

EGGS AND TOFU

SEVERAL RECIPES IN THIS COLLECTION, PARTICULARLY the Big Bowls in Chapter 7, call for poached eggs or seasoned tofu. These foods contribute substantial, high-quality protein to whatever dish they are added to, as well as comfort, wonderful flavor, and texture.

Baked Seasoned Tofu

VEG /// **MAKES 4 SERVINGS**

Thi...   ...s tofu sandwich that I enjoy at a Los Angeles restaurant called
Fo...   ...tofu like this and keep it on hand in the refrigerator for a couple
of...   ...Big Bowls (Chapter 7) and Stir-Fries (Chapter 9). It's also great
on...

1 (
fir
dr

3
p

3
c

1. Heat the oven to 375°F. Line a baking sheet with parchment. Pat the tofu dry with paper towels and cut into ½- to ¾-inch-thick slices.

2. In a large, wide bowl, whisk together all of the remaining ingredients. Pat each slice of tofu with paper towels, then dip into the marinade, making sure to coat both sides. Transfer to the baking sheet.

3. Bake the tofu for 10 to 15 minutes, until the edges are just beginning to color and the marinade sets on the surface of the tofu. Allow to cool.

*You can substitute sugar for the honey if you want to make a vegan version of this recipe.

ADVANCE PREPARATION: The marinade will keep for about 3 days in the refrigerator. The baked tofu will keep for a couple of days in the refrigerator.

Poached Eggs

MAKES 1 TO 4 POACHED EGGS

Poached eggs are building blocks that can transform just about anything into a substantial dish. Knowing that poaching eggs is always a possibility makes me confident about being able to put a comforting, simple meal on the table. I use them to enrich soups and to turn all sorts of vegetable and grain preparations, as well as salads, into main dishes. Top a bowl of grains with some well-seasoned cooked vegetables and a poached egg, maybe sprinkled with dukkah (page 137) or with feta, and it's dinner. Add a poached egg to a serving of Mediterranean Stewed Peppers (page 6) and now you have *chakchouka*, a satisfying meal. Poaching eggs is not difficult, much easier than mastering the omelet. It's all about timing. Here is the foolproof method I use.

1 to 4 large or extra-large eggs, preferably free-range organic

1 to 3 teaspoons vinegar

1. Fill a lidded skillet with water and bring to a boil. (I use an 8-inch omelet pan for 1 egg, a 10-inch pan for 2 or more.) Add 1 to 3 teaspoons vinegar to the water (less if using a small pan, more if using a larger one).

2. Break the eggs into separate teacups, then tip from the teacups into the boiling water. If I'm poaching more than one egg, I hold one teacup in each hand, and tip the eggs in by twos. Immediately cover the pan tightly and turn off the heat. Set your timer for 4 minutes. Meanwhile, place a clean dishtowel next to the pan.

3. When the timer goes off, using a slotted spoon or spatula, carefully remove the poached eggs from the water. Set on the towel to drain. If you want to rinse off the vinegar, first dip the egg into a bowl of cold water, then drain on the towel.

ADVANCE PREPARATION: If you are not using the eggs right away, you can store them in a bowl of cold water in the refrigerator. They will keep for 3 days. Drain on a dishtowel before using and reheat by placing on a slotted spoon or spatula and dipping into a bowl of hot water.

CHAPTER TWO

Soups, Big and Small

M Y MANY TEMPLATES FOR SOUPS, both hearty and light, range from thick, chunky minestrones and substantial Asian noodle bowls ("big soups") to lighter, brothy garlic soups and vegetable purees ("small soups"). Whatever the nature of the soup, it is always dinner.

The hearty minestrones rely mainly on pantry ingredients and aromatics—beans, soup pasta, or rice, canned tomatoes, onions, garlic, carrots, leeks, and celery—that are easy to stock year-round. You'll learn to make a soup base with these ingredients, then add in-season vegetables—kale or cabbage or winter squash during the cooler months, peas, beans, favas, and summer squash in spring and summer.

The other "big soups," Asian noodle bowls, are lighter and less robust than minestrones. One version, Japanese/Californian in origin, begins with subtle kombu stock or vegetable stock. The other, inspired by Vietnamese *phô,* is a very aromatic vegetable stock to which in-season vegetables and a protein (like tofu) are added. Wide or deep soup bowls are filled with cooked noodles (I use buckwheat and rice noodles) then the stock and vegetables are ladled in.

Lighter, "small soups" are still substantial enough for me to serve for dinner, especially on those evenings when we prefer a smaller meal. Pureed vegetable soups are all about vegetables in season, a way to show them off. Garlic soups are the easiest and quickest in my repertoire. They are a legacy of the time I've spent in Provence and give me great confidence that dinner is always a few cloves of garlic, an egg, a toasted slice of bread, and 20 minutes away.

Except for the Asian noodle meals, none of these recipes require stock. You can use stock for the pureed vegetable soups if you want to, but water will be fine and won't interfere with the pure flavor of the vegetables. That's why, with the exception of the kombu broths and the *phô* broth used in the Asian noodle bowls (pages 55–58), you won't find recipes for vegetarian stocks in this chapter. You will find them, however, in the risotto chapter (page 147), because that's where you'll need them.

MINESTRONE

MINESTRONE IS, LITERALLY, A "BIG SOUP," a vegetable soup that also contains beans and pasta or rice. The flavor is deep and Mediterranean, and has savory layers of garlic and onion, tomatoes, and Parmesan, along with simmered beans in some soups, lentils in others. In winter I add hearty greens like kale and cabbage, and in spring and summer I add brighter vegetables— green beans, fresh favas, or peas. You might think of this as a winter dish, but on hot Provençal days you will find their version of minestrone, *soupe au pistou,* on many a table, served warm rather than hot, and filled with the summer's bounty of vegetables.

In this chapter I'm providing three different templates for minestrone. One calls for dried beans and takes longer, but is no more difficult than the other two. Another calls for canned beans, and the third is a lentil minestrone. The advantage to using dried beans or lentils is that the beans and lentils produce a savory broth. The advantage to using canned beans is that the process is quicker.

Note: All of the minestrones can be made as vegan soups by omitting the Parmesan rind and Parmesan cheese.

Minestrone with Dried Beans

VEGAN WITHOUT THE CHEESE /// **MAKES 6 GENEROUS SERVINGS**

When I make minestrone using dried beans, I begin by simmering the soaked beans in water with a halved onion, a couple of crushed garlic cloves, and a bay leaf to obtain a savory broth. Then I make a flavorful tomato base with tomatoes and aromatics, to which I add the beans and their broth, as well as additional vegetables. You can make the base with a small or large can of tomatoes; it depends on how *tomato-y* you like your soup. I don't have a preference so I'm giving you the choice. Any number of vegetables can be added—potatoes, squash (winter or summer), cabbage, or greens work year-round, and in spring and summer it's nice to add green beans or peas, which I like to cook separately and add shortly before serving for color. Soup pasta usually goes in at the end, but rice can be used as well.

BEANS

½ pound (about 1⅛ cups) dried white beans such as navy, cannellini, or borlotti beans, washed, picked over, and soaked for at least 4 hours (or do the quick-soak method described on page 188)

2 quarts water

1 medium onion, halved and peeled

2 garlic cloves, peeled and crushed

1 bay leaf

Salt

TOMATO BASE

2 tablespoons extra virgin olive oil

1 medium onion, chopped

1 large or 2 medium carrots, diced (½-inch dice, or smaller if desired)

1 celery stalk, diced (½-inch dice, or smaller if desired)

Salt

2 tablespoons chopped fresh flat-leaf parsley

1. For the beans: Drain the soaked beans and place in a large saucepan with the water, onion, garlic, and bay leaf. Bring to a boil, reduce the heat, and simmer 30 minutes. Add salt to taste (I usually use 1 teaspoon salt per quart of water and adjust again later) and continue to simmer another 30 to 45 minutes. The beans should be just tender, or almost. Remove from the heat and use tongs to remove and discard the onion, garlic, and bay leaf.

2. Meanwhile, for the tomato base: Heat the olive oil over medium heat in a heavy soup pot or Dutch oven and add the onion, carrots, and celery. Add a pinch of salt and cook, stirring, until the vegetables are just about tender, about 5 minutes. Add the parsley and leeks and cook, stirring, until the leeks are slightly wilted, about 3 minutes. Stir in the garlic along with another generous pinch of salt. Cook, stirring, just until the garlic smells fragrant, 30 seconds to 1 minute. Stir in the tomatoes with their juice, thyme, and salt to taste. Bring to a simmer and cook, stirring often, until the tomatoes have cooked down somewhat and smell fragrant, about 10 minutes.

3. Add the beans and their broth to the tomato base and stir together.

4. To finish the soup: Add the turnips and bouquet garni and bring to a simmer. Cover and simmer over low heat for 45 minutes to 1 hour. The beans should be tender and the broth very tasty. Taste, adjust the salt, and add pepper to taste. Discard the bouquet garni.

2 leeks, white and light green parts only, halved lengthwise, cleaned well, and thinly sliced

3 to 4 garlic cloves (to taste), minced

1 (14.5- or 28-ounce, to taste) can chopped tomatoes with juice

½ teaspoon dried thyme or 1 teaspoon chopped fresh

FINISHED SOUP

2 medium turnips, peeled and diced

A bouquet garni: Parmesan rind, bay leaf, and a couple sprigs each of parsley and thyme

Freshly ground pepper

½ cup elbow macaroni or small shells

Freshly grated Parmesan for serving

5. Stir in the pasta and continue to simmer until cooked al dente, 5 to 10 minutes. Serve, topping each bowl with freshly grated Parmesan.

ADVANCE PREPARATION: The soup tastes even better a day after it's made, but don't add and simmer the pasta until you are ready to serve.

SUBSTITUTIONS AND ADDITIONS:

- *Arborio rice: Substitute ⅓ cup Arborio rice for the pasta; it will take about 15 minutes to cook.*

- *Shell beans: Shell beans are increasingly available in farmers' markets. They're the fresh version of dried beans, and have a delicious texture and flavor. You can substitute the same volume of shell beans (out of the pod) for dried beans. They do not require soaking, and require only 45 minutes of cooking in Step 1. Add salt to the water at the beginning of cooking.*

Bouquet Garni

A bouquet garni is a small bundle of herbs that seasons a soup as it simmers. My classic Mediterranean bouquet garni consists of a bay leaf and a couple of sprigs of both thyme and parsley, as well as a Parmesan rind. I tie them together with kitchen twine. You can also tie them into a cheesecloth pouch. If you do this you could also include some whole peppercorns.

Minestrone with Canned Beans

VEGAN WITHOUT THE CHEESE /// **MAKES 6 GENEROUS SERVINGS**

A minestrone using canned beans is quicker to throw together than the dried bean version, but you won't wind up with as rich a bean broth. Nevertheless the savory tomato soup base produces a soup with great depth of flavor. As in the dried bean minestrone, you have lots of choices for vegetables to add: cabbage, potatoes any time of year, winter or summer squash, fresh green beans or greens (both of which I cook separately and add shortly before serving), fresh or frozen peas.

2 tablespoons extra virgin olive oil

1 medium onion, chopped

1 large or 2 medium carrots, diced (½ inch or smaller)

1 celery stalk, diced (½ inch or smaller)

2 tablespoons chopped fresh flat-leaf parsley

Salt

2 leeks, white and light green parts only, halved, cleaned well, and sliced thin

3 to 4 garlic cloves (to taste), minced

1 (14.5- or 28-ounce, to taste) can chopped tomatoes with juice

½ teaspoon dried thyme or 1 teaspoon chopped fresh

2 quarts water

2 turnips, peeled and diced

A bouquet garni: Parmesan rind, bay leaf, and a couple sprigs each of parsley and thyme

1 (15-ounce) can cannellini or chickpeas, drained and rinsed well

½ cup elbow macaroni or small shells

Freshly ground pepper

Freshly grated Parmesan for serving

1. Heat the olive oil over medium-low heat in a large, heavy soup pot or Dutch oven and add the onion, carrots, celery, and parsley. Cook, stirring, until beginning to soften, about 3 minutes. Add a pinch of salt and continue to cook, stirring often, until just about tender, a few more minutes. Add the leeks and cook, stirring, until they begin to soften, about 3 minutes. Add the garlic, stir together until fragrant, 30 seconds to 1 minute. Stir in the tomatoes and their juice and the thyme and cook, stirring, until the tomatoes have cooked down and smell fragrant, about 10 minutes.

2. Stir in the water, turnips, and bouquet garni, and bring to a simmer. Add salt to taste (about 2 teaspoons), reduce the heat to low, cover, and simmer 45 minutes. Stir in the canned beans. Taste and adjust the salt. Discard the bouquet garni.

3. Add the pasta to the soup and simmer until the pasta is cooked al dente, 5 to 10 minutes. Grind in some pepper and taste and adjust seasonings. It should be savory and rich-tasting. Serve, topping each bowl with freshly grated Parmesan.

ADVANCE PREPARATION: This keeps for 3 or 4 days in the refrigerator, but it's best to wait until ready to serve before you add the pasta.

Minestrone with Cabbage and Winter Squash

VEGAN WITHOUT THE CHEESE /// **MAKES 6 GENEROUS SERVINGS**

The colder months bring winter squash, sometimes potatoes, and cruciferous greens like cabbage and kale to my hearty soups. Cabbage and winter squash simmer along with the soup base, sweetening the broth. I often choose chickpeas as the beans in my winter minestrones. They go well with the heartier vegetables. In this variation, I wilt cabbage with the other vegetables in the tomato base, and add the winter squash along with the beans and their liquid.

Make the *Minestrone with Dried Beans* template (page 38) with the following additional vegetables and specifications:

½ medium cabbage, chopped or shredded

1 pound winter squash, such as butternut, peeled and diced

2 to 4 additional tablespoons chopped fresh flat-leaf parsley (to taste)

1. Simmer the beans as directed in Step 1.

2. In Step 2, add the cabbage to the tomato base when you add the garlic and salt. Cook, stirring, until the cabbage has begun to wilt and the garlic smells fragrant, about 3 minutes. Continue through Step 3.

3. In Step 4, add the winter squash when you add the turnips and bouquet garni and bring to a simmer. If the broth seems low, add a little water so that everything is submerged. Cover and simmer over low heat for 1 hour.

4. In Step 5, stir in the additional parsley just before serving.

   ADVANCE PREPARATION: The soup tastes even better a day after it's made, but don't add and simmer the pasta until you are ready to serve.

Using Parmesan Rinds in Soups and Stews

Parmesan rinds can be simmered in soups and stews, giving up lots of enriching umami/Parmesan flavor. They are the vegetarian equivalent of the meat bone. I wrap mine in foil and keep them in the cheese drawer of the refrigerator, or in the freezer (I have a lot of them!). They will last for a very long time. Discard after simmering.

Minestrone with Cabbage and Winter Squash (Canned Bean Version)

VEGAN WITHOUT THE CHEESE //// **MAKES 6 GENEROUS SERVINGS**

Make the *Minestrone with Canned Beans* template (page 40) with the following additional vegetables and specifications:

½ medium cabbage, chopped or shredded

1 pound winter squash, such as butternut, peeled and diced

2 to 4 additional tablespoons chopped fresh flat-leaf parsley (to taste)

1. In Step 1, add the cabbage when you add the garlic and cook until the cabbage has begun to wilt and the garlic smells fragrant, about 3 minutes. Continue with the step.

2. In Step 2, add the winter squash when you add the turnips and bouquet garni and cook for 1 hour. Continue with the step.

4. In Step 3, stir in the additional parsley just before serving.

Minestrone with Spring and Summer Vegetables

VEGAN WITHOUT THE CHEESE //// **MAKES 6 GENEROUS SERVINGS**

Brilliant and sweet green vegetables—peas, beans, summer squash—brighten my big soups in spring and summer. In the spring, peas and favas go into the pot; they give way to green beans and a mix of green and yellow summer squash during the summer. I like white beans in these minestrones, but in mid- and especially in late summer, when fresh shell beans hit the markets, I substitute them for the dried beans. They require much less time in the pot, and nothing can beat their creamy texture.

Because I can't bear to cook my beautiful bright green vegetables until the color fades to olive, I am not traditional in my approach to minestrone and its Provençal cousin, *soupe au pistou*. I may add a small portion of the vegetables to the pot to simmer for some time so that they contribute their sweetness to the broth; but I blanch the larger portion separately and stir the beautiful produce into the pot shortly before serving.

The classic Provençal enrichment for this soup is pistou, a basil pesto without pine nuts, sometimes with a tomato thrown in (the recipe is on page 28). If I don't want to take the time to make pistou, I'll throw in a handful of slivered basil leaves or chopped parsley just before serving.

Make the *Minestrone with Dried Beans* template (page 38) with the following additional ingredients and specifications:

½ to ¾ pound summer squash (a mix of dark and light green and yellow is nice), diced

1 to 1½ pounds fresh peas or favas (or a combination), shelled and favas skinned (see page 155)

½ pound green beans or a combination of green and yellow beans, trimmed and cut into 1-inch lengths

2 to 4 tablespoons chopped fresh flat-leaf parsley or slivered basil, or ½ cup Pistou (page 28) or Parsley Pesto (page 30), for garnish

Freshly grated Parmesan for serving

1. Simmer the beans as directed in Step 1.

2. Meanwhile, make the tomato base as directed in Step 2 and add the beans and broth in Step 3.

3. In Step 4, add half the summer squash, and bring to a simmer. (If the broth seems low, add a little water so that everything is submerged.) Cover and simmer over low heat for 1 hour. Taste, adjust the salt, and add pepper to taste.

4. While the soup is simmering, separately blanch the peas and/or favas and the green beans in a pot of salted boiling water until tender but still bright green. I suggest 4 to 5 minutes for peas and green beans, the same for skinned favas unless they are very large, in which case they may need more like 6 to 8 minutes. Transfer to a bowl of cold water, drain, and set aside. Steam the remaining summer squash for about 5 minutes or until the flesh is translucent and the skin is bright.

5. Continue with Step 5, stirring in the parsley or basil (but not the pistou or pesto) and the blanched and steamed vegetables after the pasta is cooked, and simmering until the vegetables are heated through.

6. Serve, topping each bowl with freshly grated Parmesan. If using pistou or pesto, add a generous spoonful to each bowl for guests to stir in. Pass additional grated Parmesan at the table.

ADVANCE PREPARATION: The soup tastes even better a day after it's made, but don't add and simmer the pasta or add the bright green blanched and steamed vegetables until you are ready to serve.

SUBSTITUTIONS AND ADDITIONS: Substitute ⅓ cup Arborio rice for the pasta; it will take about 15 minutes to cook.

Vegetable Stock

To boost the flavor of any of the minestrones made with canned beans, you can use stock instead of water as a base. You can make a quick vegetable stock with the trimmings from your spring and summer vegetables such as squash and green bean stems and pea pods, as well as leek trimmings, carrot peels, outer layer of the onion, and parsley stems. To make the stock: Combine the vegetable trimmings, 2 quarts water, and salt to taste in a medium saucepan. Bring to a boil, reduce the heat, and simmer 20 to 30 minutes. Place a strainer over a bowl and drain. Measure out 2 quarts.

Minestrone with Spring and Summer Vegetables (Canned Bean Version)

VEGAN WITHOUT THE CHEESE /// **MAKES 6 GENEROUS SERVINGS**

Make the *Minestrone with Canned Beans* template (page 40) with the following additional vegetables and specifications:

½ to ¾ pound summer squash (a mix of dark and light green and yellow is nice), diced

1 to 1½ pounds fresh peas or favas (or a combination), shelled and favas skinned (see page 155)

½ pound green beans or a mix of green and yellow beans, trimmed and cut into 1-inch lengths

2 to 4 tablespoons chopped fresh flat-leaf parsley or slivered basil, or ½ cup Pistou (page 28) or Parsley Pesto (page 30)

1. Cook the aromatics and tomatoes as directed in Step 1.

2. While the soup is simmering, separately blanch the peas and/or favas and green beans in a pot of salted boiling water until tender but still bright green. I suggest 4 to 5 minutes for peas and green beans, the same for skinned favas unless they are very large, in which case they may need more like 6 to 8 minutes. Transfer to a bowl of cold water, drain, and set aside. Steam the summer squash for about 5 minutes or until the flesh is translucent and the skin is bright.

3. Continue with Steps 2 and 3, stirring in the parsley or basil (but not the pistou or pesto) and the blanched and steamed green vegetables after the pasta is cooked and simmering until the vegetables are heated through.

4. Serve, topping each bowl with freshly grated Parmesan. If using pistou or pesto, add a generous spoonful to each bowl for guests to stir in. Pass additional grated Parmesan at the table.

ADVANCE PREPARATION: The soup tastes even better a day after it's made, but don't add and simmer the pasta or add the bright green blanched and steamed vegetables until you are ready to serve.

SUBSTITUTIONS AND ADDITIONS: Substitute ⅓ cup Arborio rice for the pasta; it will take about 15 minutes to cook.

Lentil Minestrone

VEGAN WITHOUT THE CHEESE /// **MAKES 4 TO 6 SERVINGS**

Lentils cook more quickly than beans, so they don't require a separate pot and a separate step, and they yield a wonderful broth. Make sure to include a Parmesan rind in your bouquet garni; it helps to accentuate the umami flavor of the lentils. Brown, green, and black lentils all work well here; red lentils do not (they break down too much and do not have the same flavor as the other varieties). I tend to use brown the most often because that's the easiest to find in the supermarket.

1 to 2 tablespoons extra virgin olive oil

1 small to medium onion, chopped

1 large or 2 medium carrots, cut into ½-inch dice

1 celery stalk, cut into ½-inch dice

3 to 4 large garlic cloves (to taste), minced

Salt

1 (14- or 28-ounce, to taste) can chopped tomatoes with juice

½ teaspoon dried thyme or 1 teaspoon fresh leaves

½ pound lentils (about 1⅛ cups), picked over and rinsed

2 quarts water

A bouquet garni: Parmesan rind, bay leaf, and a few sprigs each of parsley and thyme

Freshly ground pepper

½ cup soup pasta or Arborio rice, or 1 to 1½ cups cooked rice (white or brown)

2 tablespoons chopped fresh parsley (optional)

Freshly grated Parmesan for serving

1. Heat the oil over medium heat in a heavy soup pot or Dutch oven, and add the onion, carrots, and celery. Cook, stirring, until the vegetables are just about tender, about 5 minutes. Add the garlic and a generous pinch of salt and cook, stirring, just until the garlic smells fragrant, 30 seconds to 1 minute. Stir in the tomatoes with their juice, the thyme, and salt to taste. Bring to a simmer and cook, stirring often, until the tomatoes have cooked down somewhat and smell fragrant, about 10 minutes.

2. Stir in the lentils and water and bring to a boil. Add the bouquet garni and reduce the heat to low. Season to taste with salt (about 2 teaspoons to begin with; you will probably add more later). Cover and simmer until the lentils are tender and the broth fragrant, about 1 hour. Discard the bouquet garni.

3. Season the soup with pepper and stir in the pasta or uncooked rice. Simmer until the pasta or rice is tender, another 10 to 15 minutes. (Alternatively, add cooked rice to each bowl when you serve the soup.) Taste and adjust seasonings. Stir in the parsley (if using). Serve, topping each bowlful with a generous spoonful of freshly grated Parmesan.

ADVANCE PREPARATION: The soup keeps well for about 3 days in the refrigerator. However lentil soups tend to thicken, so you will need to add more liquid when you reheat. In addition, the pasta and rice will continue to absorb liquid, so add shortly before serving if you are making the soup ahead. The soup freezes well.

Lentil Minestrone with Leeks, Cabbage, and Kale

VEGAN WITHOUT THE CHEESE /// **MAKES 4 TO 6 SERVINGS**

Lentils and kale make a delicious and attractive match—earthy, savory, vegetal. Cabbage is optional but contributes sweetness to the mix. I wilt it with the leeks and other vegetables in the tomato base, then add the kale to the simmering soup.

Make the *Lentil Minestrone* template (page 45) with the following additional vegetables and specifications:

1 or 2 leeks, cleaned and sliced

½ small head cabbage, chopped or shredded (optional)

1 generous bunch kale (preferably black kale)—about ¾ pound—stemmed, leaves washed thoroughly in 2 changes of water, and cut into strips or chopped

1. In Step 1, after softening the onion, carrots, and celery, add the leeks and a generous pinch of salt. Cook, stirring, until the leeks begin to soften, about 3 minutes. Stir in the cabbage when you add the garlic and salt. Cook, stirring, until the cabbage has begun to wilt and the garlic smells fragrant, about 3 minutes. Continue with the step.

2. In Step 2, add the kale after the lentils have cooked for 45 minutes, and cook for 15 minutes longer, until the lentils and kale are tender and the broth fragrant. Remove the bouquet garni. Taste and adjust the salt.

3. Continue the recipe with Step 3.

ADVANCE PREPARATION: This keeps well for 3 or 4 days in the refrigerator, but the pasta and rice will continue to absorb liquid. Add shortly before serving if you are making the soup ahead.

SUBSTITUTIONS AND ADDITIONS: You can substitute other greens such as chard or turnip greens for the kale.

Hurricane Soup

My sister Melodie and I refer to lentil minestrone with cabbage and kale as Hurricane Soup. I was in New York, staying at Melodie's, in late October, 2012. The day Hurricane Sandy was forecast to hit, I woke up thinking: *Must make soup.* I pulled on some clothes and rushed out to the Gristedes supermarket on 8th Avenue, about a block and a half away from my sister's brownstone in Chelsea. The Gristedes shelves were nearly bare already—I'd never seen so many empty baskets in a produce section. I managed to procure the last onion in the store, some lentils, a couple of sad carrots and leeks, and a cabbage. Melodie had a few provisions and I was able to make her a big pot of minestrone on her electric stove. We sat down to eat it not a minute too soon, as the lights went off just after dinner and didn't come back on for a week. My sister survived on that minestrone throughout the blackout; it is almost as comforting when served cold. She's been making it ever since.

ASIAN NOODLE BOWLS

PACKAGED RAMEN HAS LONG BEEN A standby for the vegetarian who doesn't cook. If you do cook, you can do so much better! I've got two templates for these noodle bowl meals. One is Japanese-Californian in spirit, the other is my vegetarian rendition of Vietnamese *phô*. They make substantial but subtly flavored one-dish meals that consist of a comforting broth, a generous portion of noodles, and vegetables in season. Protein comes in the form of tofu, edamame, or eggs.

Whereas the other soups in this chapter don't require a broth, these do, as the broth stands alone once you've slurped up your noodles and eaten your vegetables. It can be as simple as the Very Simple Kombu Broth (page 49), used in the Japanese-Californian meals in a bowl, the more complex broth for Vegetarian Phô (page 55), or the Kombu and Vegetable Broth (page 50), whose complexity is somewhere in between.

TEMPLATE

Japanese-Californian Meal in a Bowl

VEGAN /// **MAKES 4 SERVINGS**

I first enjoyed a "meal in a bowl" at a restaurant in Berkeley, California. The concept is a simple one: a bowl of comforting broth, noodles, a protein, a vegetable or two, and fresh herbs. I prefer these bowls with rich, earthy, nourishing buckwheat noodles, one of my favorite foods. The soups are warming, filling, and, at the same time, light. They go well with sake, beer, or white wine, or water or green tea.

6 to 8 cups Very Simple Kombu Broth (page 49), Kombu and Vegetable Broth (page 50), or vegetable stock such Porcini Mushroom Stock (page 151)

Soy sauce or salt (or both)

6 ounces Japanese soba noodles, cooked (page 48) and tossed with 2 teaspoons dark sesame, sunflower, or grapeseed oil

6 to 10 ounces vegetables of your choice (see variation recipes, pages 51–54)

6 to 8 ounces tofu (soft or firm), or seasoned baked tofu (homemade, page 31, or store-bought)

1 bunch scallions, thinly sliced, dark green parts kept separate

1. Bring the broth to a simmer. Taste and adjust seasoning, adding soy sauce and/or salt to taste.

2. If the noodles have been refrigerated, warm them by placing them in a strainer and dipping the strainer into the simmering broth. Then distribute the noodles among 4 deep or wide soup bowls.

3. Add the vegetables and tofu to the broth and simmer as instructed (see variation recipes, pages 51–54). Add the white and light green parts of the scallions, cover, and turn off the heat. Allow to sit for 3 minutes.

4. Ladle the soup into the bowls, taking care to distribute the tofu, vegetables, and scallions evenly. Sprinkle the dark green part of the scallions over each serving.

(continued)

ADVANCE PREPARATION: The noodles can be cooked ahead and kept in the refrigerator for a couple of days. The stock can also be made a day or two ahead.

SUBSTITUTIONS AND ADDITIONS:

- *If you wish, you can add 1 to 2 tablespoons miso to the broth when you add the tofu. After the covered soup sits for 3 minutes, stir the soup to dissolve the miso. Serve as directed.*
- *Chives or Chinese chives make a nice substitute for, or addition to, the green part of the scallions.*

How to Cook Japanese Soba Noodles the Traditional Way

Japanese soba noodles are finer and more delicate than any of the American-made brands that I've come across, and this "add-cold-water" method for cooking them works well. The noodles can be cooked ahead and added to soups, salads, and stir-fries, or just eaten as a quick meal. Bring 3 to 4 quarts water to a boil in a large pot. Add the noodles gradually, so that the water remains at a boil, and stir once with a long-handled spoon or pasta fork so that they don't stick together. Wait for the water to come back up to a rolling boil—it will bubble up, so don't fill the pot all the way—and add 1 cup of cold water. Allow the water to come back to a rolling boil and add another cup of cold water. Allow the water to come to a boil one more time and add a third cup of water. When the water comes to a boil again, the noodles should be cooked through. Drain and toss with a little sesame oil or grapeseed oil if not using right away. The noodles can be refrigerated in a plastic bag or in a covered bowl for 3 days.

Very Simple Kombu Broth

VEGAN ////

Kombu, or sea kelp, is the ingredient that gives Japanese soups their iconic flavor, which is vegetal but with a hint of the sea. It's available in natural foods stores and Asian markets, and even in some supermarkets. There is more than one way to make broth using the kombu. The first method yields a very mild broth and is made simply by soaking the kombu in warm water for a day.

MAKES 2 QUARTS

2 (4- to 6-inch) kombu strips

2 quarts warm water

Salt, sugar, and soy sauce, to taste (optional)

MAKES 5 CUPS

1 (4- to 6-inch) kombu strip

5 cups water

Salt, sugar, and soy sauce, to taste (optional)

KOMBU INFUSION

1. Wipe the strips of kombu with a damp paper towel and place in a large bowl. Add the warm water and soak for 6 to 8 hours, or overnight.

2. Remove the kombu from the water. The seaweed will be viscous and the stock slightly viscous. Discard the kombu or use in another dish. Strain the broth and refrigerate until ready to use. Season with salt, a little sugar, and soy sauce if desired.

SIMMERED KOMBU BROTH

Combine the kombu with 5 cups water in a pot. Bring to a simmer, cover, and simmer 20 minutes. Remove the kombu from the broth (discard or use in another dish). Season the broth to taste with salt, a little sugar, and soy sauce if desired.

ADVANCE PREPARATION: Kombu broth can be kept in the refrigerator for a couple of days or frozen.

Kombu and Vegetable Broth

VEGAN /// **MAKES 6½ CUPS**

This has a richer, deeper flavor than the Simple Kombu Broth and is great for meals in a bowl as well as miso soups. Dried shiitakes (black Chinese mushrooms) are the logical variety to use for an Asian broth, but I am more likely to have dried porcinis in my pantry. They yield a broth with a stronger flavor. This is based on a stock in Deborah Madison's *Vegetarian Cooking for Everyone.*

6 dried shiitake mushrooms or a small handful of dried porcinis or other dried mushrooms

1 bunch scallions, sliced, or ½ cup chopped chives

1 (4- to 6-inch) kombu strip

1 medium carrot, thinly sliced

A handful of mushroom stems or a couple of dried shiitakes (optional)

7 cups water

2 to 3 tablespoons soy sauce (to taste)

1 to 2 tablespoons rice wine or mirin (optional)

Salt and sugar (optional)

Combine all the ingredients except the salt and sugar in a saucepan and bring to a simmer. Cover and simmer 20 minutes. Line a strainer with cheesecloth and set over a bowl. Strain the broth, and season to taste with salt and a little sugar if desired.

ADVANCE PREPARATION: This will keep for a couple of days in the refrigerator and freezes well.

Japanese-Californian Meal in a Bowl with Baby Broccoli, Shiitakes, and Tofu

VEGAN //// **MAKES 4 SERVINGS**

Baby broccoli has thinner stems and more delicate, elongated flowers than regular broccoli. It pairs nicely with fresh shiitakes in this variation.

Make the *Japanese-Californian Meal in a Bowl* template (page 47) with the following vegetables and specifications:

6 fresh shiitake mushrooms, stems removed (use for broth if desired), caps thinly sliced

½ pound baby broccoli, flowers detached from the stems, stems peeled if desired and sliced ½ inch thick

At the beginning of Step 3, add the shiitakes and baby broccoli (both stems and flowers) to the broth. Simmer 3 to 4 minutes, until the broccoli is just tender. Add the tofu and continue with the recipe.

ADVANCE PREPARATION: The noodles can be cooked ahead and kept in the refrigerator for a couple of days. The stock can also be made a day or two ahead.

Japanese-Californian Meal in a Bowl with Spinach, Mushrooms, and Tofu

VEGAN /// **MAKES 4 SERVINGS**

I love spinach in anything Japanese, especially when it's barely cooked so that the leaves are just wilted but still bright green, with a bit of texture. Although bagged baby spinach is certainly the most convenient to work with, nothing beats the lush bunches of spinach you get at the farmers' market, and you get a lot more for your money. Spinach in a bag seems stingy in comparison. It's worth the time it takes to wash the sand away—and bunch spinach *does* require two good swishes in a bowl of cold water to remove all the sand.

Make the *Japanese-Californian Meal in a Bowl* template (page 47) with the following vegetables and specifications:

6 medium cremini or white mushrooms, trimmed and thinly sliced; or shiitakes, stems removed, caps thinly sliced

1 (12-ounce) bunch spinach, stemmed, washed in 2 changes of water, and torn into smaller pieces if desired; or 1 (6-ounce) bag baby spinach

Black sesame seeds for garnish (optional)

1. At the beginning of Step 3, add the mushrooms to the broth and simmer 2 minutes. Add the spinach and tofu and simmer 20 seconds. Continue with the recipe.

2. At the end of Step 4, sprinkle each serving with black sesame seeds if desired, and serve.

ADVANCE PREPARATION: The noodles can be cooked ahead and kept in the refrigerator for a couple of days. The stock can also be made a day or two ahead.

Japanese-Californian Meal in a Bowl with Sugar Snap Peas, Shiitakes, and Egg

MAKES 4 SERVINGS

In this variation I use strips of omelet instead of tofu for the protein. The sugar snap peas contribute sweet flavor and crisp texture to the soup.

Make the *Japanese-Californian Meal in a Bowl* template (page 47) with the following additional ingredients and specifications:

4 eggs

2 teaspoons grapeseed or sunflower oil

6 fresh shiitake mushrooms, stems removed (use for stock if desired), caps thinly sliced

½ pound sugar snap peas, trimmed

2 tablespoons chopped cilantro for garnish

1. Before starting the template recipe, beat 2 of the eggs in a medium or small bowl and season to taste with salt. Heat 1 teaspoon grapeseed or sunflower oil over high heat in a wok or an 8- or 10-inch nonstick skillet. When the oil feels hot when you hold your hand above it and a drop of egg sizzles and cooks within seconds of adding it to the pan, add the beaten eggs, scraping them out of the bowl with a rubber spatula. Tilt the wok or pan so that the eggs spread out, and cook until set and beginning to color, which should take less than a minute. Flip over and cook the other side for about 10 seconds, then slide out onto a plate. Repeat with the remaining oil and eggs. Roll up the omelets and cut crosswise into thin strips. Set aside.

2. Proceed with the template recipe, but in Step 3, omit the tofu and just add the shiitakes to the broth. Simmer 2 minutes. Add the sugar snap peas and simmer 2 minutes. Continue with the recipe.

3. In Step 4, after adding the broth and vegetables to each bowl, add a portion of shredded omelet. Garnish with the dark green part of the scallions and chopped cilantro, and serve.

   ADVANCE PREPARATION: The noodles can be cooked ahead and kept in the refrigerator for a couple of days. The stock can also be made a day or two ahead.

VEGETARIAN PHÔ: A VIETNAMESE MEAL IN A BOWL

PHÔ, THE HEARTY VIETNAMESE NOODLE SOUP, is another Asian noodle meal in a bowl that adapts readily to a vegetarian cuisine. Classic *phô* is made with a rich beef stock seasoned with scorched onion and ginger, sugar, fish sauce, and sweet spices like star anise and cinnamon. I make a sweet vegetable broth using lots of root vegetables, and add dried mushrooms to contribute a meaty/umami flavor. I find these soups irresistible and always make extra stock to keep in the freezer.

TEMPLATE

Vegetarian Phô

VEGAN /// **MAKES 6 SERVINGS**

This simple *phô* has the classic ingredients that you would find in a typical Vietnamese restaurant *phô*, minus the meat.

BROTH

1 ounce dried mushrooms, preferably a robust variety like porcinis

3 cups boiling water

1 large onion (about ½ pound), peeled and quartered

1 (3-inch) piece fresh ginger

1½ large leeks (1 pound), halved, cleaned, and thickly sliced

2 medium turnips (about 10 ounces), peeled and cut into wedges

3 large carrots (1 pound), peeled if desired and thickly sliced

2 ounces mushroom stems (from about 8 ounces mushrooms), or 4 dried shiitakes

1 head garlic, cut in half

2 stalks lemongrass, trimmed, smashed with the side of a knife, and sliced

Salt

1 to 1½ tablespoons sugar (to taste), preferably raw brown sugar

1. For the broth: Place the dried mushrooms in a large measuring cup or bowl and cover with the boiling water. Let sit for 20 to 30 minutes while you prepare the other ingredients.

2. Scorch the onion and ginger by holding the pieces above a gas flame with tongs, or in a dry skillet over high heat if using an electric stove. Turn the pieces of onion and the ginger until scorched black in places on all sides. When cool enough to handle, slice the ginger lengthwise.

3. Line a strainer with cheesecloth, place over a bowl, and drain the mushrooms. Squeeze them over the strainer to extract all of their flavorful juices. Set the mushrooms aside for another purpose (like adding to the *phô* later). Combine the broth with enough water to measure 3 quarts in a large soup pot.

4. To the broth, add the scorched onion and ginger, the leeks, turnips, carrots, mushroom stems, garlic, lemongrass, salt to taste, and 1 tablespoon sugar. Bring to a boil. Tie the anise pods, cloves, peppercorns, and cinnamon stick in a cheesecloth bag and add to the soup. Reduce the heat, cover, and simmer gently for 2 hours. Pour through a cheesecloth-lined strainer set over a bowl. Taste and adjust salt and sugar.

(continued)

6 star anise pods

5 whole cloves

1 tablespoon black peppercorns

1 (2- to 3-inch) cinnamon stick

FINISHED PHÔ

Vegetables of your choice (see variation recipes, page 58)

6 ounces tofu or Baked Seasoned Tofu (page 31), diced

¾ pound wide rice noodles

1 cup chopped cilantro

½ cup fresh Asian or purple basil leaves, slivered

3 shallots, sliced paper-thin, separated into rings, and soaked for 5 minutes in cold water, then drained and rinsed

4 scallions, chopped

2 cups mung bean sprouts

2 to 4 bird or serrano chiles (to taste), seeded (if desired) and finely chopped

Several sprigs fresh mint

3 to 4 limes, cut into wedges

5. To finish the *phô*: Bring the broth to a simmer in a soup pot. Add vegetables if directed in the variation recipe. Add the tofu, turn off the heat, and cover the pot to keep hot.

6. Bring a large pot of water to a boil (see Note) and add the noodles. Cook until just al dente, following the timing instructions on the package (my wide noodles take about 5 minutes). Drain and divide among 6 large soup bowls.

7. Ladle in a generous amount of hot broth, along with any additional vegetables (see variations) that have simmered in the broth and the tofu. Sprinkle on half the cilantro, half the basil, the shallots, and scallions. Pass the remaining basil, cilantro, bean sprouts, chiles, mint sprigs, and lime wedges at the table. Serve with chopsticks for the noodles and soup spoons for the broth.

NOTE: You can cook the noodles directly in the broth if you don't want to use another pot, but they will be easier to distribute among the bowls if they're cooked separately.

ADVANCE PREPARATION: The broth will keep for a few days in the refrigerator and can be frozen. The noodles can be cooked several hours ahead. Rinse them after draining and keep in a bowl. Just before serving reheat by dunking briefly into a pot of simmering water and draining (it helps to place them in a strainer or pasta pot insert).

Vegetarian Phô with Carrots, Daikon, and Tofu

VEGAN /// **MAKES 6 SERVINGS**

You can make this in the springtime with the tender young carrots that arrive in your CSA basket, or in the winter with older, large carrots, which some farmers tell me are even sweeter than their spring counterparts.

Make the *Vegetarian Phô* template (page 55) with the following additional vegetables and specifications:

1 large or 2 medium carrots, peeled if desired and cut into 2-inch julienne (about 2 cups)

1 daikon radish, peeled and cut into 2-inch julienne (about 2 cups)

In Step 5, add the carrots and daikon and simmer 2 minutes. Add the tofu. Turn off the heat and cover the pot to keep hot. Continue with the recipe.

ADVANCE PREPARATION: The broth will keep for a few days in the refrigerator and can be frozen. The noodles can be cooked several hours ahead. Rinse them after draining and keep in a bowl. Just before serving reheat by dunking briefly into a pot of simmering water and draining (it helps to place them in a strainer or pasta pot insert).

Vegetarian Phô with Kohlrabi, Golden Beets, and Beet Greens

VEGAN /// **MAKES 6 SERVINGS**

Beets and beet greens add color, sweetness, and earthiness to this nourishing *phô*. I use golden beets so that the color isn't pink, but if you don't mind pink *phô* you could use red or Chioggia beets. Make sure to peel the kohlrabi thoroughly. You need to peel away the fibrous layer underneath the skin.

Make the *Vegetarian Phô* template (page 55) with the following additional vegetables and specifications:

3 medium golden beets, peeled and cut into half-moons or julienne

2 small kohlrabi bulbs, peeled and cut into julienne

1 bunch beet greens, stemmed and washed thoroughly in 2 changes of water, then stacked and cut into ½-inch-wide strips

In Step 5, add the beets and simmer 10 to 15 minutes, until tender. Add the kohlrabi and simmer 3 minutes, until crisp-tender. Add the beet greens and simmer 2 minutes. Add the tofu. Turn off the heat and cover the pot to keep hot. Continue with the recipe.

ADVANCE PREPARATION: The broth will keep for a few days in the refrigerator and can be frozen. The noodles can be cooked several hours ahead. Rinse them after draining and keep in a bowl. Just before serving reheat by dunking briefly into a pot of simmering water and draining (it helps to place them in a strainer or pasta pot insert).

PUREED VEGETABLE SOUPS

WHEN I WAS 31, I MOVED to Paris for an "open-ended year"—and ended up staying for 12. Right away I was struck by how natural it was for people to make soup. A friend of a friend invited me for lunch the day after I arrived and served me a soup not unlike the one in the template on page 60, made with carrots, turnips, potatoes, and leeks and seasoned with salt and lots of pepper. It is more than 30 years since I ate that meal and I can still taste the soup.

In Paris, time and again I would sit down to a simple luscious pureed soup prepared, with no great fanfare, by a friend or acquaintance. It was simply what people made for dinner after work. We would chat while the soup simmered, then my host or hostess would put the contents of the soup pot through a food mill, or insert a hand blender and puree the mixture. Some cooks enriched the puree with crème fraîche while others did not.

These soups are not classic rich veloutés thickened with roux and requiring stock—the kind you learn to make in cooking school—but simple affairs made with water and vegetables that rely on potatoes or rice for thickening. The French may throw in a bouillon cube, and you can too, but stock isn't required; I only make stock when I remember to simmer the vegetable trimmings for about 30 minutes while I'm preparing my ingredients. The soup will be as good as the produce that goes into it, as long as you season it sufficiently with salt and pepper. Which is the key to just about any good simple vegetarian dish.

Garnishes for Pureed Soups

I like to garnish pureed soups with something that has a contrasting texture, like regular croutons or garlic croutons (page 65), and/or with herbs that contribute a contrasting color and/or a compatible but attention-getting flavor. It's also nice to garnish a pureed soup with a drizzle of olive oil or flavored oil, or a swirl of crème fraîche or yogurt. See individual recipes for suggestions.

Choosing a Hand Blender

The most effective hand blenders are those that have the strongest motors. Search online and read reviews. My Braun M30 is good for some things, but the motor, which is in the 200-watt range, is not nearly as effective as the heavier Wolfgang Puck hand blender I have (550 watts). Something in between would be fine.

Pureed Vegetable Soup

VEGAN //// **MAKES 4 TO 6 SERVINGS**

This simple outline calls for minimal aromatics (onion, sometimes garlic, sometimes carrots or celery), 1 to 2 pounds of vegetables (the weight varies because different vegetables will yield different volumes once cooked—think spinach vs. winter squash), seasonings, a potato or two or some rice to thicken, and 1½ to 2 quarts water or stock. Leeks, celery, and carrots will contribute to the flavor, but they will also add color, which you may or may not want if, say, you're making a puree of cauliflower soup. Sometimes the defining soup vegetables are cooked along with the onion at the beginning of the process, other times they're added with the water or stock.

1 tablespoon extra virgin olive oil

1 medium onion, chopped

Salt

1 to 2 pounds vegetable of your choice (see variation recipes, pages 61–64), chopped or diced

4 to 6 ounces starchy potato, such as a russet (½ large) or Yukon gold (1 medium), peeled and diced; or ¼ to ⅓ cup medium-grain rice, such as Arborio

6 to 8 cups (see Note) water or vegetable stock (pages 149–151)

A bouquet garni: a bay leaf and a couple sprigs each of thyme and parsley (some recipes include a Parmesan rind)

Freshly ground pepper

1. Heat the olive oil over medium heat in a large, heavy soup pot or Dutch oven and add the onion, and a generous pinch of salt. Cook, stirring, until tender, about 5 minutes. Do not allow these ingredients to brown. The pinch of salt you add with the onion should prevent this from happening, as the salt draws out liquid from the vegetables.

2. Add the vegetable(s) of choice, potatoes or rice, water, bouquet garni, and more salt (I start with 1 teaspoon salt per quart of water but I always add more), and bring to a boil. Reduce the heat, cover, and simmer until the vegetables are tender, 30 minutes to 1 hour (depending on the vegetables). Remove the bouquet garni.

3. Using a hand blender, or in batches in a regular blender, puree the soup. (If using a regular blender, fill only halfway and cover the top with a towel pulled down tight, rather than airtight with the lid, because hot soup will jump and push the top off if the blender is closed airtight.) If you have a food mill, you can also use that to puree the soup; that's the old-fashioned French way and it will give you a puree that still has a lot of texture. For a really smooth puree with no lingering fibers, after you blend the soup, put it through a medium strainer.

4. Return the soup to the pot and heat through, stirring. Season to taste with salt and pepper.

NOTE: The amount of liquid depends on the vegetable used and the desired thickness.

ADVANCE PREPARATION: This depends on the vegetable, but most pureed soups will keep for a couple of days in the refrigerator. They may require thinning out with water, stock, or milk when you reheat them, and you will want to whisk briskly to restore the consistency. If you freeze the soup, blend it again after it's thawed, before reheating it.

SUBSTITUTIONS AND ADDITIONS: Substitute unsalted butter for the olive oil in the template and in any of the recipes that follow.

VARIATION

Pureed Carrot and Leek Soup with Mint or Tarragon

VEGAN /// **MAKES 4 SERVINGS**

This is a riff on a French classic, *potage Crécy*. Butter gives way to olive oil in my version and the soup is garnished with fresh mint or with tarragon and chives, all of which I love with carrots. If you can't get hold of leeks—or just don't feel like going out and buying them—you can make a perfectly good version of this using two onions instead of one.

Make the *Pureed Vegetable Soup* template (opposite page) with the following additional ingredients and specifications:

2 medium leeks (about 1 pound), white and light green parts only, halved lengthwise, well cleaned, and thinly sliced

1½ pounds carrots, peeled if desired and thinly sliced

A bouquet garni: a couple of sprigs each of mint and parsley

Chopped fresh mint, or tarragon and/or chives, for garnish

Optional garnishes: A drizzle of olive oil or crème fraîche, toasted croutons, black sesame seeds

1. Add the leeks and carrots with a big pinch of salt in Step 1 (rather than Step 2), after you have cooked the onion. Continue to cook, stirring, until the leeks are tender, 3 to 5 minutes. Do not allow the ingredients to brown.

2. In Step 2, use ¼ cup rice, 6 cups of water or stock, and the bouquet garni. Continue with the recipe.

3. To serve, garnish each bowl with chopped fresh mint, or tarragon and/or chives. If desired, drizzle with olive oil or crème fraîche and sprinkle with black sesame seeds.

ADVANCE PREPARATION: This will keep for a couple of days in the refrigerator. It may require thinning out with water, stock, or milk when you reheat it, and you will want to whisk briskly to restore the consistency. If you freeze the soup, when you thaw it blend it again before reheating.

Pureed Sweet Potato Soup with Coconut, Apple, and Ginger

VEGAN /// **MAKES 4 SERVINGS**

In this recipe I use coconut oil to soften the onion. It's a small amount, but its flavor carries through from the beginning to the end of cooking. A beautiful marriage of flavors in a light soup that tastes rich.

Make the *Pureed Vegetable Soup* template (page 60) with the following additional ingredients and specifications:

1 tablespoon coconut oil

1 tablespoon minced fresh ginger

1 large, fairly tart apple, such as a Braeburn or Pink Lady, peeled, cored, and diced

1¼ pounds sweet potatoes, peeled and diced

½ pound carrots, peeled and diced

1 medium (about 6 ounces) Yukon gold or russet potato, peeled and diced

Thinly sliced or julienned apples tossed with a little lime juice for garnish

Coconut oil, coconut milk, crème fraîche, or plain yogurt for serving (optional)

1. In Step 1, substitute the coconut oil for the olive oil and add the minced fresh ginger after softening the onion. Cook, stirring, until fragrant, 30 seconds to 1 minute.

2. In Step 2, add the apple, sweet potatoes, carrots, potato, water or stock, and bouquet garni and simmer the soup for 45 minutes. Continue with the recipe through Step 3.

3. In Step 4, when you return the pureed soup to the pot, whisk to even out the texture. Heat through and adjust salt. Garnish with the sliced or julienned apples and a drizzle of coconut oil, coconut milk, crème fraîche, or yogurt and serve.

ADVANCE PREPARATION: This will keep for a couple of days in the refrigerator. It's best, though, when freshly made.

Pureed Spinach Soup with Middle Eastern Spices

MAKES 4 TO 6 SERVINGS

This pureed soup requires a little more rice than my template recipe calls for, because the main vegetable is spinach, which is added after the rice has cooked and has little in it to bulk up the soup. Celery and spices contribute lots of flavor, and the yogurt that's stirred in at the end adds a welcome tang that finishes the soup in a delightful way.

Make the *Pureed Vegetable Soup* template (page 60) with the following additional ingredients and specifications:

⅓ cup finely diced celery

2 large garlic cloves, minced

1½ pounds fresh spinach, stemmed and washed thoroughly in 2 changes of water

¼ teaspoon ground allspice

¼ teaspoon ground cinnamon

⅛ teaspoon ground cloves

⅛ teaspoon freshly grated nutmeg

1 scant teaspoon coriander seeds, lightly toasted and ground

1 teaspoon cornstarch

1 cup drained yogurt (see page 140) or Greek yogurt

Optional garnish: 1 small garlic clove, 1 cup drained yogurt (page 140)

¼ to ⅓ cup chopped walnuts for garnish

1. In Step 1, add the celery and garlic when you add the onion.

2. In Step 2, use ½ cup rice and water or stock. Stir in the spinach and spices after the rice is tender. Cover and simmer 5 minutes, stirring once or twice. The spinach should wilt but should retain its bright color. Proceed with Step 3.

3. After pureeing the soup, whisk 1 teaspoon cornstarch into the yogurt, and whisk into the soup. Season to taste with salt and pepper and heat through.

4. If you want a pungent, garlicky yogurt garnish, mash the small garlic clove to a paste with a pinch of salt in a mortar and pestle. Stir into 1 cup drained yogurt. Serve the soup, garnishing each bowl with a swirl of the yogurt and a sprinkling of chopped walnuts.

ADVANCE PREPARATION: You can make this several hours before you serve it but you will lose the bright green color. If you are making it ahead, the soup will look brighter if you wait until just before serving to stir in the yogurt.

GARLIC SOUP & CO.

GARLIC SOUP AND SCRAMBLED EGGS are the two meals I turn to most often when I haven't given dinner a thought until it's 6 pm and we're hungry. Assuming you have garlic and a couple of eggs (or not; you can go vegan with this), garlic soup will open up a number of possibilities for you—even if you think you have nothing on hand for dinner. Look around. Do you have some stale bread? Soup pasta? Rice? Other grains, uncooked or frozen? Is there one stalk of broccoli lingering in the produce bin in your fridge? Some peas in the freezer? Or some parsley or sage in the garden? There are many ways you can go with garlic soup, any number of vegetables you can add to make a meal of it, and a quickly prepared meal at that.

TEMPLATE

Garlic Soup

MAKES 4 SERVINGS

The bare bones Provençal garlic soup is a garlic broth with no vegetables added. I rarely have no vegetables on hand to add, however. At a minimum, peas from the freezer will work. But garlic soup can be as big or as minimal as you want it to be. Note: This is a last minute soup.

2 quarts water

3 to 6 large garlic cloves (to taste), minced or put through a press, plus 1 garlic clove, cut in half

Salt and freshly ground pepper

1 bay leaf

$\frac{1}{4}$ to $\frac{1}{2}$ teaspoon dried thyme, or a few sprigs fresh thyme, or 2 to 3 fresh sage leaves

4 thick slices country style bread or French bread, or $\frac{1}{3}$ to $\frac{1}{2}$ cup soup pasta

2 large eggs, beaten

1 tablespoon extra virgin olive oil (optional)

2 tablespoons chopped fresh flat-leaf parsley

2 to 3 tablespoons freshly grated Parmesan or Gruyère cheese

1. Bring the water to a boil in a 3- to 4-quart saucepan or soup pot. Add the minced or pressed garlic, salt (I usually use about 2 teaspoons), bay leaf, and thyme or sage. Cover and simmer 15 minutes. Taste and adjust salt.

2. Toast the bread. As soon as it's done, rub both sides with the cut clove of garlic. Set the croutons aside. If you don't have bread but do have some pasta or rice, add $\frac{1}{3}$ to $\frac{1}{2}$ cup to the soup and simmer until al dente. (Or go crazy and use both!)

3. Beat together the eggs and olive oil (if using). Spoon a ladleful of the hot soup into the eggs and stir together. Then turn off the heat under the soup and stir in the egg mixture. The eggs should cloud the soup but they shouldn't scramble. They won't if the soup isn't boiling. Stir in the parsley and pepper to taste. Discard the bay leaf.

4. Place a garlic crouton in each bowl. Ladle in the soup, sprinkle Parmesan or Gruyère over the top, and serve.

SUBSTITUTIONS AND ADDITIONS: To make the soup with poached eggs, omit the 2 beaten eggs. Instead, poach 4 eggs as directed on page 32, placing one in each bowl when you serve the soup. You can use this substitution in any of the variation recipes.

Garlic Soup with Green Vegetables

MAKES 4 SERVINGS

This is how I vary my garlic soups: I add different green vegetables. It's a great thing to do with vegetables when you don't have quite enough to make 4 side dish servings; instead they contribute to a main dish soup. If you have leftover cooked vegetables, you can just reheat them in the broth.

Make the *Garlic Soup* template (page 65) with the following additional vegetables and specifications:

6 to 8 ounces broccoli, asparagus, shelled peas, green beans, fava beans, or sugar snap peas

Break broccoli into small florets; cut asparagus into ¹/₂- to 1-inch lengths; top and tail green beans and break in half; top sugar snap peas. Add the vegetables to the soup at the end of Step 1 and simmer 5 to 10 minutes, depending on how soft you want the vegetables to be. They should remain bright. Proceed with the recipe as directed.

ADVANCE PREPARATION: This is a last-minute soup.

Garlic Soup with Greens

MAKES 4 SERVINGS

In the Mediterranean, wild greens often find their way into garlic soup. Living in Los Angeles, I'm more likely to use greens from the farmers' market or supermarket. The soup is a very nice destination for a small bunch. Sometimes I'll blanch or wilt strong-tasting greens like kale separately because though I find the strong flavors welcome in a rustic minestrone, I don't want them overpowering my simple garlic soup. To blanch kale, bring a separate pot of water to a boil, salt generously, and add the kale. Blanch for 2 to 3 minutes and transfer to a bowl of cold water. Drain, squeeze out excess water and chop coarsely or cut into slivers. If using chard or spinach just wash and chop coarsely.

Make the *Garlic Soup* template (page 65) with the following additional vegetables and specifications:

8 to 12 ounces (1 small or medium bunch) kale, chard, or spinach

Stem the greens, wash thoroughly in 2 rinses of water, and blanch if you like. Proceed with the recipe, stirring in the greens in Step 3 a few mintues before adding the eggs.

ADVANCE PREPARATION: This is a last-minute soup.

Garlic Soup with Potatoes

MAKES 4 SERVINGS

This is one of my favorite garlic soup variations. You can also add green vegetables to this variation. Don't add pasta though; the potatoes contribute enough starch. It's a very comforting soup and makes a great, quick winter meal.

Make the *Garlic Soup* template (page 65) with the following additional vegetable and specifications:

½ pound moderately starchy potatoes like Yukon golds or fingerlings

Peel, slice, or dice the potatoes and add to the water at the beginning of Step 1. Proceed with the recipe as directed.

ADVANCE PREPARATION: This is a last-minute soup.

SUBSTITUTIONS AND ADDITIONS: If you wish to also add green vegetables or greens to this version, add them at the end of Step 1, when the potatoes are tender. Simmer until the vegetables are tender and proceed with Step 2.

Garlic Soup with Rice or Whole Grains

MAKES 4 SERVINGS

I love the way cooked rice and other grains absorb the garlic broth. You can make this into a hearty soup if you use farro, spelt, brown rice, or barley, all of which you should cook separately as they take a long time and absorb a lot of liquid. White rice, bulgur, and quinoa can be cooked in the broth or cooked before. If using grains, you can omit the croutons if desired; and do not use soup pasta.

Make the *Garlic Soup* template (page 65) with the following additional ingredient and specifications:

⅓ to ½ cup uncooked white rice, medium or coarse bulgur, or quinoa (blond or red); or 1 to 1¼ cups cooked grains such as brown rice, farro, spelt, bulgur, quinoa, or barley

If using uncooked grains, add to the water at the beginning of Step 1 and simmer until tender, 15 minutes. If using cooked grains, warm and spoon into the soup bowls. Proceed with the recipe as directed.

ADVANCE PREPARATION: The soup is last minute, but cooked grains will keep for 3 or 4 days in the refrigerator.

CHAPTER THREE

Frittatas and Omelets

A FARM-FRESH EGG, WITH ITS ORANGE yolk and sturdy white, is a perfect little package of luxury. More than one, scrambled until creamy, or wrapped around vegetables in an omelet, or mixed with cooked greens, asparagus, melted onions and fennel, grated zucchini, or the leftovers of last night's risotto for a frittata, is heaven. Eggs, for me, are the ultimate comfort food.

I grew up eating eggs for breakfast—scrambled, fried, or poached, nothing more complex than that. Then one night when I was a high school senior taking a weekend break from boarding school at my history teacher's house, she prepared an eggplant and tomato frittata for me. I can still taste it. I had eaten French omelets before, but I'd never had a Mediterranean frittata, and that opened up a world of possibilities for savory egg dinners that I have not yet finished exploring.

Eggs need a good public relations firm to take on their cause. They haven't been able to redeem their reputation as a healthy food since people became so worried about the high cholesterol content of eggs in the 1970s and 1980s and then the possibility of salmonella contamination after the outbreaks in the '90s. Even though we now know that dietary cholesterol does not go directly into our bloodstream and then into our arteries when we eat it (and that saturated fats and trans fats are much more instrumental in raising blood cholesterol levels than eggs), people still eschew them (or their yolks, where most of the flavor and nutrients reside). The Harvard School of Public Health has published articles that absolve eggs of all the dietary myths we've grown up with. The fact is, they are a good source of nutrients, with 6 to 8 grams of protein (depending on the size) and micronutrients like choline, which has been linked to preserving memory, and lutein and zeaxanthin, which are good for your eyes. When I eat an egg I feel somehow that I've eaten something that is nutritionally complete. As for the salmonella, cooking eggs will kill any bacteria, and farm-fresh pastured eggs, which I recommend in any case, are not nearly as susceptible to begin with.

Whenever anybody tells me that vegetarian cooking takes too long, I pull out my omelet pan. Because eggs cook so quickly they make the perfect vegetarian convenience food. They're a wonderful vehicle for all kinds of vegetables, and also for leftovers, and they've empowered me to come home from many a late soccer game and get dinner on the table in 15 minutes.

Note: All of the eggs called for in these recipes should be large or extra-large, and preferably free-range from a small producer.

FRITTATAS

FRITTATAS MAKE QUICK AND SATISFYING DINNERS for two to six. A puffed-up frittata for two, filled with seasoned greens and Parmesan or Gruyère (or with mushrooms that have seen better days—but that I can still coax some succulence out of if I sauté them with garlic and herbs, page 11) is a go-to meal that's always a possibility, even when I think the cupboards are bare.

As for fillings, frittatas are terrific vehicles for just about any cooked vegetable. The classic Spanish frittata, *tortilla española*, is filled with sliced potatoes and chopped onions fried in copious amounts of olive oil. The iconic Provençal frittata, *truccha*, is filled with blanched Swiss chard and lots of garlic. The variety of frittatas you'll find in Italy rivals the variety of pizzas. In my home they often serve as a delicious recipient of leftover stews, ratatouille, and risottos (a favorite).

The quality of the eggs you use for frittatas really does matter. Thin-shelled, anemically pale-yolked eggs from large commercial operations, known as *battery eggs,* can't measure up against the deep yellow-orange–yolked free-range eggs I buy at the farmers' market. These eggs have more body to them too; you can tell they're stronger because the shells don't crack as easily as regular commercial eggs. The frittatas you make with fresh organic free-range eggs will be fluffier and will taste better.

TEMPLATE

Basic Frittata

MAKES ONE 2- TO 8-EGG FRITTATA

This template gives you instructions for making a range of serving sizes, from the 2-egg frittata for one to an 8-egg frittata for six—or for a crowd if you serve it as an appetizer. The technique for a frittata containing more than 4 eggs is a little different for a 2- or 4-egg frittata, because the smaller frittatas cook more quickly and don't require any slow, covered cooking. I finish larger frittatas under the broiler.

2 to 8 eggs

Salt and freshly ground pepper

1 to 2 tablespoons milk (2 percent or whole; I use 1 tablespoon for every 4 eggs)

The filling of your choice (see variation recipes, pages 73–77)

1 tablespoon extra virgin olive oil

1. Beat the eggs in a large bowl. Stir in salt and pepper to taste, the milk, and filling.

2. Heat the olive oil over medium-high heat in a heavy 8-inch nonstick skillet. Hold your hand above it; it should feel hot. Drop a bit of egg into the pan and if it sizzles and seizes at once, the pan is ready. Pour in the egg mixture. Swirl the pan to distribute the eggs and filling evenly over the surface. During the first few minutes of cooking, shake the pan gently and tilt it slightly with one hand while lifting up the edges of the frittata with a wooden or heatproof silicone spatula in your other hand, letting the eggs run underneath.

2- OR 4-EGG FRITTATA:

Use an 8-inch skillet. A 2-egg frittata will be done quickly, with just the tilting of the pan and letting the eggs run underneath until it is no longer or only slightly moist on the top (the way the French like them). Once it is set, slide it out of the pan onto a plate. If you do want to brown it on the other side you can flip it over, either with a spatula or by pushing the pan away from you, then with a quick jerk of the wrist quickly pulling it toward you and jerking the pan upward at the same time. Cook for only a few seconds on the other side, then reverse out of the pan. You will probably want to flip a 4-egg frittata and cook it on the other side. (Or you can run it under the broiler briefly, see Step 3). To

(continued)

flip it: Use a wide spatula or the jerking motion I just described. Or, slide it onto a dinner plate or a saucepan lid with a handle (this is handy; in Spain they have a special implement that looks like a lid, just for flipping tortillas), then place the pan—upside down—over the plate or lid. Being careful not to touch the pan, hold the plate (or lid) and pan together, flip the pan back to its upright position, and place on the stove. (I can do this with an 8-inch pan, but not with a larger one.) Cook on the top of the stove for another minute or two to set the eggs. Slide out of the pan onto a plate or platter. Continue with Step 4.

6- OR 8-EGG FRITTATA:

For larger frittatas, after the bottom has set, you will cover and cook the frittata over low heat before finishing under the broiler. Use a heavy 10-inch nonstick skillet. Begin cooking as directed in Step 2. Once a few layers of egg have cooked during the first couple of minutes on the stove, turn the heat down to low, cover (use a pizza pan if you don't have a lid that will fit your skillet), and cook for 10 minutes, shaking the pan gently every once in a while. From time to time, remove the lid and loosen the bottom of the frittata by sliding your spatula between the bottom of the frittata and the pan, tilting the pan and allowing egg on the top to run underneath, so that the bottom doesn't burn. It will, however, turn golden. The eggs should be just about set, with a thin wet layer on top; cook a few minutes longer if they're not.

3. Meanwhile, heat the broiler. Uncover the pan and place the frittata under the broiler, not too close to the heat, for 1 to 3 minutes, watching very carefully to make sure the top doesn't burn (it can brown in spots and puff under the broiler, but burnt eggs taste bitter). Remove from the heat, shake the pan to make sure the frittata isn't sticking, and allow it to cool for at least 5 minutes or up to 15. Loosen the edges with your spatula and carefully slide from the pan onto a large round platter.

4. Allow to cool completely if desired. Cut into wedges or into smaller bite-size diamonds. Serve hot, warm, at room temperature, or cold.

ADVANCE PREPARATION: In Mediterranean countries, frittatas are served at room temperature, which makes them perfect do-ahead dishes. They'll keep in the refrigerator for 2 to 3 days. They do not reheat well but they're good cold or at room temperature.

4-Egg Frittata with Broccoli Raab and Mushrooms

MAKES ONE 8-INCH FRITTATA, SERVING 2 TO 3

One Monday night I pulled some broccoli raab I'd blanched and frozen from the freezer, some farm-fresh eggs, mushrooms, and good Parmesan from the fridge, and put together this beautiful dinner for two. I loved the way the frittata puffed up in the 8-inch pan.

Make the *Basic Frittata* template (page 71) with the following filling ingredients and specifications:

Additional 1 tablespoon extra virgin olive oil

6 to 8 cremini mushrooms, sliced

1 garlic clove, minced

½ bunch broccoli raab, blanched (see page 5) and chopped medium-fine

1 ounce Parmesan, freshly grated (¼ cup)

1. Heat 1 tablespoon olive oil over medium-high heat in a heavy 8-inch nonstick omelet pan. When hot, add the mushrooms and cook until they begin to color and sweat, about 3 minutes. Reduce the heat to medium, add a generous pinch of salt and the garlic, and stir just until fragrant, about 30 seconds. Stir in the blanched broccoli raab. Stir together for a minute, until the mushrooms are tender. Add salt and pepper to taste, and remove from the heat.

2. In Step 1, use 4 eggs, 1 tablespoon milk, and ¼ teaspoon salt. Stir in the mushrooms, broccoli raab, and Parmesan. Wipe the omelet pan clean.

3. Proceed with Step 2, using the omelet pan, then follow the recipe instructions for a 2- to 4-egg frittata.

ADVANCE PREPARATION: Blanched broccoli raab will keep in the refrigerator for 3 days and can be frozen. The greens and mushrooms filling will also keep for 3 days but taste best when freshly seasoned. The frittata can be made a day or two ahead and served cold or at room temperature.

10-Egg Frittatas

Large 10-egg frittatas, which I make in my big heavy 12-inch nonstick skillet, are my quick go-to dishes for entertaining of all kinds, from brunch to cocktail parties to dinners. I like to cut them into small diamonds and serve them on a buffet or pass them as hors d'oeuvres. Because they're easy to transport and have great staying power, they also make great lunchbox and picnic fare. Any of the frittata recipes in this chapter can be made with 10 eggs in a 12-inch pan. You may want to increase the amount of filling proportionally, and increase the amount of milk to 3 tablespoons. The technique and timing is the same as with 8-egg frittatas.

8-Egg Frittata with Asparagus, Fresh Peas, Tarragon, and Chives

MAKES ONE 10-INCH FRITTATA, SERVING 4 TO 6

You can get asparagus pretty much year-round in natural foods markets and supermarkets, and in California it's almost always available at farmers' markets. But it's a spring and early summer vegetable in temperate climates, as are peas.

Make the *Basic Frittata* template (page 71) with the following filling ingredients and specifications:

¾ pound asparagus, trimmed

¾ cup shelled fresh peas (1 pound in the pod)

2 tablespoons chopped fresh chives

2 tablespoons chopped fresh tarragon

¼ cup freshly grated Parmesan (optional)

1. Steam the asparagus until tender, about 5 minutes. Refresh with cold water, drain, and pat dry. Cut into ½-inch slices. Steam the peas for 5 minutes, until tender.

2. In Step 1, use 8 eggs, 2 tablespoons milk, and ½ teaspoon salt. Stir in the chives, tarragon, asparagus, peas, and Parmesan (if using).

3. Proceed with Step 2, using a 10-inch skillet, then follow the recipe instructions for a 6- to 8-egg frittata.

ADVANCE PREPARATION: The asparagus can be prepared a day ahead and kept in the refrigerator. The frittata can be prepared several hours or even a day ahead, covered, and refrigerated until shortly before serving. It does not reheat well but it's good cold or at room temperature.

8-Egg Frittata with Chard or Beet Greens and Green Garlic

MAKES ONE 10-INCH FRITTATA, SERVING 4 TO 6

During most of the year, when green garlic isn't available, you can use regular garlic for this typical Provençal and Italian frittata. It can be thrown together quickly if you make a point of washing and blanching or steaming greens when you get them home from the market. It works best with the more tender greens like chard and beet greens.

Make the *Basic Frittata* template (page 71) with the following filling ingredients and specifications:

Additional 1 tablespoon extra virgin olive oil

1 bulb green garlic, papery shells removed, minced; or 2 large garlic cloves, minced

1 teaspoon minced fresh thyme (optional)

1 teaspoon minced fresh rosemary (optional)

1 generous bunch Swiss chard (any color) or beet greens (about 1 pound), wilted (see page 2) and chopped medium-fine

1. Heat 1 tablespoon oil over medium heat in a heavy 10-inch nonstick skillet and add the garlic and optional thyme and rosemary. Cook, stirring, until the garlic is fragrant, about 1 minute for green garlic, 30 seconds for regular. Stir in the chopped wilted greens. Cook, stirring, for about 1 minute, until coated with oil. Season to taste with salt and pepper and remove from the heat. Wipe the skillet clean.

2. In Step 1, use 8 eggs, 2 tablespoons milk, and ½ teaspoon salt. Stir the greens into the beaten eggs.

3. Proceed with Step 2, using the same skillet, then follow the recipe instructions for a 6- to 8-egg frittata.

   ADVANCE PREPARATION: The greens can be wilted up to 3 days ahead and the filling prepared through Step 1 several hours ahead. The frittata can be made a few hours or a day ahead and served at room temperature.

   SUBSTITUTIONS AND ADDITIONS: For a cheesy frittata, stir 2 to 3 ounces (½ to ¾ cup) crumbled feta or 2 ounces (½ cup) grated Parmesan or Gruyère (or a combination) into the beaten eggs along with the greens.

8-Egg Frittata with Onions and Walnuts

MAKES ONE 10-INCH FRITTATA, SERVING 4 TO 6

Inspired by a classic Provençal frittata but infused with a little Iranian influence (the walnuts), this is a sweet tasting frittata that I like to serve at room temperature.

Make the *Basic Frittata* template (page 71) with the following filling ingredients and specifications:

Melted Onions (page 10), made with 1 pound onions (preferably spring onions) and omitting the capers

⅓ cup finely chopped walnuts

¼ cup finely chopped fresh flat-leaf parsley

1. In Step 1, use 8 eggs, 2 tablespoons milk, and ½ teaspoon salt. Stir in the onions, walnuts, and parsley.

2. Proceed with Step 2, using a 10-inch skillet, then follow the recipe instructions for a 6- to 8-egg frittata.

ADVANCE PREPARATION: The melted onions will keep for at least 4 days in the refrigerator. The frittata can be made up to a day ahead.

8-Egg Frittata with Pipérade

MAKES ONE 10-INCH FRITTATA, SERVING 4 TO 6

Pipérade, the Basque mix of stewed sweet and hot peppers, is traditionally stirred into scrambled eggs, but this is a more portable dish that can be eaten at room temperature. The best time to make this is late summer, when the market is teeming with all sorts of sweet peppers and chiles.

Make the *Basic Frittata* template (page 71) with the following filling ingredient and specifications:

2 cups Pipérade (page 8)

1. In Step 1, use 8 eggs, 2 tablespoons milk, and ½ teaspoon salt. Stir in the pipérade.

2. Proceed with Step 2, using a 10-inch skillet, then follow the recipe instructions for a 6- to 8-egg frittata.

ADVANCE PREPARATION: The pipérade will keep for 4 to 5 days in the refrigerator. The frittata will keep in the refrigerator for 2 to 3 days.

BAKED FRITTATAS

FRITTATAS CAN ALSO BE BAKED IN the oven, as they often are in Tunisia and Greece. They puff up nicely, especially if the frittata also contains yogurt or ricotta, as many Greek and Italian frittatas do. The yogurt or ricotta can stand in for some of the eggs; you'll get the same size frittata using 6 eggs and ½ cup yogurt or ricotta as you would using 8 eggs with no yogurt or ricotta.

TEMPLATE

Baked Frittata

MAKES ONE 9- OR 10-INCH FRITTATA, SERVING 4 TO 6

In addition to the fillings for the baked frittatas that follow, you can use any of the vegetable fillings from the top-of-the-stove frittatas (pages 73–77)—and vice versa.

2 tablespoons extra virgin olive oil

6 eggs

Salt (about ½ teaspoon)

Freshly ground pepper

½ cup Greek yogurt, drained yogurt (see page 140), or fresh ricotta cheese

Filling of your choice (see recipes, pages 79–81)

1. Heat the oven to 350°F.

2. Place the olive oil in a round 2-quart baking dish or 9- or 10-inch cast iron skillet. Brush the sides of the pan with the oil and place in the oven for 5 minutes.

3. Meanwhile, whisk the eggs in a large bowl. Season with salt and pepper to taste and whisk in the yogurt or ricotta. Stir in the filling.

4. Remove the baking dish or skillet from the oven and scrape in the egg mixture. It should sizzle when it hits the baking dish. Return to the oven and bake until puffed and lightly colored, about 30 minutes. Allow to cool for at least 10 minutes before serving (it will not remain puffed). Serve hot, warm, or at room temperature.

   ADVANCE PREPARATION: Like top-of-the-stove frittatas, baked frittatas can be served hot or cooled to room temperature, so they make a good do-ahead dish. The frittata can be made a day or two ahead.

Cabbage and Gruyère Frittata Filling

MAKES ENOUGH FOR ONE 9- OR 10-INCH FRITTATA

Every once in a while I find half a head of cabbage lingering in my refrigerator crisper. It can look the worse for wear, but I cut the edges away, remove the outer leaves, chop what's left, and cook it with onion until it's sweet and tender. It makes a great filling for a baked frittata.

1 tablespoon extra virgin olive oil

½ medium onion, finely chopped

1 pound cabbage (½ medium head), cored and finely chopped

Salt and freshly ground pepper

2 tablespoons chopped fresh dill or parsley (or a combination)

2 teaspoons caraway seeds, lightly toasted and ground (optional)

2 ounces Gruyère cheese, shredded (½ cup)

1. Heat the olive oil over medium heat in a large, heavy skillet and add the onion. Cook, stirring often, until tender, about 5 minutes. Add the cabbage along with a generous pinch of salt and stir until the cabbage begins to wilt. Cover, turn the heat to medium-low, and cook, stirring often, until the vegetables are quite soft and fragrant, 10 to 15 minutes. Stir in the dill and/or parsley and the caraway seeds (if using). Season to taste with salt and pepper and remove from the heat.

2. Use the filling in the Baked Frittata template recipe (opposite page), stirring the Gruyère into the beaten eggs along with the cabbage mixture.

   ADVANCE PREPARATION: You can make the filling up to 3 days ahead. A baked frittata made with this filling is best served warm. The frittata will keep for a couple of days in the refrigerator and you can warm it in a low oven for about 15 minutes.

Fennel and Onion Frittata Filling

MAKES ENOUGH FOR ONE 9- OR 10-INCH FRITTATA

Onion and fennel sweeten as they cook slowly in olive oil. The combination is one I've enjoyed throughout the Mediterranean, from France to Greece.

1 tablespoon extra virgin olive oil

1 large sweet onion, finely chopped

1 medium fennel bulb (about ½ pound), cored and finely chopped

2 garlic cloves, minced

Salt and freshly ground pepper

2 tablespoons chopped fresh dill or fennel fronds

1. Heat the olive oil over medium heat in a large, heavy skillet. Add the onion and cook, stirring often, until tender, about 5 minutes. Add the fennel, garlic, and a generous pinch of salt. Continue to cook, stirring, until the fennel is quite tender, about 8 more minutes. Cover and simmer gently, stirring often, until the mixture has cooked down and is very soft and lightly colored, 15 to 20 minutes. It should taste sweet. Season to taste with salt and pepper and remove from the heat. Stir in the dill or chopped fennel fronds. Taste and adjust salt.

2. Use the filling in the Baked Frittata template recipe (page 78).

ADVANCE PREPARATION: You can make the filling up to 3 days ahead. A baked frittata made with this filling will keep for a couple of days in the refrigerator. Serve cold or at room temperature.

Carrot and Leek Frittata Filling

MAKES ENOUGH FOR ONE 9- OR 10-INCH FRITTATA

I never thought about using carrots as a filling for a frittata until I went to Tunisia, where they are often combined with other ingredients in baked egg dishes. In this version I combine carrots, leeks, parsley, and other fresh herbs—tarragon, marjoram, and chives.

1 tablespoon extra virgin olive oil

¾ pound carrots, peeled and cut into small dice

2 large leeks, white and light green parts only, halved lengthwise, well cleaned, and chopped

Salt and freshly ground pepper

2 garlic cloves, minced (or 1 bulb green garlic, papery skin removed, minced)

2 tablespoons water

3 tablespoons finely chopped fresh flat-leaf parsley, or a mixture of parsley, tarragon, marjoram, and chives

1. Heat the olive oil over medium heat in a large, heavy skillet. Add the carrots, leeks, and a generous pinch of salt and cook, stirring, until the vegetables begin to soften, about 5 minutes. Add the garlic and cook, stirring, until the garlic is fragrant, 30 seconds to 1 minute. Add the water, cover the pan, and let the vegetables simmer until tender, another 5 minutes. Uncover and cook off any liquid in the pan. Stir in the herbs and season to taste with salt and pepper.

2. Use the filling (with drained or Greek yogurt but not ricotta) in the Baked Frittata template recipe (page 78).

ADVANCE PREPARATION: You can make the filling a day ahead. A baked frittata made with this filling can be served hot, warm, or at room temperature and will keep for a couple of days in the refrigerator.

2-EGG OMELETS

ONE WEEKEND, WHEN I WAS STILL teaching myself to cook, I went to the store, bought four dozen eggs, came home, and didn't stop practicing making omelets until I'd used them all up. If you were serious about cooking, mastering the French omelet was a rite of passage. Julia Child was my mentor, and I also read every other French cookbook I could find for tips on how to manipulate the pan and the eggs. Everybody had a slightly different technique, but they were all clear about the fact that the pan had to be hot when you added the butter, the butter had to be hot when you added the eggs, and the eggs shouldn't be in the pan, which was in constant motion, for much longer than a minute.

TEMPLATE

2-Egg Omelet

MAKES ONE 2-EGG OMELET, SERVING 1

Today I use olive oil as often as butter for my omelets, even when I'm filling them with something very French, like Gruyère cheese (a top-10 dinner at my house). Like frittatas, 2-egg omelets can be vehicles for leftovers, for small amounts of cooked vegetables, or for something very simple like snipped fresh herbs. In some ways they're even more versatile than frittatas because you need less filling and the filling can be simple: just a little grated Gruyère or crumbled goat cheese melted into the folds of an omelet makes for a luxurious meal.

2 eggs

Salt and freshly ground pepper

2 teaspoons milk

2 to 3 teaspoons butter or olive oil (2 teaspoons is sufficient when cooking in a nonstick pan; use 3 teaspoons in a metal pan)

Filling of your choice (see variations on opposite page)

1. Break the eggs into a bowl and beat with a fork or whisk until frothy. Whisk in salt and pepper to taste and the milk.

2. Heat a heavy 8-inch nonstick omelet pan over medium-high heat. Add the butter or olive oil. When the butter stops foaming or the oil feels hot when you hold your hand above it, pour the eggs right into the middle of the pan, scraping in every last bit with a heatproof silicone spatula. Swirl the pan to distribute the eggs evenly over the surface. During the first few seconds of cooking, constantly shake the pan gently and tilt it slightly with one hand while lifting up the edges of the omelet with the spatula in your other hand, letting the eggs run underneath.

3. As soon as the eggs are set on the bottom, sprinkle the filling over the middle of the egg "pancake," then move the pan away from you and quickly jerk it back towards you so that the omelet folds over onto itself. If you don't like your omelet runny in the middle (I do), jerk the pan again so that the omelet folds over

once more. Cook, shaking the pan for another 30 seconds or longer, to taste. Tilt the pan and roll the omelet out onto a plate.

Another way to make a 2-egg omelet is to flip it over before adding the filling. Do this with the same motion, moving the pan away then quickly jerking it back towards you, but lift your hand slightly as you begin to jerk the pan back. The omelet will flip over onto the other side, like a pancake. Place the filling in the middle, then use your spatula to fold one side over, then the other side, and roll the omelet out of the pan.

VARIATION: FRESH HERB OMELET

To make the classic French *omelette aux fines herbes*, beat 1 tablespoon finely minced fresh herbs such as parsley, tarragon, chives, or chervil (a combination is nice) into the eggs when you beat them in the bowl. Make the omelet as directed (without any filling) and sprinkle more herbs over the top of the finished omelet if desired.

VARIATION: MUSHROOM OMELET

Fill the omelet with ¼ cup either Pan-Cooked Mushrooms (page 11) or Mushroom Ragout (page 12). Add a teaspoon of freshly grated Parmesan if desired. Sprinkle the finished omelet with finely chopped fresh parsley.

VARIATION: SPINACH OR GREENS OMELET

Fill the omelet with ¼ cup finely chopped wilted spinach or greens (see page 3), seasoned with salt, pepper, and garlic if desired. Add a teaspoon of freshly grated Parmesan if desired.

VARIATION: SPINACH AND MUSHROOM OMELET

One of my favorite fillings. Make the Pan-Cooked Mushrooms (page 11) and at the end of cooking add 1 cup finely chopped wilted spinach (see page 3) and toss together. Fill the omelet with ¼ cup of this mixture along with 1 tablespoon freshly grated Parmesan or Gruyère.

CHAPTER FOUR

Gratins

THINK *GRATIN* WAS ONE OF my son's first words, so often do I make them for dinner. A vegetable gratin is simply a vegetable casserole that is baked in the oven in a heavy baking dish (preferably earthenware or enameled cast iron) until the top and sides are browned, or *gratinéed*. The French word *grater* means to scrape—that's where our word "grate" comes from—and if a gratin is properly baked, you will want to scrape the delicious browned bits off the sides of the dish and eat them.

I make two basic types of gratin. One is sort of like a vegetable quiche without a crust and without as much custard as a quiche. Mine are on the light side—I use 2 percent or whole milk instead of cream, and not an overwhelming amount of cheese. The other is Provençal, bound with rice and eggs, and sometimes a small amount of milk. Provençal gratins are called *tians* after the earthenware dish they're made in. I sometimes substitute other grains for the rice, but rice works best. Millet is also a good choice. Whatever type of gratin I make, the vegetables are always the focus.

As for fillings, the gratin I make most often is filled with seasoned wilted greens (see page 88). Greens of one type or another are a weekly purchase at the farmers' market and if they don't end up somewhere else, they'll always end up in a gratin.

Quiche-Without-a-Crust Gratin

MAKES 4 TO 6 SERVINGS

One reason why I always stock Gruyère cheese in my refrigerator is that it is so easy to make a gratin using this template, with any number of vegetables as the filling.

3 eggs

¾ cup milk (2 percent or whole)

Salt and freshly ground pepper

2 to 3 ounces Gruyère cheese, shredded (½ to ¾ cup), to taste

½ to 1 ounce Parmesan, grated (2 to 4 tablespoons), optional

Prepared vegetables of your choice, usually 1 to 2 pounds, cooked in olive oil or roasted (sometimes blanched first), with aromatics like onion, garlic, and herbs (thyme, rosemary, parsley) and seasoned (see variation recipes, pages 88–91)

1. Heat the oven to 375°F. Oil a 2-quart baking dish, preferably earthenware or enameled cast iron, with olive oil.

2. Beat the eggs in a large bowl. Beat in the milk and about $\frac{1}{2}$ teaspoon salt. Stir in the shredded Gruyère, grated Parmesan (if using), pepper to taste, and prepared vegetables. Combine thoroughly. Transfer to the prepared baking dish, scraping out every last bit with a rubber spatula.

3. Bake the gratin until the sides are browned, the top is browned in places, and the gratin is sizzling, 35 to 45 minutes. Let sit for 10 minutes or longer before serving.

ADVANCE PREPARATION: Gratins keep for a few days in the refrigerator and they're good cold or at room temperature. Reheat if you wish in a medium oven for about 15 minutes.

SUBSTITUTIONS AND ADDITIONS: Substitute goat cheese for the Gruyère.

Leftovers Gratin

Leftover vegetable dishes make great fillings for gratins. Say you've got some Mushroom Ragout (page 12), some corn on the cob, or a mess of greens from last night's dinner. One to two cups will suffice but more will work too. Mix up the ingredients in either gratin template and stir in your leftovers. Bake in an oiled baking dish as directed.

Provençal Gratin (Tian)

MAKES 4 TO 6 SERVINGS

Provençal *tians* are hearty gratins bound with eggs and rice. They are great cold as well as hot and the leftovers will slice up nicely, making them great lunchbox fare. I also cut the leftovers into small triangles and serve them as hors d'oeuvres.

2 or 3 eggs, (to taste)

½ cup milk (2 percent or whole), optional

Salt and freshly ground pepper

1 cup cooked rice, preferably medium- or short-grain, such as Arborio

2 to 3 ounces Gruyère cheese, shredded (½ to ¾ cup), to taste

Prepared vegetables of your choice (usually 1 to 2 pounds), cooked in olive oil or roasted (sometimes blanched first), with aromatics like onion, garlic, and herbs (thyme, rosemary, parsley) and seasoned (see variation recipes, pages 88–91)

¼ cup breadcrumbs, or a mixture of breadcrumbs and freshly grated Parmesan

1 to 2 tablespoons extra virgin olive oil for the top

1. Heat the oven to 375°F. Oil a 2-quart baking dish, preferably earthenware or enameled cast iron, with olive oil.

2. Beat the eggs in a large bowl. Beat in the milk (if using) and about ½ teaspoon salt. Stir in the rice, shredded Gruyère, pepper to taste, and prepared vegetables. Combine thoroughly. Transfer to the prepared baking dish, scraping out every last bit with a rubber spatula.

3. Top the gratin with the breadcrumbs (or breadcrumbs and Parmesan) and drizzle with the olive oil. You can also toss the breadcrumbs with the olive oil before spreading them on top of the mixture.

4. Bake the gratin until the sides are browned, the top is browned in places, and the gratin is sizzling, 35 to 45 minutes. Let sit for 10 minutes or longer before serving.

ADVANCE PREPARATION: Gratins keep for a few days in the refrigerator and they're good cold or at room temperature. Reheat, if you wish, in a medium oven for about 15 minutes.

SUBSTITUTIONS AND ADDITIONS:

- *Substitute 1 cup of another cooked grain, such as barley, quinoa, or millet, for the rice.*
- *Substitute goat cheese for the Gruyère.*
- *Substitute 1 ounce freshly grated Parmesan for 1 ounce of the Gruyère.*

Greens Gratin

MAKES 4 TO 6 SERVINGS

If getting your family to eat greens is challenging, try putting greens in a gratin. I make these just about every week because I buy greens every week. If you get into the habit of blanching or steaming greens when you bring them home, it won't take much time to throw this together. The recipe works for just about any type of green. I use chard quite often and beet greens even more often, because every time I buy beets at the farmers' market I choose the ones with the greens attached, which you should do as well. Choose the beets for the look of the greens as much as for the beetroots. If you're standing next to a customer who wants her greens cut off, ask the vendor for them so you can make this gratin. If I'm making the gratin with chard, I use the stems as well as the greens in the gratin if the stems are wide and meaty.

Make the *Quiche-Without-a-Crust Gratin* template (page 86) with the following vegetables and specifications:

2 generous bunches beet greens or chard (1½ to 2 pounds), wilted (see page 3)

1 tablespoon extra virgin olive oil

1 medium or ½ large onion, chopped

Salt and freshly ground pepper

2 large garlic cloves, minced

1 teaspoon each fresh thyme leaves and chopped fresh rosemary (optional but recommended)

1. If using chard with wide stalks, before wilting (when you strip the leaves from the stalks), retain the stalks and rinse them and cut into small dice. Heat the olive oil in a medium skillet over medium heat and add the onion and chard stalks if using. Cook, stirring often, until tender and just beginning to color, 5 to 8 minutes. Add a generous pinch of salt and the garlic and cook until fragrant, another 30 seconds to a minute, then stir in the herbs and the greens. Stir together for a minute, just until the greens are well mixed with the aromatics and coated with oil. Season to taste with salt and pepper.

2. Proceed with the gratin template recipe, adding the sautéed greens in Step 2.

NOTE: You can make this gratin with a smaller amount of greens. If you only have one bunch and need a home for them, make a gratin anyway.

ADVANCE PREPARATION: The blanched greens keep for 3 or 4 days in the refrigerator and can be frozen. The gratin will keep for a few days in the refrigerator and is good both cold and at room temperature. Reheat, if you wish, in a medium oven for about 15 minutes.

SUBSTITUTIONS AND ADDITIONS: The sautéed greens and aromatics also work with the Provençal Gratin template recipe (page 87)

Winter Squash Gratin

MAKES 4 TO 6 SERVINGS

A gratin makes a lovely home for winter squash, and there are many ways you can vary the theme. You can mash the roasted squash and whisk it with the eggs and milk (see Mashed Winter Squash substitution, below), or you can dice it, as I do here, because I love the look of a gratin made with little squares of roasted winter squash. Winter squash is compatible with a number of herbs—sage, thyme, and rosemary speak of Provence, mint of Greece. However I go with this gratin, it's a dinner we enjoy on a regular basis.

Make the *Quiche-Without-a-Crust Gratin* template (page 86) with the following vegetables and specifications:

1 tablespoon extra virgin olive oil

1 small onion, finely chopped

Salt

2 garlic cloves, minced

2 to 3 teaspoons fresh thyme leaves or chopped fresh sage

Roasted Winter Squash (page 15), preferably butternut, using 1½ to 2 pounds squash, cut in small dice

1. Heat the olive oil over medium heat in a medium skillet. Add the onion and cook, stirring often, until tender, about 5 minutes. Add a generous pinch of salt, the garlic, and thyme or sage and cook, stirring, until fragrant, another 30 seconds to 1 minute. Stir in the roasted squash and remove from the heat.

2. Proceed with the gratin template recipe, adding the squash mixture in Step 2.

ADVANCE PREPARATION: The roasted squash will keep for 2 or 3 days in the refrigerator. The finished gratin will also keep for 2 or 3 days. It's good at room temperature or you can reheat it.

VARIATION: MASHED WINTER SQUASH GRATIN

Instead of dicing the squash in the Roasted Winter Squash recipe (page 15), follow the directions in the Note to roast and mash chunks of squash. Whisk the mashed squash into the beaten eggs and milk in Step 2 of the template recipe.

VARIATION: GREEK WINTER SQUASH GRATIN

In the template, substitute feta for the Gruyère. With the squash, substitute 2 tablespoons or more chopped fresh mint for the thyme or sage. If desired, stir 1 cup cooked bulgur (see page 132) into the egg and milk mixture along with the squash and other ingredients in Step 2 of the template recipe.

VARIATION: PROVENÇAL WINTER SQUASH GRATIN

The roasted squash mixture here also works with the Provençal Gratin template (page 87). Follow the template recipe as directed, adding the roasted squash, which can be either diced or mashed, in Step 2.

Provençal Cabbage and Rice Gratin

MAKES 4 TO 6 SERVINGS

You can do so many things with a large head of humble cabbage; it's the perfect vegetable for a frugal cook. I season this with dill, which isn't Provençal, but goes wonderfully with cabbage.

Make the *Provençal Gratin* template (page 87) with the following vegetables and specifications:

Additional 2 tablespoons extra virgin olive oil

1 medium onion, finely chopped

Salt and freshly ground pepper

2 large garlic cloves, minced

1 small or ½ large head of cabbage, cored and chopped or shredded (4 cups)

2 to 4 tablespoons chopped fresh dill, to taste

2 tablespoons chopped fresh flat-leaf parsley

1. Heat the 2 tablespoons olive oil over medium heat in a large, heavy skillet. Add the onion and a pinch of salt and cook, stirring, until soft and beginning to color, about 8 minutes. Add the garlic and stir together until fragrant, 30 seconds to 1 minute. Stir in the cabbage and another generous pinch of salt. Cook, stirring, until the cabbage wilts, about 5 minutes. Turn the heat to low, cover, and continue to cook, stirring often, until the cabbage is very tender, sweet, and fragrant, 8 to 10 minutes. Stir in the dill, parsley, and salt and pepper to taste.

2. Proceed with the gratin template recipe, adding the cabbage mixture in Step 2.

ADVANCE PREPARATION: The cabbage filling will keep for a few days in the refrigerator. The baked gratin will keep for 3 or 4 days and is good hot or cold. Reheat in a medium oven.

Broccoli Raab Gratin with Red Pepper Lattice

MAKES 4 SERVINGS

I particularly like the broccoli raab in this Provençal gratin because the mix of chopped stems and leaves introduces a range of textures. I use 4 eggs instead of 2 or 3 for a fluffier gratin, and leave out the breadcrumbs because the roasted pepper lattice makes such a beautiful topping.

Make the *Provençal Gratin* template (page 87) with the following additional ingredients and specifications:

Additional 1 tablespoon extra virgin olive oil

1 to 2 garlic cloves (to taste), minced

1 small bunch broccoli raab (about ¾ pound), blanched (see page 5) and chopped medium-fine

2 teaspoons chopped fresh rosemary, or 1 teaspoon each chopped fresh rosemary and thyme

Salt and freshly ground pepper

Additional 1 or 2 eggs (4 eggs total)

1 large red bell pepper, roasted (see page 8) and cut lengthwise into thin strips

1. Heat the 1 tablespoon olive oil over medium heat in a large, heavy skillet. Add the garlic and cook, stirring, until fragrant and sizzling, about 30 seconds. Add the chopped broccoli raab and herbs. Season to taste with salt and pepper. Stir over medium heat for about a minute, until the broccoli raab is infused with the garlic, oil, and herbs.

2. Proceed with the template recipe, using 4 eggs total and adding the broccoli raab in Step 2.

3. In Step 3, omit the breadcrumbs. Smooth the top of the gratin and arrange the red pepper strips in a lattice design on top. Drizzle with olive oil before baking.

ADVANCE PREPARATION: The blanched seasoned broccoli raab will keep for about 3 days in the refrigerator. The gratin will keep in the refrigerator for 3 or 4 days.

Savory Bread Pudding

MAKES 4 TO 6 SERVINGS

If you find yourself on a regular basis with stale bread on your hands, you'll appreciate this template. I love bread but we don't always finish a loaf before it gets hard, and I hate to throw out food. Not a problem: I make savory bread pudding, which is really a kind of gratin. The stale bread is soaked in milk, then layered or mixed with vegetables and baked in a custard. The savory bread pudding browns in the oven on the sides and the top, like any good gratin, which is why I'm including the template in this chapter.

¼ to ½ pound stale or day-old bread

1 large garlic clove, cut in half

1½ to 1¾ cups milk (2 percent or whole), depending on how hard the bread is

Salt and freshly ground pepper

4 eggs

Vegetables and aromatics of your choice (see variation recipes, pages 93–95)

2 to 3 ounces Gruyère cheese, shredded (½ to ¾ cup), to taste

1. Prepare the bread: If the bread is still soft, slice it and toast it lightly. Rub all the slices, front and back, with the cut clove of garlic. If the bread is stale but not too hard to slice, slice it, don't bother toasting it, and rub the slices with garlic. Cut the sliced bread into cubes if desired. If the bread is too hard to cut safely, place the whole chunk in a bowl with 1 cup of the milk. Refrigerate for 1 hour or longer, turning the bread in the milk every once in a while. Break the bread up with your hands. Using a wooden spoon, whisk, or immersion blender, mash or beat the soaked bread so that the mixture turns into a mush.

2. In a large bowl, beat together the milk (or remaining milk, if you soaked the bread) and eggs. Add ½ teaspoon salt, a few twists of the pepper mill, and the bread, along with any milk remaining in the bowl. Toss together and let sit for 15 to 30 minutes.

3. Meanwhile, heat the oven to 350°F. Rub the sides of a 2-quart baking dish or gratin with the cut side of a garlic clove. Oil or butter the dish.

4. Stir the vegetables into the bread mixture along with the Gruyère (or arrange in the prepared dish according to the directions in the specific variation recipes that follow). Scrape the bread mixture into the prepared baking dish.

5. Bake until puffed and browned, 40 to 45 minutes. Remove from the oven and serve hot or warm.

    ADVANCE PREPARATION: Bread puddings can be assembled hours before baking. They can also be baked ahead and reheated, but they will lose the puff.

Savory Bread Pudding with Mushrooms

MAKES 4 TO 6 SERVINGS

This gratin always shows up at Thanksgiving, a favorite among the vegetarians at the table. It's got the comforting elements of a stuffing and the satisfying elements of a main dish. If you use wild mushrooms, the bread pudding will be particularly delicious.

Make the *Savory Bread Pudding* template (opposite page) with the following additional ingredients and specifications:

½ recipe Mushroom Ragout (page 12) or 1 recipe Pan-Cooked Mushrooms (page 11) made with 1 pound mushrooms

Proceed with the template recipe, stirring the mushrooms into the bread mixture in Step 3.

Savory Bread Pudding with Tomatoes

MAKES 4 TO 6 SERVINGS

A great bread pudding for summer. You can use any type of tomato for this, though try not to use tomatoes that are too juicy as they can diffuse the custard, resulting in a watery pudding.

Make the *Savory Bread Pudding* template (opposite page) with the following additional ingredients and specifications:

1½ pounds tomatoes, sliced

Salt and freshly ground pepper

1 teaspoon fresh thyme leaves

1 tablespoon extra virgin olive oil

3 to 4 tablespoons freshly grated Parmesan

1. Proceed with the template recipe through Step 3, beating the Gruyère into the eggs.

2. In Step 4, spoon half the bread mixture into the baking dish. Top with half of the sliced tomatoes. Add the remaining bread mixture, smooth over the tomatoes, and top with the remaining sliced tomatoes. Sprinkle with salt, pepper, and the fresh thyme, and drizzle on the olive oil. Sprinkle the Parmesan over the top, and bake as directed in Step 5.

Savory Bread Pudding with Tomatoes and Goat Cheese

MAKES 4 TO 6 SERVINGS

This is just like the preceding savory bread pudding, with goat cheese standing in for the Gruyère.

Make the *Savory Bread Pudding* template (page 92) with the following additional ingredients and specifications:

4 ounces goat cheese, crumbled (1 cup)

1½ pounds tomatoes, sliced

1 teaspoon fresh thyme

1 tablespoon extra virgin olive oil

1. Proceed with the template recipe through Step 3, beating ½ cup of the goat cheese into the eggs in Step 2.

2. In Step 4, omit the Gruyère. Spoon half the bread mixture into the baking dish. Top with half of the sliced tomatoes. Add the remaining bread mixture, smoothing it over the tomatoes. Top with the remaining sliced tomatoes. Sprinkle the top layer with the remaining goat cheese and fresh thyme. Drizzle with the olive oil, and bake as directed in Step 5.

CHAPTER FIVE

Pasta

WHEN I HAVEN'T REALLY PLANNED dinner and it's time to get some food on the table, how many times have I posed this question: "What do you want for dinner—pasta, omelet, or scrambled eggs?" I have no problem with cooking and eating pasta often, as long as vegetables are part of the equation. When I'm with Italian friends, that's the way I live, and I'm very happy living that way.

Although there are thousands of ways to prepare pasta, I've narrowed my pasta templates down to four basic recipes. In the first template, I combine pasta, tomato sauce (either marinara or uncooked tomato sauce), and vegetables that are simply blanched in the water I've set up for the pasta. In the second template are pastas that don't require a tomato sauce; here pasta is tossed with a more complex vegetable preparation, then moistened with some of the pasta cooking water. The last two templates are for lasagnas, one with a tomato sauce and the other with béchamel.

Pasta with Tomato Sauce and Blanched Vegetables

VEGAN WITHOUT THE CHEESE ///

This simple template is one of the most predictably satisfying dinners you can serve: pasta tossed with a delicious tomato sauce—cooked or uncooked—and a vegetable in season, cooked in the same water that you'll use for your pasta. In spring it might be peas, sugar snaps, asparagus, favas, or green beans. In summer it'll definitely be green beans, sometimes corn. In the fall and winter I'll use broccoli or cauliflower (or both), chopped blanched greens, sometimes combined with chickpeas. The instructions in the template are very simple—I do nothing more than blanch or steam the vegetables, then toss with the pasta and tomato sauce. The depth of flavor comes from the tomato sauce. When using a marinara sauce, depending on the quantity of pasta you are making, you can toss the noodles and vegetables right in the pan with the sauce—if the pan is big enough. Or you can warm your sauce in a small saucepan and use a big pasta bowl to toss together the pasta, sauce, and vegetables. If I'm making pasta for two or three people or if I'm thawing frozen marinara sauce, I'll use a microwave-safe bowl that's large enough to accommodate the pasta to thaw my sauce, then toss the pasta, vegetables, and tomato sauce together in that bowl.

Salt

1 portion (see chart, page 100) vegetables for each serving

3 to 4 tablespoons marinara sauce (pages 24 to 27) or Uncooked Tomato Sauce (page 23) for each serving (maybe a little more than ¼ cup for the uncooked sauce—I leave that up to you)

2 to 4 ounces dried pasta for each serving (see Note)

Drizzle of olive oil (optional)

Freshly grated Parmesan for serving

1. Bring a large pot of water to a boil while you prepare your vegetables (see the chart on page 100). If there are just two of you, it can be a large saucepan, but if you're serving more than two, use a pasta pot (most have an 8-quart capacity). When the water comes to a boil, salt generously. Add the vegetables to the boiling water. See the cooking times in the chart—they aren't very long. The vegetables should be tender but not mushy. Fill a bowl with cold water. With a mesh skimmer, strainer, or spider, transfer the vegetables to the cold water. Drain in a colander or strainer.

2. Heat the sauce in a saucepan or skillet over medium heat, or in a large microwave-safe bowl in the microwave. Bring the water back to a boil and add the pasta. Refer to the package for timing suggestions, and a minute or so before the suggested time remove a piece, rinse briefly with cold water so you don't burn your tongue (the only time you should ever rinse pasta), and take a bite. It should be cooked through but resist your teeth a little bit in the middle (al dente). If you want the vegetables really hot, drop them back into the pot along with the pasta for a few seconds.

3. Drain the pasta and vegetables (if in the water); you may need to hold onto some cooking water, depending on the recipe. Or scoop out the pasta (and vegetables) with a strainer or skimmer—or lift out if you're using a pasta pot with an insert—and transfer to the pan or bowl with the sauce. Drizzle in a little bit of olive oil if desired and add the cooked vegetables if they aren't there. Toss together the pasta, vegetables, and sauce and serve, passing Parmesan for sprinkling.

NOTE: Unless you routinely cook pasta by the pound, I highly recommend using a scale to measure pasta. It makes it so easy to figure out portions. I count 3 ounces for a main dish as a rule. However I've recently learned that for hungry teenage boys I should figure on 4 ounces. Two ounces are probably enough for small children. I find that 3 to 4 tablespoons of marinara works with 3- or 4-ounce servings of pasta, but if you're only serving 2 ounces of pasta per person, then cut it back to 2 to 3 tablespoons per serving.

SUBSTITUTIONS AND ADDITIONS: Drain and rinse a 15-ounce can of chickpeas, white beans, or borlotti beans (I like chickpeas best). Add to the tomato sauce and heat through, then toss with the pasta and vegetables. Or simply substitute the beans for the vegetables.

Kids, Vegetables, and Tomato Sauce

Pasta with tomato sauce may strike you as very ordinary, but in my family it's a fundamental part of our diet. When I'm making dinner for kids who don't eat vegetables, I'm comforted by the fact that they actually are eating a lot of vegetables—tomatoes—when they eat pasta with my marinara sauce, even if they push aside the green stuff.

Prep and Timing for Blanching Vegetables

These are the vegetables that I serve most often with tomato sauce and pasta. They're the usual suspects, vegetables that I'm most likely to have on hand (depending on the season) and that are easy to procure. Prep and cooking here is simple—they're blanched in the pot you'll use for the pasta (or you can steam them, but why get out an extra pot?). Then they're tossed with the pasta and your unforgettable marinara sauce.

VEGETABLE	PORTION SIZE	HOW TO PREPARE	STEAMING OR BLANCHING TIME
Asparagus	2 to 5 spears, depending on the thickness	Snap off woody ends. Examine flower end and make sure there are no rotten pieces. Cut into ½- to 1-inch lengths after steaming or blanching.	4 to 5 minutes, depending on the thickness.
Beans, fresh (green, yellow, romano)	1½ to 2 ounces, or 1 handful	Snap off stem end; string if necessary. If you want smaller lengths, cook first then cut.	4 to 5 minutes
Broccoli	1 handful florets	Cut crowns from stems; break into smaller florets. Reserve stems for another purpose.	Blanch: 2½ minutes (once cooked, broccoli gets mushy quickly) Steam: 4 minutes
Broccoli raab (rapini)	1½ to 2 ounces	Cut away tough stem ends at bottom. Separate thick stems from flowers and greens. Coarsely chop after blanching.	5 minutes for thick stems, 3 minutes for flowers and greens
Cauliflower	1 handful florets	Core and break or cut into florets.	5 minutes
Chard or beet greens	2 to 3 ounces	Stem; wash leaves in 2 changes of water. Coarsely or finely chop after wilting. If desired, briefly sauté with garlic.	Blanch: 1 minute Steam: 2 minutes
Corn, off or on the cob	⅓ to ½ ear	Remove the kernels before or after steaming or boiling.	4 to 5 minutes
Fava beans	6 to 8 ounces (unshelled weight)	Once shelled, drop the beans into a pot of boiling water and boil small beans for 1 to 2 minutes (3 to 5 minutes for bigger, harder beans). Transfer to a bowl of ice water and drain. Slip off the skins by flicking off the edge of the bean at the dark spot where the bean was attached to the pod and gently squeezing out the bean.	1 to 2 minutes for small beans, up to 5 minutes for larger starchier beans
Kale	2 to 3 ounces	Stem; wash leaves in 2 changes of water. Coarsely or finely chop after wilting.	Blanch: 2 to 4 minutes Steam: 3 to 4 minutes
Peas, English shell	4 ounces (unshelled weight), or 3 to 4 tablespoons shelled	Remove from pods.	4 to 5 minutes
Peas, sugar snap	1½ to 2 ounces	Snap off stem end and string if desired.	3 minutes

Pasta with Vegetables (No Tomato Sauce)

VEGAN WITHOUT THE CHEESE /// **MAKES 4 SERVINGS**

Beautiful produce that is cooked until tender, finished with garlic and olive oil, and seasoned with aromatics, stock, or wine (or not) wants to be at the center of the plate, and often begs nothing more than to be tossed with pasta. There's an easy way to make a meal of this, even if you have no stock on hand. The pasta cooking water, which has become starchy from the pasta, serves as a sort of sauce, moistening and stretching the vegetable preparation. Add the pasta and some good Parmesan and toss it all together: That's a wonderful dinner.

This bare bones template requires four ingredients: a vegetable, extra virgin olive oil, garlic, and pasta (well okay: salt too). Cheese completes it, and it's part of my template, but if you adhere to a vegan diet, you'll enjoy this pasta without it. The choice of vegetables is fairly limitless. Greens of all kinds work well; mushrooms like the Pan-Cooked Mushrooms on page 11 are a favorite standby. There have been times when I've pulled together a delicious meal based on this template with nothing more than the one red pepper I found in the fridge upon returning from a trip, or even with the peas in my freezer. But of course the dish will stand out if you use terrific produce.

You can then become more elaborate, cooking the vegetables into a ragout with shallots or onions, herbs, and stock. Or toss your cooked pasta and vegetables with a creamier cheese like fresh ricotta or goat cheese. Some vegetables—mushrooms and peppers—should be cooked in the pan only, whereas others— greens and spinach, cauliflower, beans, peas, and favas—should be blanched first in the pasta pot, then finished in the pan with aromatics. But it all begins with the produce, the pasta, and the cooking water.

The weight or volume of vegetables and the way they're prepared will be specific to each recipe (like the frittata fillings in Chapter 3). Usually a pound of vegetables will work for four people, but this can vary. Three-fourths of a pound of mushrooms can be stretched into a ragout that's sufficient, whereas 1 pound of fava beans, once shelled and skinned, can look pretty skimpy. A bunch of greens can vary in weight from $\frac{1}{2}$ to $1\frac{1}{4}$ pounds. The thing is to cook different vegetables as much as possible to get a sense of what quantities work for you and your family.

Vegetables and aromatics of your choice (see variation recipes, pages 103–105)

Salt

¾ to 1 pound dried pasta

1 tablespoon extra virgin olive oil for tossing the pasta

2 ounces freshly grated Parmesan, a mix of Parmesan and Pecorino Romano, or other cheese (½ cup)

1. Bring a large pot of water to a boil for the vegetables and pasta.

2. Prepare the vegetables as directed in the variation recipe, then blanch if directed (keeping the pot of water on the heat for boiling the pasta). Then sauté the vegetables with the indicated aromatics. (If you plan on tossing the pasta with the vegetables in their pan, make sure to sauté the vegetables in a pan that is large enough to accommodate everything. For example, my 12-inch skillet is big enough to accommodate pasta for 2 or 3, but beyond that I really need a big pasta bowl.) Keep the vegetables warm.

(continued)

3. When the water in the large pot returns to a boil, salt generously (if you have not already), but keep in mind that you'll be tossing some of this water with your finished pasta dish, so it should not be unpalatably salty; you can salt a little less than "salty as the ocean" but not so much less that the pasta and vegetables will taste bland. Add the pasta and cook al dente, using the timing instructions on the package as a guide, but checking the pasta a minute before the time indicated is up.

4. With a ladle, transfer $1/2$ cup of the pasta cooking water to the pan or bowl with the vegetables and $1/2$ cup of the cooking water to a small bowl, in case you need more to moisten the pasta. Drain the pasta and toss at once with the vegetables, olive oil, and cheese. If the mixture seems dry, stir in some or all of the pasta water you set aside. Serve hot.

ADVANCE PREPARATION: Most of the vegetables can be prepped and cooked several hours or even a day or two before you cook the pasta. Indeed, this template should be used for all manner of leftovers. Reheat gently. You may need to add a bit more pasta cooking water as liquid evaporates in the refrigerator.

Perciatelli with Broccoli Raab and Red Pepper Flakes

VEGAN WITHOUT THE CHEESE /// **MAKES 4 SERVINGS**

This is modeled on a classic Apulian dish (see Orecchiette with Broccoli Raab, below), but here, the broccoli raab is coursely chopped and it works better with the tubular perciatelli or bucatini. You have the option of using ricotta salata, Pecorino Romano, Parmesan, or goat cheese.

Make the *Pasta with Vegetables (No Tomato Sauce)* template (page 101) with the following additional ingredients and specifications:

1 generous bunch broccoli raab (1 to 1¼ pounds)

Additional 1 tablespoon extra virgin olive oil

2 garlic cloves, minced

½ teaspoon red pepper flakes

Salt and freshly ground pepper

1. Blanch the broccoli raab (see page 100) in a large pot of salted boiling water, keeping the pot of water over heat for the pasta. Coarsely chop and place in a bowl lined with paper towels.

2. Heat 1 tablespoon olive oil over medium heat in a large, heavy skillet or wide saucepan and add the garlic and red pepper flakes. As soon as the garlic begins to sizzle and smell fragrant, add the broccoli raab and salt and black pepper to taste. Stir together for a couple of minutes, until the greens are nicely infused with garlic and olive oil. Season to taste with more salt and black pepper, if you wish (the red pepper flakes have already contributed some spice). Remove from the heat and keep warm (you can also do this step while the pasta is cooking).

3. Bring the water you used for blanching the broccoli raab back to a boil. Proceed with Steps 3 and 4 of the template recipe, using perciatelli or bucatini pasta, and topping the finished dish with 2 to 3 ounces of freshly grated ricotta salata, Pecorino Romano, Parmesan (or a mix), or 2 ounces crumbled goat cheese.

ADVANCE PREPARATION: You can prepare this dish through Step 2 and keep the cooked greens in the refrigerator for up to 3 days. Reheat in a skillet, adding a little more oil and cooking water from the pasta to moisten.

SUBSTITUTIONS AND ADDITIONS: Substitute other greens such as kale, beet greens, or Swiss chard for the broccoli raab.

VARIATION: ORECCHIETTE WITH BROCCOLI RAAB

For the iconic Apulian dish, use orecchiette for the pasta and chop the broccoli raab very fine, so that the pieces will settle into the "little ear"-shaped pasta.

Pasta with Peas, Fava Beans, Green Garlic, and Herbs

VEGAN WITHOUT THE CHEESE /// **MAKES 4 TO 6 SERVINGS**

Your time is well spent when you shell peas, skin fava beans, and serve them up with pasta. Fava beans, especially, require some work, and their yield, once skinned, can disappoint given that a pound of favas in the pod looks like quite a lot. That's why they're a perfect vegetable to toss with pasta. Their flavor and texture surprises the palate with every bite. I love to use penne with either of these vegetables, but especially with peas, because sometimes the peas get hidden inside the tubes of pasta. Fusilli is a good choice if you're using only fava beans, as the beans can lodge in the spirals of the corkscrews.

Make the *Pasta with Vegetables (No Tomato Sauce)* template (page 101) with the following additional ingredients and specifications:

2 pounds fava beans, shelled

1 pound fresh peas, shelled (about ¾ cup)

Additional 1 tablespoon extra virgin olive oil

1 bulb green garlic, papery shells discarded, minced

1 tablespoon minced chives

4 large basil leaves, torn into small pieces or cut into slivers

1. Fill a bowl with cold water. Blach the favas in a large pot of salted boiling water until tender: Small beans will take 1 minute, medium beans 2 to 3 minutes, and large beans 4 to 5 minutes. Using a skimmer or a strainer, transfer the favas to the bowl of cold water. Allow the beans to cool for several minutes, then slip off their skins by pinching off the eye of the skin and squeezing gently. Set aside in a bowl.

2. Add the peas to the boiling water and blanch for 4 minutes, until just tender. Scoop them out of the water and add to the fava beans.

3. Heat 1 tablespoon olive oil over medium-low heat in a large, heavy skillet and add the green garlic. Cook gently, stirring, until translucent, 2 to 3 minutes. Stir in the favas, peas, chives, and basil. (You can also do this step while the pasta is cooking).

4. Bring the water in the pot back to a boil. Proceed with Steps 3 and 4 of the template recipe, using penne or fusilli pasta and Parmesan.

ADVANCE PREPARATION: You can prepare the vegetables through Step 3 several hours before cooking the pasta.

SUBSTITUTIONS AND ADDITIONS:

• *Substitute goat cheese or fresh ricotta for the Parmesan. Mix it with the ½ cup pasta cooking water until creamy, then toss with the pasta and vegetables.*

• *Instead of a mix of favas and peas, use 3 pounds favas only or 2 pounds peas only.*

TWO TEMPLATES FOR LASAGNA

LASAGNA IS IN ESSENCE A GRATIN, a layered casserole of pasta, vegetables, and/or sauce and cheese that's baked until bubbling. But it belongs in the pasta chapter because we always think of it as pasta.

You may think of this dish as an elaborate operation, and indeed it can be if you make your own fresh lasagna noodles and a traditional, long-simmering Bolognese *ragù*. But no-cook lasagna noodles have transformed the process of making this dish, and a simple marinara sauce requires far less time than a Bolognese sauce. My lasagna can be a family weeknight meal, but it's also impressive enough to serve for a dinner party. No matter that vegetarian lasagna is easy, it always strikes guests as impressive, and families always love Mom's lasagna. If you master one of the marinara sauces on pages 24–27 or the béchamel in the template recipe, you're more than halfway there. (My lasagnas require one or the other, but not both, as a traditional lasagna Bolognese would.)

I've seen my fair share of heavy, rich vegetarian lasagnas, laden with mozzarella cheese that some cooks think the casserole requires, perhaps to compensate for the absence of meat. I don't think this is necessary, although fresh mozzarella—the kind that comes in a little water if it's packaged, not the rubbery dry logs or blocks—has a place in some of my recipes. The bare bones of my tomato sauce lasagnas are the tomato sauce itself, no-boil lasagna noodles, ricotta cheese (fresh, good-quality ricotta that you can find in good Italian delis, not the gummy industrial ricotta you get at the supermarket) mixed with an egg, and Parmesan. Sometimes I add some mozzarella to this simple mix, but more often I add vegetables and no additional cheese. It's the vegetables that define these lasagnas.

Lasagna with Tomato Sauce and Vegetables

MAKES 6 SERVINGS

You can make this as is, with no additional vegetables. But it does make a wonderful vehicle for all kinds of produce. My favorites are spinach, roasted cauliflower, roasted broccoli, and roasted eggplant.

8 ounces ricotta cheese (about 1 cup)

2 tablespoons water

1 egg

Pinch (tiny!) of cinnamon

Salt and freshly ground pepper

2⅓ cups marinara sauce (pages 24–27)

½ pound (more or less) no-boil lasagna noodles (the precise number of noodles depends on the size and shape of your baking dish)

Vegetable preparation of your choice (see filling recipes, pages 108–109)

4 ounces freshly grated Parmesan (1 cup)

1 tablespoon extra virgin olive oil for drizzling (optional)

1. Heat the oven to 350°F. Lightly oil or butter a rectangular baking dish. It should have a capacity of at least 2 quarts.

2. Blend together the ricotta, water, egg, cinnamon, and salt and pepper to taste.

3. Spread a thin layer (about ⅓ cup) of marinara sauce over the bottom of the baking dish. Top with a layer of lasagna noodles. Top the noodles with half of the ricotta/egg mixture and spread in a thin layer with a rubber spatula. Top the ricotta with half of the vegetable filling, then top the vegetables with about ⅔ cup marinara sauce and about ⅓ cup Parmesan. Repeat the layers, then add a final layer of lasagna noodles topped with the remaining marinara sauce and Parmesan. If desired, drizzle a tablespoon of olive oil over the top.

4. Cover the baking dish *tightly* with foil (it's important to crimp the foil tightly against the edges of the pan so that the dish is sealed and the lasagna noodles steam and don't dry out). Bake until the noodles are tender and the mixture is bubbling, about 40 minutes. Uncover and, if you wish, bake until the top begins to brown, another 5 to 10 minutes; but make sure that the noodles are completely covered with sauce or they will dry out. Remove from the heat and allow to sit for 5 to 10 minutes before serving.

ADVANCE PREPARATION: You can assemble this up to a day ahead and refrigerate, or freeze for a month. Transfer directly from the freezer to the preheated oven and add 10 to 15 minutes to the baking time. The lasagna can be baked several hours ahead and reheated in a medium oven.

SUBSTITUTIONS AND ADDITIONS: If you want more cheese in your lasagna, add two layers of shredded fresh mozzarella (about 6 ounces total) either in place of or on top of the vegetables.

■■■

Lasagna with Roasted Broccoli or Cauliflower

MAKES 6 SERVINGS

It's worth the extra time it takes to roast broccoli or cauliflower (rather than steaming or blanching) for this lasagna. Roasting coaxes out a layer of flavor that is not lost in the winter dish. The roasted vegetables also contribute great texture.

Make the *Lasagna with Tomato Sauce and Vegetables* template (page 107) with the following vegetables and specifications:

Roasted Broccoli (page 18) or Roasted Cauliflower (page 19), using about 1½ pounds (about ¾ medium head), or a mix of both

¼ to ½ teaspoon red pepper flakes

1. Cut the roasted broccoli and/or cauliflower into small pieces and toss with the red pepper flakes. Divide into 2 equal portions.

2. Proceed with the template recipe as directed.

ADVANCE PREPARATION: You can assemble this lasagna up to a day ahead and refrigerate, or freeze for a month. Transfer directly from the freezer to the preheated oven and add 10 to 15 minutes to the baking time. The lasagna can be baked several hours ahead and reheated in a medium oven.

Casserole Layers: Getting Organized

Before you begin to assemble your lasagna, it helps to have a good idea of the quantities of each element you'll need for the layers. It's very frustrating to get to the last layer of your casserole and not have enough sauce for the top. So figure on the following:

3½ layers of tomato sauce (the half layer is for the bottom of the dish, a very thin layer to coat the bottom, about ⅓ cup; divide the rest of the sauce into 3 equal portions, approximately ⅔ cup each)

3 layers of lasagna noodles (divide into 3 equal portions)

3 layers of Parmesan (⅓ cup each)

2 layers of ricotta/egg mixture (divide into 2 equal portions)

2 layers of vegetables (divide into 2 equal portions)

Spinach Lasagna

MAKES 6 SERVINGS

This is an easy way to work more greens into your diet. It's a classic that remains a family favorite.

Make the *Lasagna with Tomato Sauce and Vegetables* template (page 107) with the following vegetables and specifications:

1 generous bunch spinach (1 pound)

Additional 1 tablespoon extra virgin olive oil

1 garlic clove, minced

Salt and freshly ground pepper

1. Stem the spinach, wash thoroughly in 2 changes of water, and wilt (see page 3). Finely chop.

2. Heat the olive oil over medium heat in a medium skillet and add the garlic. Cook until the garlic begins to sizzle and smell fragrant, 30 seconds to a minute. Add the spinach and salt and pepper to taste. Stir and toss in the pan for about a minute, until nicely infused with the oil and garlic. Remove from the heat.

3. Proceed with the template recipe, stirring the chopped spinach into the ricotta mixture at the end of Step 2 instead of layering it in the lasagna.

ADVANCE PREPARATION: You can assemble this lasagna up to a day ahead and refrigerate, or freeze for a month. Transfer directly from the freezer to the preheated oven and add 10 to 15 minutes to the baking time. The lasagna can be baked several hours ahead and reheated in a medium oven.

SUBSTITUTIONS AND ADDITIONS: Substitute Swiss chard or beet greens for the spinach.

Lasagna with Vegetables and Herbed Béchamel

MAKES 6 SERVINGS

Certain vegetables don't require a tomato sauce to show off in lasagna, while some (beets) would even clash with tomato sauce. In the spring, when asparagus, artichokes, and fava beans are so sweet and delicate, I want to embellish them only with a béchamel enhanced with fresh herbs and Parmesan cheese. These are less rustic, more elegant, than the tomato-based lasagnas, and the béchamel takes no more time to make than a marinara (less, in fact). But it can't be made too far ahead, so these can't be made on a whim the way the tomato lasagnas can when you have marinara sauce stashed in the freezer.

2 tablespoons extra virgin olive oil (or 1 tablespoon olive oil and 1 tablespoon unsalted butter); plus 1 tablespoon olive oil, for drizzling (optional)

2 tablespoons minced shallot or onion

2 tablespoons sifted all-purpose flour

3 cups milk (1 percent, 2 percent, or whole)

Pinch (very small) of freshly grated nutmeg

Salt and freshly ground pepper

4 ounces Parmesan, grated (1 cup)

¼ cup finely chopped fresh herbs, such as parsley, tarragon, chives

½ pound (more or less) no-boil lasagna noodles (depends on the size and shape of your baking dish)

Vegetable preparation of your choice (see variation recipes, pages 112–115)

1. To make the béchamel, heat the oil (or oil and butter) over medium heat in a heavy medium saucepan. Add the shallot or onion and cook, stirring, until softened, about 3 minutes. Stir in the flour and cook, stirring, until smooth and bubbling, but not browned, about 3 minutes. It should have the texture of wet sand at low tide. Whisk in the milk all at once and bring to a simmer. Whisking all the while, simmer until the mixture begins to thicken. Turn the heat to very low and simmer, stirring often with a whisk and scraping the bottom and edges of the pan with a heat-proof spatula, until the sauce is thick and has lost its raw flour taste, 10 to 15 minutes. Season with the nutmeg and salt and pepper to taste. Strain while hot into a large measuring cup or a medium bowl. Stir in ¼ cup of the Parmesan and the fresh herbs.

2. Heat the oven to 350°F. Oil or butter a rectangular baking dish. It should have a capacity of at least 2 quarts. Spread a thin layer (about ⅓ cup) of béchamel over the bottom. Top with a layer of lasagna noodles. Spoon about ⅓ cup béchamel over the noodles. Top with half of the vegetables and sprinkle with about ⅓ cup of the Parmesan. Repeat the layers, then end with a layer of lasagna noodles topped with béchamel and Parmesan. Make sure the noodles are well coated with béchamel so they will be sure to soften during baking. If desired, drizzle 1 tablespoon olive oil over the top.

3. Cover the baking dish *tightly* with foil (it's important to crimp the foil tightly against the edges of the pan so that the dish is sealed and the lasagna noodles steam and don't dry out). Bake until the noodles are tender and the mixture is bubbling, 30 to 40 minutes. Uncover and, if you wish, bake until the top begins to brown, another 5 to 10 minutes, but make sure that the noodles are completely covered with béchamel. Remove from the heat and allow to sit for 5 minutes before serving.

ADVANCE PREPARATION: You can assemble this up to a day ahead and refrigerate, or freeze for a month. The lasagna can be baked several hours ahead and reheated in a medium oven.

Béchamel

Béchamel is the classic white sauce that is one of the "mother sauces" in traditional French cooking. It also exists in Italian cuisine (*besciamella*). It is made by whisking milk into a paste of flour and butter called a *roux*. When the mixture reaches the boiling point it thickens into a smooth sauce, which is simmered until there is no longer any trace of a raw flour taste. Although this white sauce is often referred to as a cream sauce, there is rarely any cream in it. What causes it to be creamy and rich is the suspension of the roux in liquid.

Though the classic French béchamel and Italian *besciamella* are made with butter, Provençal cooks often use olive oil, and olive oil béchamel is delicious. That's the sauce I use for my vegetarian lasagnas (though I give you the choice of using a combination of the two). The lasagnas don't include lots of heavy cheese, just vegetables, pasta, béchamel, and Parmesan.

If you're new to cooking you may have steered away from French sauces, but they are not difficult at all to make. The first step is making the roux—the flour and olive oil (or butter) paste. You simply combine the two ingredients and stir over medium heat for 3 to 5 minutes, until the mixture has a texture resembling wet sand at low tide and no longer has a raw floury taste. Then you whisk in the milk and whisk until the sauce thickens. It will do so as soon as it reaches a simmer. Then it's just a question of simmering the sauce for 10 to 15 minutes, until the sauce is velvety and has no floury taste. In cooking school, they tell you that you must simmer the sauce for at least 20 minutes in order for the roux to be properly dispersed in the liquid and reach its maximum viscosity. But I've found 10 to 15 minutes to be sufficient for this amount of béchamel.

Lasagna with Roasted Beets, Beet Greens, and Herbed Béchamel

MAKES 6 SERVINGS

Beets may not work with tomato sauce, but they are delicious in this lasagna with béchamel. A surprising lasagna that everybody always raves about, this is probably the only pink lasagna you'll ever see (that is, unless you use golden beets). Roast the beets and prepare the greens ahead so you can assemble this quickly.

Make the *Lasagna with Vegetables and Herbed Béchamel* template (page 110) with the following vegetables and specifications:

2 bunches medium beets (or 6 beets), any color, with their greens

1. Remove the greens from the beets. Roast the beets (see page 20), peel, and slice. Divide the sliced roasted beets into 2 equal portions. Wash the greens, wilt (see page 3), and chop.

2. Proceed with the template recipe, but in Step 2, after spreading a thin layer of béchamel on the bottom of the dish, stir the chopped beet greens into the remaining béchamel. Layer the sliced beets as directed in the template.

ADVANCE PREPARATION: Roasted beets and wilted greens will keep for 3 or 4 days in the refrigerator. You can assemble this up to a day ahead and refrigerate, or freeze for a month. The lasagna can be baked several hours ahead and reheated in a medium oven.

NOTE: Refer to "Casserole Layers" on page 108 for suggestions on organizing the components of your lasagna, substituting béchamel for tomato sauce.

Asparagus and Herb Lasagna

MAKES 6 SERVINGS

In this variation I replace some of the milk in the béchamel with the asparagus stock from blanching the asparagus and simmering the stems. For the herbs, I like a mix of tarragon, parsley, and chives.

Make the *Lasagna with Vegetables and Herbed Béchamel* template (page 110) with the following ingredients and specifications:

2 pounds asparagus

4 large garlic cloves, peeled and crushed

Salt

Additional ¼ cup finely chopped fresh herbs, such as tarragon, chervil, parsley, chives, basil

1. Trim the asparagus by breaking off the woody ends. Place the trimmed ends and the garlic in a medium saucepan and add 2 quarts water. Bring to a boil, add 1 teaspoon salt, reduce the heat, and simmer, partially covered, for 30 minutes. Scoop out the stems and garlic and discard.

2. Fill a bowl with ice and water. Bring the saucepan of cooking liquid back to a boil and add the asparagus stalks. Blanch until tender but not mushy: Thick asparagus stalks will take 4 to 5 minutes, medium and thin asparagus 3 minutes. Transfer, using a skimmer or tongs, to the bowl of ice water. Do not discard the cooking water. Drain the asparagus and dry on a clean dish towel. If the asparagus stalks are thick, cut in half lengthwise first, then cut all of the asparagus into ¾-inch lengths. Set aside.

3. When making the béchamel in Step 1 of the template recipe, use just 2 cups milk and combine the milk with 1 cup of the asparagus stock. Add the additional ¼ cup herbs with the other herbs at the end of the step.

4. In Step 2, after spreading a thin layer of béchamel over the bottom of the dish, stir the asparagus into the remaining béchamel (instead of layering with the lasagna). Continue with the recipe.

ADVANCE PREPARATION: You can assemble this up to a day or two before you bake it. Wrap tightly in plastic and refrigerate.

CHAPTER SIX

Polenta

THIS IS A SHORT CHAPTER, but polenta deserves its own place in my panoply of vegetarian main dishes. I don't think about polenta for months on end, then one day I throw some in the oven, thaw some tomato sauce (or make some), and we sit down to one of our favorite meals. For those who cannot eat wheat and so have said good-bye to pasta, polenta may be your magic bullet. That's why I've put this chapter right after the pasta chapter.

This delicious cornmeal porridge has risen from its humble origins to appear on the fanciest of restaurant menus, usually served as an accompaniment to meat. But in my house it's the main event, a vehicle for simple toppings like marinara sauce or more complex bean or vegetable ragouts. I almost always stir cheese into my polenta, but it isn't a necessary component; if you follow a vegan diet you can omit the cheese and substitute olive oil for the butter—you won't miss the cheese. I serve it hot from the oven while still soft, or I let it cool, then slice it and layer it gratin style in a baking dish, or sear it in a pan or on a grill.

Oven-Baked Polenta

MAKES 4 SERVINGS

I don't cook polenta in the traditional Italian way, stirring it slowly on top of the stove until I get a blister on the inside of my thumb. I use the easier, unsupervised oven method, tried and true for many years. You can get it started in the oven and go on to make the rest of your meal during the hour and 10 minutes of baking.

1 cup polenta

1 quart water

1 teaspoon salt

Topping of your choice (opposite page)

1 tablespoon unsalted butter

1. Heat the oven to 350°F. Combine the polenta, water, and salt in a 2-quart baking dish (it can be square, round, or oval). Stir together and place in the oven. Bake 1 hour. While the polenta is baking, prepare the topping (unless it's one of the suggested bean dishes, which should be prepared ahead).

2. Remove the polenta from the oven and stir in the butter, stirring well with a fork or a spatula. Return to the oven for 10 more minutes. Remove from the oven and stir again. Carefully taste a little bit of the polenta; if the grains are not completely soft, return to the oven for 10 more minutes.

3. Serve right away for soft polenta, or let sit 5 minutes or longer for a stiffer polenta. To serve, spoon onto a plate, make a depression in the middle, and serve with the topping of your choice. I recommend about $\frac{1}{4}$ cup marinara sauce per serving, and about twice that amount of other toppings.

NOTE: The recipe is easily doubled: Use a 3-quart baking dish for a double recipe.

ADVANCE PREPARATION: If you want soft polenta you must serve it right after you remove it from the oven, as it stiffens quickly. If you're going to use it for a gratin or to grill slices, you can keep it in the refrigerator for 2 to 3 days.

VARIATION: POLENTA WITH PARMESAN

When you remove the polenta from the oven, immediately stir in $1\frac{1}{2}$ to 2 ounces ($\frac{1}{3}$ to $\frac{1}{2}$ cup) freshly grated Parmesan. I also like to grind a little black pepper over the top.

Polenta Gratin

MAKES 4 SERVINGS

I love having firm polenta on hand. It's a great excuse for making a delicious gratin.

Make the *Oven-Baked Polenta* template (opposite page) with the following additional ingredients and specifications:

1 to 2 cups topping of your choice (any of the toppings suggested for polenta, below)

¼ to ½ cup freshly grated Gruyère or Parmesan cheese, or a mix

1 tablespoon extra virgin olive oil

1. Make the polenta as directed. Line a rimmed baking sheet or baking dish with plastic wrap or parchment and lightly oil the plastic wrap or parchment. Spoon the hot polenta onto the sheet and spread out so it is about $\frac{1}{2}$ inch thick. Allow it to cool at room temperature until stiff, about 15 minutes, or cover and chill.

2. Heat the oven to 375°F. Oil a 2-quart gratin or baking dish. Cut the polenta into squares or rectangles, or use a round cookie cutter and cut into rounds. Arrange the polenta in the dish, overlapping the pieces slightly. Spread the topping over the polenta in an even layer. Sprinkle with the cheese and drizzle with the olive oil. Bake until the mixture is bubbling and the cheese has melted, 20 to 25 minutes. Serve hot.

ADVANCE PREPARATION: You can assemble a polenta gratin up to a day ahead and refrigerate until ready to bake. You can also refrigerate the oven-baked polenta (after you've spread out to cool) for a day or two, before you assemble the gratin.

Polenta Toppings

Here are the toppings I like best, both with soft polenta and with polenta gratin:

Marinara sauce (using fresh or canned tomatoes; pages 24–27)

Marinara sauce (pages 24–27) with blanched or steamed greens (see page 3)

Mushroom Ragout (page 12)

Mediterranean Stewed Peppers (page 6)

Any simmered bean or lentil dish in Chapter 10 (page 185)

Grilled Polenta

When you grill slices of polenta, they become crispy on the edges but remain moist in the middle. The grilled slices go beautifully with the same toppings I serve with oven-baked polenta.

Make the *Oven-Baked Polenta* template (page 118) with the following additional ingredients and specifications:

Extra virgin olive oil for brushing

Topping of your choice (page 119)

1. Make the polenta as directed. Allow to cool in the baking dish, or for thinner slices spread into a lined rimmed baking sheet or baking dish as directed in the Polenta Gratin recipe (page 119), making a layer that is ¾ to 1 inch thick. Allow to cool and, if there is time, refrigerate for an hour or more so that the squares are quite stiff. You can also line a loaf pan with plastic and spread the polenta in the pan. When completely cooled, unmold and slice the polenta.

2. Heat a grill pan or an outdoor grill. Oil the pan or grill rack. Cut the chilled polenta into squares and brush lightly with olive oil on both sides. Grill for 3 to 4 minutes on each side, until grill marks appear. You can also sear the squares in a heavy pan, using enough oil to coat the bottom of the pan. Serve with any of the polenta toppings.

Millet Polenta

MAKES 6 SERVINGS

Deborah Madison, in her wonderful cookbook *Vegetable Literacy*, puts a new spin on millet for me that may have changed my millet cooking life forever. She suggests treating it like polenta, which it kind of resembles when it's cooked, with most of the grains breaking down to a mush while others remain crunchy. I'd always been a bit flummoxed by this uneven cooking and the texture of the broken down millet (it's a bit chalky). But serving it like a polenta makes perfect sense. You can serve it soft, right after it's cooked, or let it set up and then slice it and crisp the slices or use them in gratins, as I do with cornmeal polenta. The millet polenta is prepared in almost the same way as cornmeal polenta, but to coax more flavor out of the millet, I toast it in a dry skillet first, then bake it in the same skillet. You can use water or vegetable stock for the liquid.

1 cup millet

4 cups water or vegetable stock (pages 149–151)

1 teaspoon salt

1 to 2 tablespoons butter, (to taste)

½ cup freshly grated Parmesan (optional)

Freshly ground pepper

Polenta topping of your choice (see page 119), optional

1. Heat the oven to 350°F. Heat a 9- or 10-inch cast iron skillet (see Note) over medium-high heat. Add the millet and toast, stirring or shaking the pan, until the grains begin to pop and smell sort of like popcorn. Add the water or stock and salt.

2. Transfer the pan to the hot oven and bake for 25 minutes. Give the millet a stir and bake for another 25 minutes. There should still be some liquid in the pan. Stir in the butter and bake until the millet is thick and no more water or stock is visible in the pan, another 5 to 10 minutes.

3. Stir in the Parmesan (if using) and serve right away, with your choice of topping. Or allow to cool and spread in another pan or baking dish, or a small plastic-lined baking sheet (see cornmeal polenta recipes pages 119–120) and let cool until stiff. Cut into squares, slices, or rounds, which you can grill, pan-sear, or layer in a gratin.

ADVANCE PREPARATION: The firm millet will keep for 2 or 3 days in the refrigerator.

NOTE: If you don't have a heavy ovenproof skillet, toast the millet in another skillet on top of the stove until the grains smell toasty and begin to pop, then transfer to a 2-quart baking dish and proceed with the recipe.

CHAPTER SEVEN

Whole Grains and Big Bowls

W HENEVER I'M IN PORTLAND, OREGON, I try to get to the downtown pod of food trucks, my favorite destination (well, maybe tied with the Sunday farmers' market). I walk around the block looking for the longest lines, which I figure will lead me to the best food. One long line that intrigued me the first time I was there was the one snaking from a booth called The Whole Bowl. Unlike the other food trucks, which are more ethnic, Whole Bowl offerings appeared to be a throwback to the '70s—copious servings of brown rice with black beans, avocado, some vegetables, and salsa. Why then the long lines?

Comfort is the answer. A generous serving of grains topped with tasty vegetables—blanched greens finished in a skillet with garlic, rosemary, and thyme; roasted carrots, winter squash, or cauliflower bathed in the North African herb sauce chermoula or sprinkled with a Middle Eastern spice mix; simmered black beans with amaranth, spiced up with salsa and sprinkled with queso fresco—can be very comforting indeed. If some thought and effort goes into the food that tops the grains, it can also be memorable. Whenever I post these types of meals in my "Recipes for Health" column on nytimes.com, the recipes go to the top of the Most E-Mailed list; they have the same appeal as The Whole Bowl that draws a crowd in the Portland pod of food trucks.

Big Bowls suit families. The kids can eat each element separately, as kids are wont to do. But I like to stir everything together. If there's a poached egg sitting on top of the combo, I'll break it up so that the yolk runs over the vegetables and grains, and every bite is a complex surprise.

This chapter differs from the other chapters in the book because the Big Bowl instructions, such as they are, are not part of a recipe or template, but a set of guidelines for building the bowl. It's followed by instructions for cooking a variety of grains. Rather than variations on a template, the dishes in this chapter are stand-alone recipes for grain, vegetable, and condiment combos.

Though I call for specific grains in the recipes, pretty much any grain and vegetable or bean combination works, so you can substitute one grain for another if you wish. Every year I see new varieties of rice, quinoa, barley, and wheat hitting the market. They're all worth trying. Each of you will have your favorites, whether it's quinoa or bulgur, red rice or purple jasmine rice, basmati or plain old brown rice (which will always be high on my list). Noodles work as well: I've devoted this chapter to grains, but know that you can substitute soba noodles, whole wheat noodles, or rice noodles in any of the Big Bowls.

HOW TO BUILD A BIG BOWL

EACH ELEMENT OF A BIG BOWL is a side dish, but when you combine everything, the sum of the parts is a main dish. The grains are the vehicles for the vegetables. If the vegetables are simply cooked, no recipe is required; but here they're roasted, pan-cooked, or simmered with other ingredients that render them so tasty that they get all your attention. You want them at the center of the plate . . . or bowl. To supplement the grains and vegetables there's sometimes a protein element—tofu, poached eggs, beans, or cheese—though not always. I am not one who feels that a meal is not a meal without a high-protein food. Finally, there's a finish to the dish, something flavorful like a salsa, pesto, or the spiced nut and seed mix called dukkah. Grated or crumbled cheeses like feta and Parmesan can also count as finishes, as do chopped fresh herbs.

Big Bowl Building Blocks

GRAINS OR RICE	VEGETABLES AND/OR BEANS	SUPPLEMENTAL PROTEIN	SAUCES, SALSAS, AND/OR CONDIMENTS
Any of the grains featured on pages 128–135	Wilted Greens or Broccoli Raab (page 3) briefly sautéed in olive oil with garlic, thyme, and rosemary	Baked Seasoned Tofu (page 31)	Marinara sauce (pages 24–27)
Cooked soba noodles (see page 48), whole wheat noodles, or rice noodles	Roasted Peppers (page 8)	Poached Eggs (page 32)	Uncooked Tomato Sauce (page 23)
	Pan-Cooked Mushrooms (page 11)	Grated or crumbled cheese, such as feta, goat, queso fresco, Gruyère, or Parmesan	Basil or parsley pesto (pages 29 and 30)
	Roasted winter squash, eggplant, cauliflower, or broccoli (pages 18–21)	Canned beans such as chickpeas, drained and rinsed	Chermoula (page 143)
	Any of the bean recipes in Chapter 10 (page 185)	Drained yogurt or garlic yogurt	Salsa Fresca (page 205)
	Any of the vegetable and bean stews in Chapter 13 (page 249)		Chopped nuts or seeds such as walnuts or sesame seeds
			Salsa Ranchera (page 206)
			Fresh Tomatillo Salsa (page 208)
			Harissa (page 254)
			Preserved Lemons (page 260)
			Dukkah (page 137)
			Chopped fresh herbs (parsley, tarragon, basil, dill, chives, sage)
			Extra virgin olive oil

Assemble Your Bowl

1. Spoon the grains into deep or wide bowls, or onto plates. I usually serve ³⁄₄ to 1 cup of cooked grains per serving for these dishes. You can serve as little as ¹⁄₂ cup and as much as 1¹⁄₂ cups.
2. Place vegetables and/or beans on top of the grains.
3. If using seasoned tofu, arrange beside or on top of the vegetables. If using poached eggs, place on top of the vegetables. (If there is a tomato sauce, it can go under or over the egg.)
4. Spoon, sprinkle, or arrange supplemental beans, cheese, yogurt, and condiments, including sauces and salsas, on top.

(ALMOST) EVERY GRAIN IN THE BOOK

EVERY TIME I THINK I'VE COOKED every grain there is, another one appears at Whole Foods Market or in the Bob's Red Mill catalog. Or I find out that Alter Eco, a company devoted to Fair Trade production of foods and textiles, is launching a new and colorful variety of rice or quinoa that I've never seen before and can't wait to cook.

I don't love every grain, and not every grain that comes onto the market works well for the Big Bowls in this chapter. Tiny grains, like amaranth and teff, tend to cook up to a mush, and though that might work for a breakfast cereal or as a cooked grain to bulk up a gratin, I don't much care for them when served on their own. Millet, which I've finally grown to like, I prefer when prepared like polenta (see page 121), because it tends to break down during cooking.

Over the decades that I've been working with whole grains, I've changed my cooking methods for some of them more than once. Quinoa is a case in point. There are a few ways to cook it. You can cook it in $1\frac{1}{2}$ to 2 times its volume of water (depending on the type; blond quinoa requires less water than black or red quinoa), or you can cook it in abundant water, like pasta, then drain it. The grains are fluffier when you cook it this way, but you have to be careful not to let them get waterlogged. I may change my cooking methods again, but I've cataloged the grains I use in the pages that follow. If you find that you have better luck following instructions on a package, which may differ from these, by all means use the method that works best for you.

How to Make Dry, Fluffy Grains

I learned this technique for rice pilaf from Clifford A. Wright and find that it's a great trick to use with just about any grain to achieve a dry, fluffy result. When the grains are cooked, drain them if necessary and return to the pot. Place a clean dry dishtowel across the top of the pot and return the lid. Let sit undisturbed for 10 to 15 minutes (or longer, until you're ready to serve). The towel absorbs steam and the grains will be dry and fluffy instead of sticky and clumpy or waterlogged.

White Rice and Basmati Rice

Rice can be cooked many ways, but I'm giving you the technique that I find to be most reliable, whether I'm cooking regular Carolina rice, basmati rice, or jasmine rice. The amount of liquid will affect the texture of your rice. A ratio of 2 parts liquid to 1 part rice produces soft, tender rice. You will get chewier rice if you use less liquid, say 1½ parts liquid to 1 part rice. In Asia, where the rice is fluffy but dry, most cooks don't use measures and proportions at all. Instead, they use this trick: They determine the amount of liquid to use by covering the rice with enough water to rise above the rice by the length of the first joint of your index finger.

Basmati rice is traditionally soaked for 30 minutes or up to 2 hours before cooking. The raw grains are brittle, and soaking them gives them the chance to absorb a little water, so that they won't break during cooking. But the truth is, I never remember to do this and my rice turns out fine.

1 cup basmati rice or long- to medium-grain white rice

1½ to 2 cups water

½ to ¾ teaspoon salt (or to taste)

1. Place the rice in a bowl in the sink and rinse under cool running water and drain several times, until the water runs clear or almost clear. If using basmati rice and you remember and have the time, soak for 30 minutes; but don't worry if you skip this step. Drain.

2. Combine the water, rice, and salt in a heavy 2- or 3-quart saucepan with a tight-fitting lid. Bring to a boil, reduce the heat to low, and cover. Simmer until all of the liquid has been absorbed, 12 to 15 minutes. Turn off the heat.

3. Uncover the rice and place a clean dishtowel over the top of the pan (it should not be touching the rice). Replace the lid and allow to sit for at least 10 minutes, undisturbed. Serve.

VARIATION: MIDDLE EASTERN PILAF

After Step 1, heat 1 to 2 tablespoons butter or oil in the heavy 2- or 3-quart saucepan over medium heat. If desired, add ¼ to ½ cup finely chopped onion and cook, stirring, until it begins to soften, about 3 minutes. Add the rice and cook, stirring, for 2 to 3 minutes, until the rice is sizzling and the grains are separate. Add the water and the salt and continue with the recipe.

VARIATION:

Substitute stock or broth for the water.

ADVANCE PREPARATION: Cooked rice, all types, will keep for 3 days in the refrigerator and can be frozen. Spread the rice in a lightly oiled 2-quart baking dish and allow to cool completely, uncovered. To reheat, cover with foil and place in a 325°F oven for 20 minutes.

Brown Rice

There are many shapes and sizes and varieties of brown rice now available in natural foods stores. I went to Whole Foods to check this out one day and found long-grain, medium-grain, and short-grain brown rice, Calrose brown rice, sprouted brown rice, brown basmati rice, brown jasmine rice, and sticky brown rice, just to name a few.

I cook all of the various types of brown rice the same way I cook white rice, but for 40 to 45 minutes, until all of the water has been absorbed by the rice, by which time the rice will be cooked through and chewy/tender. I don't rinse brown rice as many times as basmati rice because there isn't as much starch that needs to be rinsed away. Some package instructions say to use $2\frac{1}{2}$ cups water for 1 cup rice, but the results are too mushy when I use that much water. However, if I'm scaling down a recipe and cooking only $\frac{1}{2}$ cup of rice (I rarely cook that small a quantity), 1 cup of water won't be quite enough, so I use $1\frac{1}{4}$ cups.

New Rice Varieties

The method for cooking all of these varieties is the same as for white and brown rice. See the chart on page 131 for rice and liquid measures, cooking times, and yields.

LUNDBERG WEHANI: A reddish brown whole-grain rice developed by Lundberg Family Farms in California. The grains have a slightly chewy texture and nutty, savory flavor.

LUNDBERG BLACK JAPONICA RICE: A combination of medium-grain mahogany rice and short-grain black rice, grown in the same field by Lundberg Family Farms. When cooked it looks like black rice and has a chewy texture.

RUBY RED RICE: A rich, earthy-tasting, red long-grain rice distributed by Alter Eco, a French company that specializes in the distribution of Fair Trade products (including terrific chocolates). The package says to cook 1 part rice in $2\frac{1}{2}$ parts water, but I find that a ratio of 1 to 2 works better. The texture of the cooked rice is soft.

THAI STICKY PURPLE RICE: Alter Eco packages this medley of Khao Nio Dam rice and Thai white rice. The purple color dominates, a beautiful dark, fragrant mixture with a sticky texture.

BHUTANESE RED RICE: A beautiful medium-grain red rice imported from Bhutan by Lotus Foods, this has a nutty flavor and a chewy texture that is slightly sticky.

FORBIDDEN RICE: This is a black rice imported from China by Lotus Foods. The cooked rice is dark purple and quite beautiful, with a chewy texture.

Wild Rice

MAKES 3 CUPS

While technically a grass and not related to rice, we put wild rice in the same category. It used to be very rare and expensive, but Lundberg cultivates it now and it's easy to come by. I've always loved the nutty, musty-earthy flavor and the look of wild rice. Interestingly, when I lived in France I brought some back from a trip to Minnesota to cook for my French friends, and they didn't like it at all. They thought it was ugly!

It's important when you cook wild rice to cook it long enough so that the grains begin to splay, to burst at one end or even all the way through. Otherwise you don't get the full flavor of the rice: It feels hard, like it's withholding something within that shell, and it is! I cook it in abundant stock or water; the liquid that isn't absorbed by the rice is quite tasty and has some texture from the starch in the rice. Don't throw the liquid away: It makes a nice addition to a stock, and can be used in multigrain risottos (page 160–162) or to cook your next batch of wild rice.

3½ cups vegetable stock (pages 149–151) or water

1 teaspoon salt

1 cup wild rice

1. Bring the stock or water to a boil in a large saucepan and add the salt and rice. Reduce the heat, cover, and simmer until the rice grains are tender and beginning to splay, 40 to 45 minutes.

2. Set a strainer over a bowl and drain the rice. Return it to the saucepan, cover the saucepan with a dishtowel, replace the lid, and let sit until ready to serve.

ADVANCE PREPARATION: Wild rice will keep in the refrigerator for about 3 days and can be frozen.

Cooking Rice at a Glance

Each type of rice yields a different amount when cooked (see below). Basmati expands to a good three times its original volume, so 1 cup of rice yields 3 cups cooked rice, which can feed four people if eaten as a side dish. But if it's at the center of your plate (or bowl, or the stir-fried rice dishes in Chapter 9), 1 cup would feed two, perhaps with a little left over. When you begin to make meals out of the Big Bowls in this chapter you will settle upon a quantity that works best for you and the members of your family.

1 CUP RICE	SALT	WATER OR STOCK	SIMMERING TIME (COVERED)	YIELD
White (medium- and long-grain)	½ to ¾ teaspoon	1½ to 2 cups	15 minutes	2 cups
Basmati	½ to ¾ teaspoon	1½ to 2 cups	15 minutes	3 cups
Brown basmati	½ to ¾ teaspoon	2 cups	35 to 40 minutes	3 cups
Brown (short-, medium-, and long-grain)	½ to ¾ teaspoon	2 cups	40 to 45 minutes	2 cups
Wild rice	1 teaspoon	3½ cups	40 to 45 minutes	3 cups
Lundberg Wehani	½ to ¾ teaspoon	2 cups	50 to 60 minutes	3 cups
Lundberg Black Japonica	½ to ¾ teaspoon	2 cups	40 minutes	3 cups
Ruby Red	½ to ¾ teaspoon	2 cups	30 minutes	3 cups
Thai Sticky Purple	½ to ¾ teaspoon	2 cups	25 minutes	3 cups
Bhutanese Red	½ to ¾ teaspoon	1½ cups	20 minutes	3 cups
Forbidden Rice	½ to ¾ teaspoon	2 cups	30 to 40 minutes	3 cups

Bulgur

MAKES 2 CUPS

Bulgur is a Middle Eastern staple made from durum wheat. It's made by boiling hard wheat berries until they are about to crack open, then allowing them to dry, at which point the outer bran layers are rubbed off and the grains are ground. Bulgur comes in one of four grades—fine (#1), medium (#2), coarse (#3), and very coarse (#4). The different grinds are used for specific types of dishes. Pilafs are made with medium, coarse, and very coarse bulgur. Tabouli and kibbe are made with fine bulgur.

This is a convenient grain to have on hand in your pantry. It's easy to find in natural foods stores and in Middle Eastern markets. Don't confuse it with cracked wheat, which is another product made from raw wheat berries. Because bulgur is made from precooked wheat berries, it takes only about 20 minutes to reconstitute, just by soaking or by simmering. I usually simmer coarse bulgur and soak medium and fine bulgur in boiling water to reconstitute. The grain has a wonderful nutty flavor and a light texture.

1 cup coarse, medium, or fine bulgur

½ to ¾ teaspoon salt

2 cups water

COARSE BULGUR

Bring the water to a boil in a medium saucepan and add the bulgur and salt. When the water returns to a boil, reduce the heat, cover, and simmer until the water has been absorbed, about 20 minutes. Remove from the heat, remove the lid, and cover the pot with a dishtowel. Return the lid and allow to sit undisturbed for 10 minutes.

FINE OR MEDIUM BULGUR

1. Place the bulgur in a bowl and add the salt. Swish in the bowl to distribute the salt. Pour on 2 cups hot or boiling water and allow the bulgur to sit until softened, about 20 minutes.

2. Transfer the bulgur to a strainer set in your sink and press it against the strainer to remove excess water.

ADVANCE PREPARATION: Reconstituted bulgur will keep for 3 days in the refrigerator and can be frozen.

Farro, Spelt, and Kamut

MAKES 3 CUPS FARRO OR SPELT, 2½ CUPS KAMUT

There are several varieties of whole-grain wheat available in natural foods stores and online. In addition to wheat berries from North American wheat, it's now easy to get hold of ancient strains—farro, spelt, and Kamut. There is some argument in the food community about whether or not spelt and farro are exactly the same botanical strain of wheat. From my point of view, it doesn't really matter, as I find them to be interchangeable in cooking. They're long-cooking, nutty-tasting, chewy, hearty grains that contribute to a very satisfying dinner in a bowl.

Deborah Madison tells us in her book *Vegetable Literacy* that the ancient varieties of wheat have fewer chromosomes and lower levels of gluten proteins than the modern wheat that is the source of flour in the United States. People with full-blown celiac disease cannot tolerate even a little bit of gluten, but some people with mild gluten (or wheat) intolerance do better with these grains, as well as with barley, which also contains gluten and is another ancient grain. The ancient varieties of wheat have a good nutritional profile, better than that of modern wheat. Kamut, for example, is higher in protein than many whole grains.

Wheat berries of all kinds will cook faster and will be softer if you soak them before cooking. You can cover them with boiling water and soak them for an hour, or you can soak them overnight in water from the tap. It's important to cook wheat berries until they begin to splay, or burst at one end. That way they'll absorb the flavors of whatever you're serving them with and they'll be easier to chew and digest.

1 cup wheat berries (any variety: farro, spelt, Kamut)

Boiling water

1 quart water

¾ to 1 teaspoon salt

1. Place the wheat berries in a bowl and cover with boiling water. Soak for 1 hour and drain. Alternatively, soak overnight in cold water to cover.

2. Combine the drained wheat berries with 1 quart of water in a saucepan. Bring to a boil and add the salt. Reduce the heat, cover, and simmer until the grains are tender and just beginning to splay at one end, about 50 minutes. Turn off the heat and leave the grains to soak and swell further in the cooking water for 15 minutes. Drain off excess water (set the strainer over a bowl to catch the liquid and add to stocks if desired; it will have a pleasant flavor and a nice texture). Return the wheat berries to the pot. Cover the pot with a dishtowel, return the lid, and let sit until ready to serve.

ADVANCE PREPARATION: Cooked wheat berries will keep for 3 to 4 days in the refrigerator and freeze well.

Barley

MAKES 3 CUPS

Barley is a chewy, hearty grain born to accompany mushrooms in soups and pilafs. It goes well with many other vegetables as well—peas and greens, onions and leeks are favorites. Most of the barley we get in stores has had its husk removed and is called pearled barley; it has lost some nutrients by being pearled, but it cooks up a little faster than whole unpearled barley. I like to toast barley before cooking it.

1 cup barley

3 to 4 cups water or vegetable stock (pages 149–151)

¾ to 1 teaspoon salt

1. Heat a medium saucepan over medium heat and add the barley. Toast it in the pan, stirring the grains until they begin to smell a little bit like popcorn.

2. Add the water or stock and bring to a boil. Add the salt, reduce the heat, cover, and simmer until the barley is tender (it will always be chewy), 45 to 50 minutes.

3. Drain off any liquid remaining in the pot through a strainer set over a bowl (the liquid can be added to stocks). Return the barley to the pot, cover the pot with a towel, and return the lid. Allow to sit for 10 to 15 minutes before serving.

ADVANCE PREPARATION: Cooked barley will keep for 3 days in the refrigerator and freezes well.

Toasting Grains

Some grains benefit from toasting in a dry skillet, or sometimes in oil, or on a baking sheet in the oven, before simmering. Quinoa, barley, and millet are the grains I most often toast first. Just stir in the pan over medium-high heat, either dry or using 1 tablespoon oil for each cup of grain, until they begin to smell a little bit like popcorn, then add water or stock and follow the basic cooking directions. If you toast in the oven, put the grain on a baking sheet and place in a 325°F oven for 10 to 15 minutes, until you get that faint popcorn aroma.

Quinoa

MAKES 3½ CUPS BLOND AND RAINBOW QUINOA, 2½ CUPS RED AND BLACK QUINOA

Quinoa has become so popular in the United States that, once exclusively grown in Bolivia and Peru, it is now being grown in the western states. It's a high-protein grain, light and grassy. There are three varieties—blond, black, and red—that are sometimes packaged together as "rainbow quinoa." The black and red varieties have a smaller, tighter grain and even more nutrients than the blond variety because of the anthocyanins in the red and black pigments. They take a little longer to cook than the blond variety.

There is more than one way to cook quinoa. Toasting it first adds depth to the flavor. Rinse the quinoa thoroughly, then toast in the oven or a dry skillet (see opposite page) if you like. You can cook quinoa in abundant water, and drain it, like pasta, or cook it like rice. I find that the quinoa is slightly fluffier when I cook it like pasta, perhaps because the grains have more room to swell.

1 cup quinoa

1 quart water

1 teaspoon salt

PASTA METHOD

1. Toast the quinoa if desired (see opposite page).

2. Bring the water to a boil in a large saucepan and add the salt and quinoa. Bring back to a boil and cook blond quinoa for 15 minutes, until you see a little thread emerge from the grain. Cook red and black (and rainbow) quinoa for 20 minutes; you will see the thread in red quinoa, but not black, but you will see that the grain has burst.

3. Drain the quinoa and shake the strainer well to remove excess water. Return the quinoa to the pot. Cover the pot with a dishtowel and return the lid. Let sit for 15 minutes or longer.

1 cup quinoa

1½ cups water for blond and red quinoa, 2 cups water for black and rainbow quinoa

½ to ¾ teaspoon salt

RICE METHOD

1. Toast the quinoa if desired (see opposite page).

2. Combine the quinoa, water, and salt in a medium saucepan and bring to a boil. Cover, reduce the heat, and simmer until there is no longer any liquid in the pot and the white and red quinoa display a thread spiral. Blond quinoa will take 15 minutes; black, red, and rainbow quinoa will take 20 minutes,

3. Turn off the heat, remove the lid, and place a dishtowel over the pot. Return the lid and let sit for 10 to 15 minutes.

Black or Wehani Rice with Sweet Pepper Ragout and Poached Eggs

MAKES 4 TO 6 SERVINGS

You don't have to use black rice for this but it does look beautiful against the red peppers. Adding a poached egg makes this comforting dish much like the North African dish Chakchouka (page 8), with the addition of grains making it a meal. Use any of the versions of the stewed peppers on page 6, but include enough sweet red pepper so that you get the color against the rice. Sometimes I sprinkle the Middle Eastern spice mix called dukkah over the poached egg.

1 cup Black Japonica, Wehani Rice, or Forbidden Rice, cooked (see page 129)

Mediterranean Stewed Peppers (page 6), any version

4 to 6 eggs, poached (see page 32)

Salt and freshly ground pepper

1 to 2 tablespoons chopped fresh parsley, basil, marjoram, or chives (to taste)

2 to 3 ounces crumbled feta cheese or freshly grated Parmesan (½ to ¾ cup)

Dukkah (opposite) for sprinkling (optional)

1. Distribute the rice among 4 to 6 bowls or plates. Top with the stewed peppers.

2. Set the poached eggs on top of the peppers and rice.

3. Season the eggs with salt and pepper and sprinkle the herbs over the mix. Sprinkle on the cheese and optional dukkah and serve.

ADVANCE PREPARATION: The stewed peppers will keep for about 5 days in the refrigerator. The cooked rice will keep for 3 days and freezes well.

Dukkah

MAKES ABOUT 1¼ CUPS

This Middle Eastern nut and spice mix has become a staple in my home. I sprinkle it on all sorts of vegetable preparations, on yogurt, sometimes just into the palm of my hand to eat as a snack. In the Middle East, bread and raw vegetables are dipped into olive oil and then dipped into or sprinkled with dukkah. I like to sprinkle it over vegetables and grains and use it often in Big Bowls. The mix has many variations, differing from cook to cook and country to country throughout the Middle East.

½ cup unsalted peanuts, almonds, or hazelnuts (or a combination), lightly toasted

¼ cup sesame seeds, lightly toasted

2 tablespoons coriander seeds

1 tablespoon cumin seeds

2 teaspoons nigella seeds

1 teaspoon ground sumac

½ teaspoon kosher salt or coarse sea salt (or to taste)

Chop the nuts very fine. Mix with the toasted sesame seeds in a bowl. In a dry skillet over medium-high heat, lightly toast the coriander seeds, shaking the pan constantly, just until fragrant, usually no more than 3 minutes. Immediately transfer to a spice mill and allow to cool. In the same skillet, toast the cumin seeds just until fragrant. Transfer to the spice mill and allow to cool. When the spices have cooled, grind and add to the bowl with the nuts and sesame seeds. Add the nigella seeds, sumac, and salt and mix together.

ADVANCE PREPARATION: Dukkah will keep for at least a month in a jar if you keep it in the freezer.

SUBSTITUTIONS AND ADDITIONS: Add to or substitute for the nuts and spices listed:

- *¹/₂ cup chickpea flour, lightly toasted*
- *¹/₂ cup pumpkin seeds, toasted*
- *¹/₄ cup shredded coconut, lightly toasted*
- *1 to 2 tablespoons dried mint*
- *1 to 2 tablespoons dill seeds*
- *1 to 2 tablespoons fennel seeds*
- *¹/₂ to 1 teaspoon cayenne, chili powder, or Aleppo pepper*
- *¹/₄ to ¹/₂ teaspoon ground black pepper*

Wild Rice with Seared Brussels Sprouts, Winter Squash, and Tofu

VEGAN /// **MAKES 4 SERVINGS**

When I pan-cook Brussels sprouts and squash we sometimes can't even wait until we put together a Big Bowl; the vegetables are just too tempting. But if you can wait, make a meal of them with grains and baked seasoned tofu. Wild rice is perfect with this medley. Make sure you turn on your exhaust fan before you begin cooking the Brussels sprouts as the oil becomes quite hot; I have set off my smoke alarm when I neglected to turn on the fan.

Baked Seasoned Tofu (page 31; retain marinade)

4 to 6 tablespoons extra virgin olive oil, as needed

½ pound Brussels sprouts, trimmed and halved lengthwise through the stem end

Salt and freshly ground pepper

1 pound peeled, seeded winter squash, such as kabocha or butternut, cut into ¼-inch-thick, 2- or 3-inch-long slices

2 to 3 tablespoons chopped fresh mint

1 cup wild rice, cooked (see page 130)

1. Heat the oven to 250°F. Place the baked seasoned tofu in a baking dish, add its marinade, and warm in the oven while you cook the Brussels sprouts and squash.

2. Heat 2 tablespoons of the oil over medium-high heat in a large, heavy skillet, preferably cast iron. When it is rippling, place the Brussels sprouts in the oil, cut side down. Turn the heat to medium and sear on one side until nicely browned, 2 to 3 minutes. Turn the Brussels sprouts over and cook on the other side until nicely browned and tender, 3 to 5 minutes. Don't worry if some of the leaves are charred dark brown or black. Transfer to a baking sheet or baking dish, season with salt and pepper (try not to eat them up right away), and keep warm in the low oven.

3. Heat another 2 tablespoons olive oil over medium-high heat in the same skillet. Add one layer of squash slices and cook until lightly browned on the first side, about 3 minutes. Flip over and cook until lightly browned on the other side and tender all the way through. Season to taste with salt and pepper and transfer to the pan with the Brussels sprouts. If you cannot cook all of the squash at once, heat the remaining oil and cook another batch. Sprinkle the chopped mint over the vegetables.

4. Cut the tofu into strips. Spoon the wild rice into bowls or onto plates and spoon a little of the tofu marinade over the rice. Top with the seared vegetables and strips of tofu and serve.

ADVANCE PREPARATION: The wild rice will keep for about 3 days in the refrigerator and freezes well. The tofu will keep for a couple of days in the refrigerator and can be reheated in a medium oven.

Farro with Mushroom Ragout and Spinach

VEGAN WITHOUT THE CHEESE /// **MAKES 6 SERVINGS**

Farro, or any of the other varieties of whole wheat berries (such as spelt, Kamut, and wheat berries), is a perfect vehicle for my savory Mushroom Ragout. The hearty grains stand up to the meaty essence of the mushrooms. If you don't have the time to make the ragout, then do the quicker Pan-Cooked Mushrooms on page 11 (you'll need a double recipe for 6 people). The mixture begs for some dark green produce, but nothing too robust, as we already have that with the mushrooms. Spinach is perfect. Chard would also work.

1 generous bunch spinach (more if desired), stemmed, washed thoroughly in 2 changes of water, and coarsely chopped; or 2 bags baby spinach

2 teaspoons extra virgin olive oil

Salt and freshly ground pepper

1 cup farro, cooked (see page 133)

Mushroom Ragout (page 12)

2 to 3 ounces shredded Gruyère or Parmesan cheese (½ to ¾ cup)

1. Steam the spinach for 1 minute, just until it wilts. Transfer to a bowl and toss with the olive oil. Season with salt and pepper to taste.

2. Spoon the farro into wide bowls or onto plates. Stir the spinach into the mushroom ragout and spoon onto the grains; or, top the farro with the mushrooms and arrange a clump of cooked spinach on one side or on top. Sprinkle Gruyère or Parmesan over the top and serve hot.

ADVANCE PREPARATION: The ragout can be made up to 3 or 4 days before you wish to serve it. Keep in the refrigerator. Reheat gently on top of the stove. The wheat berries will keep for 3 days in the refrigerator and freeze well. The spinach can be wilted a day or 2 ahead as well and reheated with the olive oil in a small skillet.

Drained Yogurt

Thick Greek-style yogurt isn't difficult to find these days. But you can also make your own drained yogurt, which is a little thicker. To make 1 cup of drained yogurt you will need 2 cups of plain yogurt. It can be low-fat or whole-milk yogurt, but not nonfat.

Line a strainer with a double thickness of cheesecloth and set over a bowl. Place 2 cups yogurt in the strainer and refrigerate for at least 2 hours, preferably 4 hours or overnight. Transfer the drained yogurt to a covered container and refrigerate.

ADVANCE PREPARATION: Drained yogurt will last through the sell-by date on your yogurt container. It will continue to give up water in the container, which you can simply pour off.

Big Grain Bowl with Black Beans, Greens, and Avocado

VEGAN WITHOUT THE CHEESE /// **MAKES 4 TO 6 SERVINGS**

The iconic Whole Bowl that draws long lines at the food truck pod in central Portland consists of brown rice and black beans, avocado, and salsa. This version takes that Portland bowl up a notch.

3 cups cooked grains (see pages 128–135), such as brown or red rice, quinoa, or barley

Black Beans with Amaranth, Spinach, or Chard (page 189)

1 or 2 Hass avocados, sliced or diced

Chopped cilantro

Salsa Fresca (page 205)

Crumbled feta cheese or queso fresco

Spoon the grains into deep or wide bowls. Top with the black beans and greens. Garnish with avocado and cilantro. Add a spoonful of salsa, sprinkle feta or queso fresco over the top, and serve.

ADVANCE PREPARATION: Both the cooked beans and cooked grains will keep for 3 days in the refrigerator and freeze well.

Garlic Yogurt

This is a typical condiment for many Turkish, Greek, and Middle Eastern dishes. You can also stir in chopped fresh herbs such as mint, dill, or parsley, and/or finely chopped or grated cucumber.

1 to 2 plump garlic cloves (or more to taste)

¼ to ½ teaspoon salt

1 to 2 cups drained yogurt (opposite) or Greek-style yogurt

Cut the garlic cloves in half lengthwise. Discard any green shoots running down the middle. Combine the garlic and salt in a mortar and crush the garlic with the pestle. Then grind and mash until the garlic is reduced to a puree. Stir into the yogurt.

ADVANCE PREPARATION: I don't like making this too far in advance because the garlic becomes stronger and more acrid once it is exposed to the air.

Big Bowl with Roasted Beets, Beet Greens, and Garlic Yogurt

MAKES 4 SERVINGS

Roasted beets served with their greens and topped with garlicky yogurt is one of my favorite Greek dishes. It's served as a *mezze* (starter) in Greece, but here it's a component of a main-dish Big Bowl. I like beets and their greens with lighter grains like bulgur or quinoa, but I wouldn't say no to just about any grain topped with this combination. A dark rice like Bhutanese red rice or Wehani would also be good. Black or red rice will appeal if you don't like the look of the grains stained with beets (I like it). If you can, use two different colors of beets, such as red beets and Chioggias. In this dish, rather than season the greens with garlic as I usually do, the garlic is in the pungent yogurt that goes on top.

2 bunches beets with generous greens (2 different colors, if possible)

2 tablespoons chopped fresh dill, parsley, or mint

2 tablespoons extra virgin olive oil

Salt and freshly ground pepper

1 to 1½ cups bulgur, quinoa, or rice, cooked

1 to 2 tablespoons fresh lemon juice (or more to taste)

1 cup Garlic Yogurt (page 141)

3 tablespoons chopped walnuts

1. Cut away the greens from the beets. Roast the beets (see page 20) and allow to cool in the covered baking dish. Cut away the ends and slip off the skins. Dice the beets, toss with half the chopped fresh herbs, and set aside.

2. While the beets are in the oven, stem the greens and wash in at least 2 changes of water. Chop coarsely and place in a bowl.

3. Heat a large wide skillet over high heat. Add the greens by the handful, stirring each handful until the greens wilt in the water left after washing. Once one batch has wilted, add another until all of the greens are wilted. Add 1 tablespoon of the olive oil and turn the heat down to low. Season with salt and pepper, cover, and simmer for 5 minutes. The greens should be tender but still bright. Stir in the remaining chopped herbs and turn off the heat.

4. Distribute the grains among 4 bowls or plates. Reheat the greens in the pan (if necessary) and add 1 tablespoon lemon juice. Toss together and distribute among the bowls or plates. Top with the diced beets. Drizzle on the remaining 1 tablespoon olive oil and squeeze on another tablespoon of lemon juice, or more to taste. Place spoonfuls of the garlic yogurt over the tops of the beets and beet greens, sprinkle on the walnuts, and serve.

ADVANCE PREPARATION: The roasted beets will keep for 4 to 5 days in the refrigerator, as will the wilted greens, but don't add the lemon juice until you're ready to serve because the color will quickly go from bright to drab. The cooked grains will keep for about 3 days in the refrigerator.

Chermoula

MAKES ABOUT 1 CUP

Chermoula is a pungent Moroccan herb sauce that is traditionally used as a marinade and accompaniment for grilled fish. I think it's delicious with roasted vegetables; it's a great condiment for Big Bowls (it also makes a terrific sandwich relish). The herbs don't need to be ground into a paste as they are in a pesto, but can instead be finely chopped in a food processor (in fact, the word is derived from the word *sharmula*, which means to tear lightly—thank you, Clifford A. Wright).

2 cups cilantro leaves (2 large bunches)

1½ cups flat-leaf parsley leaves (1 large bunch)

3 to 4 garlic cloves (to taste), halved, green shoots removed

½ teaspoon salt (plus more to taste)

2 teaspoons cumin seeds, lightly toasted and ground

1 teaspoon sweet paprika

½ teaspoon coriander seeds, lightly toasted and ground

⅛ teaspoon cayenne (or more to taste)

⅓ to ½ cup extra virgin olive oil (to taste)

¼ cup fresh lemon juice

1. Start by coarsely chopping the cilantro and parsley leaves on a cutting board.

2. Turn on a food processor and drop in the garlic. When it is chopped and adhering to the sides of the bowl, scrape down the bowl and add the chopped herbs, salt, and spices. Pulse together several times until the herbs are finely chopped, then turn on the machine and slowly add ⅓ cup olive oil and the lemon juice. When all of the oil and the lemon juice have been added, stop the machine, taste, and adjust seasoning. Add more olive oil or salt if desired.

ADVANCE PREPARATION: This is best when it is freshest, but you can pour a film of olive oil over the top and keep it for a few days in a jar in the refrigerator.

Basmati Rice with Roasted Vegetables, Chermoula, and Chickpeas

VEGAN WITHOUT THE EGGS /// **MAKES 4 TO 6 SERVINGS**

I love to toss roasted vegetables with chermoula, the Moroccan herb relish made with cilantro, parsley, olive oil, lemon juice, and spices. It's delicious with sweet vegetables like winter squash, carrots, and parsnips. You can steam the rice and make the chermoula while the vegetables are roasting. This can be a vegan dish with the chickpeas only, or you can top the bowl with a poached egg.

2 to 2½ pounds mixed root vegetables (such as carrots, parsnips, turnips, fennel, shallots), trimmed, peeled, and cut into 1-inch pieces; or 2½ pounds winter squash, peeled and cut into ½- to 1-inch dice

2 to 3 tablespoons extra virgin olive oil (to taste)

Salt and freshly ground pepper

½ to 1 cup Chermoula (page 143), to taste

1 (15-ounce) can chickpeas, drained and rinsed; or 1½ cups cooked chickpeas

1 cup basmati rice, cooked (see page 128)

4 eggs, poached (see page 32), optional

1. Toss the vegetables with the olive oil and salt and pepper to taste. Roast following the directions on page 15.

2. Transfer the vegetables to a bowl, add the chermoula and chickpeas, and toss together.

3. Spoon the rice into bowls or onto plates. Top with the vegetables and chickpeas. If desired, top the vegetables with a poached egg. Season the egg with salt and pepper and serve.

ADVANCE PREPARATION: The chermoula can be made a day ahead. The cooked rice will keep for 3 days in the refrigerator.

SUBSTITUTIONS AND ADDITIONS: Substitute 2 to 2½ pounds cauliflower for the root vegetables or squash (or add a smaller quantity) and roast following the recipe on page 19.

CHAPTER EIGHT

Risotto

ISOTTO IS ONE OF THE easiest of dinners to pull together if you have stock on hand, yet it also always strikes me as something fancy, a luxurious dish I can make on short notice for a small dinner party (small because making more than a double recipe of risotto can be tricky as the rice can become gummy if not served right away). It has that luxurious air about it because it's creamy, even though there's no cream in it. The starch from short-grain Italian rice leaches into the stock as you stir risotto, and that is what makes it creamy.

The stock is very important to the richness of the dish, so make a flavorful vegetable or garlic stock for your vegetarian risottos. For some risottos a stock that's based on the vegetable that is at the heart of your risotto makes the most sense—a mushroom stock (page 151) for a mushroom risotto, for example. But this doesn't always work; some vegetables (like greens and cruciferous vegetables) don't make good stock. Both the simple vegetable stock (page 149) and garlic stock (page 150) are good, rich-tasting broths to use with any of the risottos in this chapter.

In recent years I've been making classic risottos with Arborio rice (Carnaroli and French

Camargue rice also work), but also I've taken to combining Arborio rice with other heartier, less-starchy whole grains for mixed-grains risottos. I begin making these risottos following my template, starting with a small amount of Arborio, which is needed to get the right creamy texture, and at the end I stir in a greater amount of other cooked whole grains. Templates for both types of risotto are in this chapter.

THE IMPORTANCE OF STOCK

I DON'T OFTEN USE STOCKS WHEN I make soups, but you will need them for risottos, so I've placed them in this chapter. If you aren't vegetarian, you can use chicken stock (preferably homemade), otherwise it's easy to make vegetable stocks.

You can try boxed vegetarian stocks, but I haven't found one I like. They taste like stale onions and garlic to me. Some bouillon that comes in cubes is acceptable, but most of them are full of salt and additives. You can come up with something much better just by simmering vegetable trimmings or a couple of heads of garlic (cut in half across the middle) with a bouquet garni for 30 minutes. Dried mushrooms and mushroom stems also make a robust, meaty stock.

The three stocks that follow are simple. Unlike meat stocks, they're ready in an hour or less. The simple vegetable stock has a sweet flavor; the garlic stock has a deeper, richer flavor that stands in well for chicken stock; and the mushroom stock has a rich, umami/meaty flavor. In addition to these, some of the risotto recipes will instruct you to simmer the vegetable trimmings to create a stock: pea pods when using fresh peas, for example, or asparagus stems for asparagus risotto.

A note on seasoning: The recipes instruct you to make sure that your stock is well seasoned, and this is important. But make sure not to oversalt, because the stock reduces during the course of the risotto making process and it can become too salty if you're not careful.

Simple Vegetable Stock

MAKES ABOUT 7 CUPS

This is a very easy, mild, almost sweet-tasting stock in which the vegetables are just thrown into the pot with water and a bouquet garni. You can add other trimmings, but don't use potatoes because they'll cloud the stock. The reason there are so many carrots is that they give the stock a very sweet flavor.

2 quarts water

1 onion, quartered

3 large carrots, thickly sliced

1 celery stalk, sliced

4 to 8 garlic cloves (to taste), crushed and peeled

1 leek, white and green parts (unless you want a clearer stock, in which case don't use the dark green parts), cleaned and sliced

A bouquet garni: a bay leaf, a couple of sprigs each thyme and parsley, and a fresh sage leaf tied with a string or in cheesecloth

Salt

CHOICE OF VEGETABLE TRIMMINGS

Chard stalks, sliced

Parsley stems, sliced

Leek greens, cleaned and sliced

Mushroom stems

Scallion trimmings

Combine the water with all of remaining ingredients in a large soup pot, pasta pot, or Dutch oven and bring to a boil. Reduce the heat, cover partially, and simmer gently for 30 minutes. Strain through a fine strainer. Taste and adjust salt.

ADVANCE PREPARATION: This is best used within a day of being made, but you can freeze it.

Garlic Stock

MAKES ABOUT 2 QUARTS

Whole cloves of garlic, uncut and simmered gently for an hour with aromatics, yield a mild, sweet-tasting, comforting stock that makes an ideal vegetarian stand-in for chicken stock.

2 heads garlic

2 quarts water

1 tablespoon extra virgin olive oil

A bouquet garni: a bay leaf, a couple of sprigs each thyme and parsley, and a fresh sage leaf tied with a string or in cheesecloth

Salt

1. Fill a medium saucepan with water and bring to a boil. Fill a bowl with ice and water. Separate the heads of garlic into cloves and drop them into the boiling water. Blanch for 30 seconds, then transfer to the ice water. Allow to cool for a few minutes, then drain and remove the skins from the garlic cloves. They'll be loose and easy to remove.

2. Combine the 2 quarts water with the garlic cloves and remaining ingredients in a large saucepan and bring to a gentle boil. Reduce the heat, cover, and simmer 1 hour. Strain. Taste and adjust salt.

ADVANCE PREPARATION: This can be made a day ahead and freezes well. It's at its best, however, if used the day it's made.

SUBSTITUTIONS AND ADDITIONS: For a more pronounced flavor, instead of blanching the garlic cloves to peel them, crush with the flat side of a knife and peel, the way you do when you're going to mince the garlic. The skins will easily pop away from the cloves when you crush them. You can also cut the heads in half horizontally and not peel the garlic at all.

Porcini Mushroom Stock

MAKES ABOUT 6 CUPS

Dried porcinis are a great source for a robust vegetarian stock. Actually any dried mushrooms will work, but porcinis are my favorite. Whenever you use dried porcinis in a recipe, if the recipe doesn't call for the soaking water always strain it and freeze for stocks.

1 ounce dried porcini mushrooms (about 1 cup) or other dried mushrooms

2 cups boiling water

¼ to ½ pound fresh button or cremini mushrooms, quartered; or whole mushroom stems

1 head garlic, cut in half horizontally

A bouquet garni: a few sprigs each parsley and thyme, a bay leaf, and 10 peppercorns tied in cheesecloth

Salt

1. Place the dried porcinis in a bowl and cover with the boiling water. Let sit for 30 minutes. Agitate the mushrooms from time to time to release sand. Line a strainer with cheesecloth and place over a 1-quart measuring cup. Drain the mushrooms through the strainer and squeeze them dry over the strainer. Set aside the mushrooms for another use.

2. Combine the mushroom stock with enough water to make 7 cups and place in a saucepan. Add the remaining ingredients and bring to a boil. Reduce the heat, cover, and simmer 30 minutes. Strain. Taste and adjust salt.

ADVANCE PREPARATION: You can make this a day ahead and refrigerate. It freezes well.

Arborio Risotto

MAKES 4 TO 5 SERVINGS

When and how you introduce the vegetables that define your risotto will be recipe-specific (see the variation recipes, pages 154–158). Sometimes the rice is cooked along with a vegetable ragout of sorts, as in the Eggplant and Tomato Risotto on page 157 or the Barley and Arborio Risotto with Mushrooms on page 161. In other vegetable risottos, the vegetables are introduced halfway through the cooking so you don't overcook them. No matter how the ingredients that define your risotto are prepared, the basic method for the rice is always the same and the end result should be creamy, not stodgy, the rice al dente.

7 cups well-seasoned Simple Vegetable Stock, Garlic Stock, or Porcini Mushroom Stock (pages 149–151)

2 tablespoons extra virgin olive oil

½ cup minced onion

Salt and freshly ground pepper

1½ cups Arborio rice

1 to 2 garlic cloves (to taste), minced

½ cup dry white wine, such as pinot grigio or sauvignon blanc

¼ to ½ cup freshly grated Parmesan (1 to 2 ounces)

1. Bring the stock to a simmer over low heat in a saucepan, with a ladle nearby or in the pot. Make sure the stock is well seasoned.

2. Heat the olive oil over medium heat in a wide, heavy skillet or a wide, heavy saucepan. Add the onion and a generous pinch of salt and cook gently until it is just tender, 3 to 5 minutes. Do not brown.

3. Add the rice and garlic and stir until the grains separate and begin to crackle. Add the wine. It should bubble right away, but it shouldn't evaporate too quickly. Stir until it is no longer visible in the pan.

4. Begin adding the simmering stock, a couple of ladlefuls (about $^{1}/_{2}$ cup) at a time. The stock should just cover the rice, and should be bubbling, not too slowly but not too quickly. Cook, stirring often, until it is just about absorbed. Add another ladleful or two of the stock and continue to cook in this fashion, adding more stock and stirring when the rice is almost dry. You do not have to stir constantly, but stir often and when you do, stir vigorously, because it's the stirring that coaxes the starch out of the rice, and the starch is what makes risotto creamy. When the rice is no longer hard in the middle but is still chewy (al dente), usually in 20 to 25 minutes, it is done. Taste now and adjust seasoning.

5. Add another ladleful of stock to the rice. Stir in the Parmesan and pepper to taste and remove from the heat. The mixture should be creamy (add more stock if it isn't). Serve right away in

wide soup bowls or on plates, spreading the risotto in a thin layer rather than a mound.

ADVANCE PREPARATION: You can begin up to several hours before serving. Proceed with the recipe and cook halfway through Step 4, that is, for about 15 minutes. The rice should still be hard in the middle when you remove it from the heat, and there should not be any liquid in the pan. Spread the risotto in an even layer in the pan and keep it away from the heat until you resume cooking. If the pan is not wide enough for you to spread the rice in a thin layer, then transfer it to a baking sheet. Fifteen minutes before serving, bring the remaining stock back to a simmer and reheat the rice. Resume cooking as directed.

Saffron Risotto with Fresh Favas and Green Garlic

MAKES 4 TO 5 SERVINGS

If you get a CSA basket you may receive lots of green garlic and favas in the spring (early spring if you live in California, later in more temperate climates). I can't resist buying both when I go to the farmers' market. Risotto is a perfect vehicle for these vegetables. The saffron makes this risotto all the more luxurious, both to the palate and to the eye.

Make the *Arborio Risotto* template (page 152) with the following additional ingredients and specifications:

1 bulb green garlic, papery layers removed, minced

Generous pinch saffron threads

2½ pounds fava beans in the pods, shelled and skinned (opposite page)

2 tablespoons chopped fresh parsley, tarragon, or chives, or a combination

1. At the end of Step 2 of the template recipe, add the green garlic to the onion and cook, stirring, until fragrant, about a minute.

2. Continue with Step 3, but just before you add the wine, rub the saffron between your thumb and fingers and stir into the rice. Stir in the wine and proceed with the recipe, adding the favas in Step 4 after the first 15 minutes of cooking and stirring the risotto.

3. Finish the risotto, adding the herbs with the Parmesan and pepper with the last ladleful of stock.

ADVANCE PREPARATION: The favas can be skinned up to 2 days ahead of time. Keep in the refrigerator. For the risotto, see advance preparation notes (page 153) in the template recipe.

VARIATION:

Add ½ pound asparagus, trimmed and cut into ¾-inch lengths, along with the fava beans and proceed as directed in the recipe.

How to Skin Fava Beans

Before you begin to shell (shuck) the favas, put a medium pot of water on the stove over high heat. By the time the water comes to a boil, you'll have finished shucking the beans. Place the shucked beans in a bowl and fill another bowl with ice water.

When the water in the pot comes to a boil, add salt to taste and drop in the shelled fava beans. If the beans are about the size of your thumbnail or the first joint of your thumb, boil them for 2 minutes. If they are smaller than that, boil for 1 minute. Using a skimmer or a strainer, transfer the beans from the boiling water directly to the ice water. Allow them to cool for a minute or two in the ice water and drain. Don't drain the boiling water until you've skinned a bean and ascertained whether or not it's cooked enough for you. I like them just barely cooked through unless they're very starchy, which is sometimes the case if the beans are large or beginning to dry out.

To slip off their skins, pinch off the eye of the skin, where it was joined to the pod, and gently squeeze out the bean. This will go more quickly if you hold several beans in one hand and use your other thumbnail and forefinger to pinch off the eyes, one after another, then squeeze the beans one after another right into a bowl or into your "pinching" hand.

Eggplant and Tomato Risotto

MAKES 4 TO 5 SERVINGS

This is a summer risotto that is best when made with sweet long Asian eggplants from the farmers' market. I roast the eggplant first so that it won't require so much oil.

Make the *Arborio Risotto* template (page 152) with the following additional ingredients and specifications:

1 large or 2 medium eggplants (about 14 ounces), preferably a long variety, cut into ½-inch dice

Additional 1 tablespoon extra virgin olive oil

1 pound tomatoes, grated (see Note); or peeled, seeded, and diced

Pinch sugar

2 teaspoons fresh thyme leaves

Salt

2 to 4 tablespoons minced fresh parsley or 1 to 2 tablespoons slivered fresh basil (to taste)

1. Season the eggplant with salt, toss with the 1 tablespoon olive oil, and roast following the instructions on page 21.

2. In Step 3 of the template recipe, before you add the wine, stir in the tomatoes, sugar, thyme, and salt to taste and cook, stirring, until the tomatoes have cooked down and coat the rice, 5 to 10 minutes.

3. Continue with recipe, adding the roasted eggplant just before you start adding the simmering stock to the rice in Step 4. Add the parsley or basil when you add the Parmesan and last ladleful of stock in Step 5.

NOTE: To grate tomatoes, cut the tomato in half along the equator. Squeeze out the seeds into a strainer set over a wide bowl and rub the seed pods against the strainer to catch the sweet pulp that surrounds the seeds. Set a box grater in the bowl. Cup the halved tomato in your hand and rub against the large holes of a box grater. The skin will protect your hand.

ADVANCE PREPARATION: You can roast the eggplant up to a day ahead of time. For the risotto, see advance preparation notes (page 153) in the template recipe.

Risotto with Roasted Squash and Wilted Red Onions

MAKES 4 TO 5 SERVINGS

The two vegetables in this risotto are sweet. The squash caramelizes as it roasts and the onions are cooked down until they become very soft and incredibly sweet. If you get into the habit of roasting squash and slow-cooking onions from time to time, you can make this risotto very quickly. This isn't the first winter squash risotto I've published, but I'm always tweaking the recipe.

Make the *Arborio Risotto* template (page 152) with the following additional ingredients and specifications:

1 large red onion, quartered lengthwise and cut across the grain into thin slices

2 teaspoons chopped fresh sage

Roasted Winter Squash (page 15), using 1½ pounds winter squash cut into ½-inch dice

2 tablespoons chopped fresh flat-leaf parsley

1. In Step 2 of the template recipe, omit the ½ cup minced onion and use the thinly sliced red onion instead. After cooking for 3 to 5 minutes, cover the onions, reduce the heat to low, and simmer, stirring often, until very soft and sweet, 10 to 20 minutes longer. Add the minced garlic (2 cloves) to the onions (instead of adding with the rice) and cook, stirring, for about a minute. Turn the heat up to medium and add the rice. Cook, stirring, until the grains of rice are separate. Continue with the recipe, adding the wine in Step 3.

2. In Step 4, add the sage with the second addition of stock. Then, about 10 minutes before the risotto is done, add half of the roasted squash. Finish cooking the risotto, taste and adjust seasonings.

3. In Step 5, add the remaining roasted squash when you add the last ladleful of stock to the rice. Stir in the parsley when you add the Parmesan and pepper.

ADVANCE PREPARATION: The roasted squash will keep for 3 or 4 days in the refrigerator. For the risotto, see advance preparation notes (page 153) in the template recipe.

MULTIGRAIN RISOTTOS

A RISOTTO SHOULD BE A CREAMY, comforting dish in which the grains are suspended in a reduced stock that is instrumental in flavoring the grains. You can't get that kind of creaminess with most grains because they don't release their starch in the same way that short-grain Italian rice (and French rice from the Camargue) does. Some grains do give up some of their starch when cooked until tender in abundant water (wheat berries and wild rice do, for example), but they take longer to cook than rice.

If you want to make a creamy risotto with whole grains, the way to do it is to cook the whole grains separately and then stir them into a risotto made in the traditional way with Arborio rice, just less of it—$2/3$ cup as opposed to $1\frac{1}{2}$ cups. If there is a nice starchy stock left over from cooking your grains, add it to the stock you are using for your risotto. It will contribute great texture to the dish. Stir in the cooked grains along with that last ladleful of stock when the risotto is just about ready. The resulting multigrain risotto will have a wonderful variety of textures and pleasing contrasting colors. If you follow my lead and keep cooked grains on hand in the freezer you can make these dishes often.

Multigrain Risotto

MAKES 5 TO 6 SERVINGS

The first steps in this template are identical to those in Arborio Risotto (page 152). You might not use all the stock when you make this, but sometimes when I set out with only 4 cups of stock I run short, so the recipes call for more than you might use. You can always freeze what's left over.

5 to 6 cups well-seasoned Simple Vegetable Stock, Garlic Stock, or Porcini Mushroom Stock (pages 149–151), plus any cooking liquid left over from cooking the grains (you may not use all of it)

2 tablespoons extra virgin olive oil

½ cup minced onion

Salt and freshly ground pepper

⅔ cup Arborio rice

1 to 2 garlic cloves (to taste), minced

½ cup dry white wine, such as pinot grigio or sauvignon blanc

3 cups cooked whole grains, such as wild rice, black rice, red rice, barley, or farro (see pages 128–135)

¼ to ½ cup freshly grated Parmesan (1 to 2 ounces)

1. Bring the stock to a simmer in a saucepan over low heat, with a ladle nearby or in the pot. Make sure that it is well seasoned.

2. Heat the olive oil over medium heat in a wide, heavy skillet or a wide, heavy saucepan. Add the onion and a generous pinch of salt and cook gently until it is just tender, 3 to 5 minutes. Do not brown.

3. Add the rice and garlic and stir until the grains separate and begin to crackle. Add the wine. It should bubble right away, but it shouldn't evaporate too quickly. Stir until it is no longer visible in the pan.

4. Begin adding the simmering stock, a couple of ladlefuls (about ½ cup) at a time. The stock should just cover the rice, and should be bubbling, not too slowly but not too quickly. Cook, stirring often, until it is just about absorbed. Add another ladleful or two of the stock and continue to cook in this fashion, adding more stock and stirring when the rice is almost dry. You do not have to stir constantly, but stir often and when you do, stir vigorously, because it's the stirring that coaxes the starch out of the rice, and the starch is what makes risotto creamy. When the rice is no longer hard in the middle but is still chewy (al dente), usually in 20 to 25 minutes, it is done. Taste now and adjust seasoning.

5. Add another ladleful of stock to the rice. Stir in the cooked whole grains and heat through. Add the Parmesan and pepper to taste and remove from the heat. The mixture should be creamy (add more stock if it isn't). Serve right away in wide soup bowls or on plates, spreading the risotto in a thin layer rather than a mound.

ADVANCE PREPARATION: Most cooked grains keep for 3 days in the refrigerator and freeze well. For the risotto, see advance preparation notes (page 153) in the Arborio Risotto template recipe.

Barley and Arborio Risotto with Mushrooms

MAKES 5 TO 6 SERVINGS

Mushroom risotto is one of my favorites, and mushroom and barley soup is also a favorite, so I put the two together. The resulting risotto makes a hearty winter meal. If you're looking for something vegetarian to serve to staunch meat eaters, this is your dish.

Make the *Multigrain Risotto* template (opposite page) with the following additional ingredients and specifications:

1 ounce (about 1 cup) dried mushrooms, preferably porcinis

About 3½ cups boiling water

1 pound fresh cultivated or wild mushrooms, cleaned, trimmed, and cut into thick slices

½ to 1 teaspoon chopped fresh rosemary, or ¼ to ½ teaspoon crumbled dried (to taste)

½ to 1 teaspoon fresh thyme leaves, or ¼ to ½ teaspoon dried (to taste)

3 cups cooked barley (see page 134); if there is any cooking liquid left over, add it to the stock

2 to 4 tablespoons minced fresh flat-leaf parsley

1. Place the dried mushrooms in a bowl or 1-quart measuring cup and add boiling water to measure up to the quart line on the cup. Let sit for 20 minutes. Line a strainer with cheesecloth or with a double thickness of paper towels, place it over a bowl, and drain the mushrooms. Squeeze the mushrooms over the strainer to extract all the liquid, then, away from the bowl, rinse them in several changes of water to remove sand. Squeeze out excess water. Chop coarsely and set aside.

2. Use only 2½ to 3 cups of the stock called for in the template recipe. Combine the mushroom soaking liquid with enough stock to make 6 cups. Taste and adjust the salt. It should be well seasoned. Transfer to a saucepan and bring to a simmer.

3. Proceed with the template recipe, but in Step 2, use just 1 tablespoon olive oil to cook the onion. When the onion has softened, add the reconstituted dried and the fresh mushrooms. Cook, stirring, until the fresh mushrooms begin to release liquid. Use 2 cloves minced garlic, and add it here (instead of with the rice) along with the rosemary and thyme. Cook, stirring, until the mushroom liquid has just about evaporated.

4. In Step 3, add the remaining 1 tablespoon oil with the rice.

5. Proceed with Step 4 as directed. In Step 5, stir in the parsley with the cooked barley and finish the risotto.

ADVANCE PREPARATION: The cooked barley freezes well and keeps in the refrigerator for 3 days. You can prepare this recipe through Step 3 several hours before serving. See advance preparation notes (page 153) in the Arborio Risotto template recipe.

SUBSTITUTIONS AND ADDITIONS: Substitute cooked farro (see page 133) for the barley.

Arborio and Black Rice Risotto with Brussels Sprouts and Lemon Zest

MAKES 5 TO 6 SERVINGS

Brussels sprouts have enjoyed renewed favor over the years as cooks have been treating them with respect, searing and roasting them rather than overcooking them. In this beautiful black and white and green mixed-grains risotto, you sear the Brussels sprouts first and set them aside until halfway through the cooking of the risotto. The dish is finished off with lemon zest and a splash of lemon juice, one of my favorite ways to enrich a risotto.

Make the *Multigrain Risotto* template (page 160) with the following additional ingredients and specifications:

Additional 1 tablespoon extra virgin olive oil

Salt and freshly ground pepper

3 cups cooked black rice (see page 131)

1 pound Brussels sprouts, trimmed and quartered

1 tablespoon grated lemon zest

1 tablespoon fresh lemon juice

2 to 4 tablespoons minced fresh flat-leaf parsley, or a combination of parsley and dill

1. Heat 2 tablespoons olive oil over medium-high heat in a wide, heavy skillet. Sear the Brussels sprouts just until beginning to brown, 3 to 5 minutes, stirring and shaking the pan. Transfer to a plate or bowl. Season to taste with salt and pepper.

2. Proceed with the template recipe, using just 1 tablespoon olive oil for the onion in Step 2. Add the Brussels sprouts after the first 10 minutes of stirring and cooking the rice in Step 4.

3. In Step 5, stir in the cooked black rice when you add the last ladleful of stock. Add the lemon zest, juice, and parsley when you add the Parmesan.

ADVANCE PREPARATION: The cooked black rice will keep for 3 days in the refrigerator. You can sear the Brussels sprouts hours before you begin the risotto. For the risotto, see advance preparation notes (page 153) in the Arborio Risotto template recipe.

CHAPTER NINE

Stir-Fries

STIR-FRIES ARE ALWAYS POPULAR IN our house. I used to look at the long lists of ingredients in stir-fry recipes and my mind would drift to dishes that to me seemed simpler by virtue of their shorter ingredient lists. But now I understand that although a bit of time goes into stir-fry prep, it's all at the front end of the recipe and it can be leisurely, a time to visit with your kids, have a glass of wine with your partner, catch up on the news. The actual cooking takes place in minutes. So if you can rearrange your thinking so that you don't find a recipe daunting if a number of ingredients are involved (most of which you will have on hand in a good pantry), stir-fries can find a place in your repertoire at least once a week, if not more often.

When I began cooking vegetarian food in the 1970s we did a lot of stir-fries—without knowing much about Chinese food—and served them with brown rice. My earliest stir-fry recipes weren't anything like the more authentically Chinese dishes I've learned to make in more recent years, but they tasted good then, and probably they'd taste good now, as they did have the essential elements of a good stir-fry— garlic, ginger, soy sauce, usually a glaze made with a cornstarch slurry, and lots of fresh vegetables.

I drifted away from Asian cooking when I moved to Paris in 1981 and became more serious about the cuisines of the Mediterranean. But not too long ago I was reintroduced to stir-frying by my friend and colleague Grace Young, whose wonderful book *Stir-Frying to the Sky's Edge* taught me all the things I'm about to tell you.

There are three or four main elements to a vegetarian stir-fry: The aromatics (usually ginger and garlic, sometimes chiles); the protein if included (for you, that will be tofu or eggs); most importantly here, the vegetables; and finally, a liquid seasoning element (which can be but doesn't have to be a sauce or a slurry that thickens when it's heated) and additional seasonings which invariably include salt and sugar. You cook the grains or noodles that will be served with the stir-fry and prepare all of the stir-fry ingredients before you begin stir-frying. The elements for the liquid component, which include soy sauce, Chinese rice wine or dry sherry, and stock or water, are combined in one dish and seasoning elements in others.

Vegetables for stir-fries are cut uniformly so that they take the same amount of time to cook. Carrots, for example, will be sliced very thin or cut into julienne as will red peppers and broccoli stems (broccoli stems are peeled first). Some green vegetables are blanched very briefly before being stir-fried. It's important that the vegetables, tofu, and other solids that go into a stir-fry are dry. If you wash vegetables, drain them well on paper towels so that they can sear properly in the wok. Otherwise they'll stew or steam and you won't get that wonderful seared flavor that is unique to stir-fries. See specific recipes for more details. Before you begin, set the table, and call your family to dinner so that they'll be ready for it when you pull the wok off the stove.

STIR-FRYING TOOLS

THE TWO THINGS YOU'LL NEED if you're planning on stir-fries becoming a regular part of your repertoire are a good wok and a long-handled metal spatula with a slightly contoured edge. I also have a Chinese (or wok) skimmer, which is a wide-mesh brass strainer with a long bamboo handle. This I use in all of my cooking (for pasta, for blanching vegetables, and for deep-frying), not just in stir-fries.

I cannot overemphasize the benefits of using a wok rather than a skillet for stir-frying. And the wok to buy is a carbon-steel, 14-inch flat-bottomed

How to Season a Wok

These are the directions that Grace Young gives in her essential book, *Stir-Frying to the Sky's Edge*. It's an infinitely simpler method than the all-day process I vaguely remember using with my first wok decades ago. You will need peanut or vegetable oil, fresh ginger, and 1 bunch of scallions.

All carbon-steel woks have an anti-rust coating applied at the factory that must be removed first. Then the wok must then be "seasoned" so that it won't rust.

1. To remove the anti-rust coating, scour the wok with a stainless steel scouring pad and hot, soapy water, using lots of elbow grease. Scour both inside and out, and rinse with hot water. This is the only time in your wok's life that you will scour it like this.

2. Open your kitchen windows and turn on your exhaust fan. Put your wok on a burner and heat over low heat until all of the water on the wok evaporates. There may be a faint smell of the residue from the coating, and the metal inside the wok may change color. This is normal. Allow the wok to cool.

3. Heat the wok over high heat until a drop of water evaporates within a second or two when added to the wok. Add 2 tablespoons peanut or vegetable oil, $\frac{1}{2}$ cup unpeeled sliced ginger, and 1 bunch scallions cut into 2-inch pieces (make sure they are dry). Reduce the heat to medium and stir-fry for 5 minutes, pressing the ingredients into all surfaces of the wok, from top to bottom, as you stir-fry. Continue to stir-fry for another 10 to 15 minutes, adding more oil if the mixture becomes dry. Eventually the ginger and scallions will become brown and crusty. Remove the wok from the heat. Allow the ginger and scallions to cool in the wok, then discard.

4. Rinse the wok with hot water and the soft side of a sponge, *without* any soap. Place it back on a burner and heat over low heat until there is no longer any water visible in the wok. Remove from the heat. The wok is now ready for cooking. It will be slightly mottled, and the more you stir-fry the more of a dark patina it will acquire. This is the wok's natural nonstick surface. Never use a scouring pad or the rough side of a sponge on your wok. Use hot water and, only if necessary, a small amount of liquid soap. Always dry the wok over low heat before putting away.

wok. They are not very expensive. You'll find that anything smaller will be too small; food will spill out of it when you stir-fry, especially when you're making rice or noodles. A wok really can't be too big, even if you're not cooking much in it.

You want carbon steel because that's the material that will heat up and cool down the most efficiently and give you that wonderful seared flavor that we love about stir-fries. It's easy to "season" a carbon-steel wok, which effectively transforms it into a nonstick pan but with much better cooking properties than nonstick woks (or other nonstick pans) have. Woks require high heat, and carbon-steel woks are much more economical, durable, and safer than the heavy-duty nonstick pans that can stand up to high heat.

The reason you want to seek out a flat-bottomed wok is that a wok with a rounded bottom (like my first wok) will not sit properly on a burner on a Western stove; it wobbles when you stir-fry and you have to hold it steady. Also a flat-bottomed wok heats up more efficiently, giving you a hot flat surface and cooler sides to push food to if necessary. Woks with a long, heatproof handle are much easier to use than the type with two small handles attached at the sides (also like my first wok). The small handles get hot, so you have to use a pot holder to hold onto them, which is dangerous as the pot holder can get perilously close to the flame.

My First Wok

I still have my first wok. I got it when I was about 21, my first serious item of cookware. I spent a day curing the heavy, carbon-steel two-handled bowl-shaped vessel, and it still has its beautiful black patina. The wok was my main cooking pot during my early passionate days of cooking; it has lived with me in South Texas and in Austin; in Paris and Provence; and in Berkeley and now in Los Angeles, where it hangs on a big baker's rack with my other pots and pans. It isn't the wok I use now, but it has only recently been replaced by a flat-bottomed version with a long wooden handle, and I will never part with it.

Stir-Fried Tofu and Vegetables

VEGAN /// **MAKES 4 SERVINGS**

This template for a main-dish vegetarian stir-fry includes tofu, my most frequent protein choice. The liquids—soy sauce, Chinese rice wine or sherry, and water or vegetable stock—are those I always use in stir-fries, sometimes in conjunction with other liquid ingredients. I always begin cooking my stir-fried tofu and vegetables by searing the tofu. Then I add the aromatics, the vegetables, and the liquid seasonings. Because this is a book of main-dish recipes, the portions are large. If you're preparing other dishes, then the recipes will serve more people.

It's very important to read stir-fry recipes through twice before you begin. You won't have time to be reading a recipe as you stir-fry—it all happens in 5 minutes or less. So you'll want to know beforehand the order in which you'll be adding items to the wok, and have them arranged in that order.

1 (14-ounce) package firm tofu, drained and cut into 2 × ¾ × ¼-inch dominoes

1 to 2 tablespoons soy sauce (to taste)

1 tablespoon Shao-hsing rice wine or dry sherry

¼ cup Simple Vegetable Stock (page 149) or water

¼ to ½ teaspoon salt (to taste)

⅛ to ¼ teaspoon freshly ground pepper (to taste)

¼ to ½ teaspoon sugar (to taste)

Slurry: 1 teaspoon cornstarch or arrowroot dissolved in 2 tablespoons stock or water (see Note on page 170)

2 tablespoons peanut, sunflower, or grapeseed oil

2 to 3 teaspoons minced garlic (to taste)

2 to 3 teaspoons minced ginger (to taste)

Vegetables of your choice (see variation recipes on pages 171–173)

1. Place the tofu dominoes on paper towels. Place another paper towel on top and let sit while you prepare the remaining ingredients.

2. In a small bowl or measuring cup, combine the soy sauce, rice wine or sherry, and stock or water. In another small container, combine the salt, pepper, and sugar. If using (see Note on page 170), make the slurry in another bowl and stir well. Have all the ingredients within arm's length of your pan.

3. Heat a 14-inch flat-bottomed wok or 12-inch stainless-steel skillet over high heat until a drop of water evaporates within a second or two when added to the pan. Swirl in 1 tablespoon of the oil by adding it to the sides of the wok and swirling the wok, then add the tofu. Sear for 30 seconds without stirring, then stir-fry until lightly colored, 1 to 2 minutes. Remove the tofu to a plate.

4. Swirl in the remaining 1 tablespoon oil, add the garlic and ginger, and stir-fry for no more than 10 seconds. Add the vegetables and stir-fry for 1 minute. Add the salt, pepper, and sugar, toss together, and add the soy sauce mixture. Stir-fry until the vegetables are crisp-tender, 1 to 2 minutes. Return the tofu to the wok (along with the slurry if called for in the variation). Stir together for 1 minute (or if using the slurry, just until lightly glazed). Serve with hot grains or noodles.

(continued)

NOTE: Some stir-fries are finished with a glaze, created by adding a slurry—cornstarch or arrowroot dissolved in a small amount of water or stock—at the end of cooking. The liquid in the wok will thicken when the slurry is introduced and heated to the boiling point. Other, dryer stir-fries do not include a slurry. Instructions for including or omitting the slurry will be in the Variations.

ADVANCE PREPARATION: Stir-fries are last-minute dishes as far as cooking goes, but you can prepare all of your ingredients hours in advance. Keep in the refrigerator until 15 to 30 minutes before you cook.

VARIATION: STIR-FRIED VEGETABLES (WITHOUT TOFU)

Stir-fries don't require tofu to qualify as a main dish. Many of the vegetarian dishes in this book are low in high-protein foods but completely satisfying. Use the template recipe, but skip Steps 1 and 3, omitting the tofu and 1 tablespoon of the oil.

Garlic, Ginger, and a Very Hot Wok

Every time I make a stir-fry, whenever I add the garlic and ginger to my hot wok I'm afraid I'm going to ruin the dish as I watch it quickly cook to a point that would be unacceptable in a Mediterranean dish. But the stir-fry never tastes like burnt garlic. The aromatics are in the hot oil for no more than 10 seconds (usually less) before the other vegetables are introduced to the wok, and the moisture in the vegetables has a sort of deglazing effect. As you stir-fry, the garlic and ginger will go up the sides of the wok and be cooled by the other ingredients.

Stir-Fried Tofu with Shiitakes and Chinese Broccoli

VEGAN /// MAKES 4 SERVINGS

Chinese broccoli qualifies as a vegetable that is both hard and soft; the stems are hard, the leaves soft. So the two need to be separated for cooking since the stems take a minute or so longer to cook than the leaves. I like to briefly blanch the stems first.

Make the *Stir-Fried Tofu and Vegetables* template (page 169) with the following additional ingredients and specifications:

6 ounces fresh shiitake mushrooms

2 cups water

1 pound Chinese broccoli

Salt

½ teaspoon red pepper flakes (optional)

1 bunch scallions, chopped, dark green parts separated (optional)

2 tablespoons chopped cilantro (optional)

1. Remove the stems from the mushrooms and quarter the caps. Simmer the stems in the 2 cups water for 20 minutes to make a light mushroom stock. Strain and measure out ¼ cup (freeze the rest in ice trays).

2. Separate the broccoli leaves from the stems, rinse the leaves, and pat dry or spin in a salad spinner (they should not be wet). Trim away the ends of the stems and cut the stems in half lengthwise if thicker than ½ inch. Cut into 2-inch lengths. Bring a medium saucepan full of water to a boil, add 1 teaspoon salt, and drop in the broccoli stems. As soon as the water comes back up to a boil (30 seconds to a minute), transfer the stems to a bowl of cold water and drain. Drain again on dishtowels or paper towels and pat dry.

3. Proceed with Steps 1 through 3 of the template recipe, making the slurry in Step 2.

4. In Step 4, add the red pepper flakes (if using) with the ginger and garlic. Stir-fry for no more than 10 seconds, then add the mushroom caps and stir-fry for 30 seconds. Pour in the mushroom stock and stir-fry for 1 minute, until the mushrooms are tender and the stock has evaporated. Add the broccoli stems and stir-fry for 1 minute. Continue, adding the broccoli leaves with the salt, pepper, and sugar. Add the soy sauce mixture and return the tofu to the wok along with the optional scallions (white and light green parts only). Stir-fry for 1 to 2 minutes, until the vegetables are crisp-tender. Stir in the optional cilantro

(continued)

and dark green scallion ends along with the slurry and stir-fry for about 30 seconds, just until the tofu and vegetables are lightly glazed. Remove from the heat and serve with hot grains or noodles.

ADVANCE PREPARATION: Stir-fries are last-minute dishes as far as cooking goes, but you can prepare all of your ingredients hours in advance. Keep in the refrigerator until 15 to 30 minutes before you cook.

SUBSTITUTIONS AND ADDITIONS:

- *Substitute thick-stemmed asparagus for the Chinese broccoli. Snap off the woody stems and cut on the diagonal in 2-inch lengths. Blanch just until the water in the pot comes back to a boil after adding the asparagus and transfer to a bowl of cold water. Drain and dry on dishtowels or paper towels. Omit Step 2*
- *Substitute bok choy for the Chinese broccoli. Slice the bok choy crosswise into 3/4-inch pieces. Omit Step 2.*
- *You can make this dish without the tofu. Use just 1 tablespoon oil.*

Bok Choy

What I love about bok choy is that it has two distinctive features—moist, crunchy stems and cruciferous leafy greens—like two vegetables in one. Sold both as bok choy and baby bok choy, the vegetable can range in size from 3 inches long to 8 inches. The small, dwarf bok choy, which is about 3 inches long, is the most tender. Just trim the ends and cut in half. I cut larger bok choy into 2-inch pieces. After you rinse it, be sure to spin it dry in a salad spinner so that it sears properly in the wok.

Stir-Fried Tofu, Amaranth Greens, Sweet Red Pepper, and Green Garlic

VEGAN /// **MAKES 4 SERVINGS**

A number of farmers at our California farmers' markets sell beautiful lush bunches of amaranth greens in the spring. The leaves are dark red and green and the stems are tender enough to include in a stir-fry. If you can't find amaranth, substitute beet greens or red chard.

Make the *Stir-Fried Tofu and Vegetables* template (page 169) with the following additional ingredients and specifications:

1 generous bunch amaranth greens, about 1 pound

1 bulb green garlic, papery shells removed, minced

1 hot green chile, such as a serrano, jalapeño, or Thai green chile, minced

1 large red bell pepper, cut into 2-inch julienne

1 tablespoon sesame seeds

2 teaspoons dark sesame oil

1. Wash the amaranth, spin dry, and trim away the thick ends of the stems. Cut the bottom thicker parts of the stems into ½-inch lengths. Stem the leaves that have long stringy stems (discard these stems) and chop coarsely. Place the cut thick stems and leaves together in a large bowl.

2. Proceed with Steps 1 through 3 of the template recipe. (Do not make the slurry.)

3. In Step 4, use the green garlic in place of the regular garlic. Add the green garlic and chile with the ginger and stir-fry for no more than 10 seconds. Add the bell pepper and stir-fry until crisp-tender, 1 to 2 minutes. Add the amaranth stems and leaves and sesame seeds with the salt, pepper, and sugar and stir-fry until the leaves have wilted and the stems are crisp-tender, 1 to 2 minutes. Return the tofu to the wok along with the soy sauce mixture and sesame oil and stir-fry 30 seconds. Remove from the heat. Serve with rice or noodles.

ADVANCE PREPARATION: Stir-fries are last-minute dishes as far as cooking goes, but you can prepare all of your ingredients hours in advance. Keep in the refrigerator until 15 to 30 minutes before you cook.

STIR-FRIED RICE

STIR-FRIED RICE MAKES A COMFORTING MEAL, with the deep, satisfying flavors of seared rice with ginger, soy sauce, and garlic, stir-fried onion or scallions, and if I have it on hand, cilantro. I almost always include eggs, which are first cooked like a pancake and cut into slivers. The vegetables vary with the seasons, though a good stir-fried rice can be ultra-simple, with nothing more than carrots, scallions, and eggs. I like to throw in peas or edamame as well, and have no qualms about using the frozen ones that I sometimes find lingering in my freezer.

This is an ideal dish to make if you have leftover rice. In fact, using cold rice is the key to successful stir-fried rice of any kind. Just-cooked rice will be too mushy. It's a good idea to be in the habit of cooking a pot of rice regularly so you have some on hand for stir-fries and other dishes (Big Bowls, gratins, etc.). I prefer brown rice for Chinese-style vegetarian stir-fried rice because it has such a nutty flavor; so do a number of other whole-grain rice varietals on the market like Wehani, black rice, and red Bhutanese, as long as they're not too sticky. When you cook rice, if you cover the pot with a towel when the rice is done and let it sit for 10 to 15 minutes (see page 126), then fluff it and allow it to cool, the texture will be perfect.

I count on 1 to 1½ cups of cooked rice per serving when I make fried rice. Each type of rice has a different yield. Check the chart on page 131 to determine how much uncooked rice you'll need to yield the amounts called for in the recipes.

Chinese-Style Stir-Fried Brown Rice

VEGAN WITHOUT THE EGGS /// **MAKES 2 TO 3 SERVINGS**

This template makes a delicious and substantial main dish even without additional vegetables. The seasonings—ginger, garlic, soy sauce—are characteristically Chinese (as opposed to seasonings that would be used in Thai or Malaysian fried rice dishes, which usually include fish sauce and/or chile sauce).

2 eggs

Salt

2 teaspoons plus 2 tablespoons peanut, sunflower, or grapeseed oil

2 to 3 teaspoons minced garlic (to taste)

2 to 3 teaspoons minced fresh ginger (to taste)

1 to 2 cups diced carrots or red bell pepper (¼-inch dice), or a mix

3 cups cooked brown rice (see page 129), either chilled or at room temperature

1 bunch scallions, sliced, dark green parts separated

1 to 2 tablespoons soy sauce (to taste)

1 cup thawed frozen peas or shelled edamame

⅛ to ¼ teaspoon ground pepper (to taste), preferably white pepper

½ cup chopped cilantro

1. Beat the eggs in a bowl and season with a pinch of salt. Prepare the other ingredients and place in separate bowls within arm's reach of your wok.

2. Heat a 14-inch flat-bottomed wok or a 12-inch skillet over high heat until a drop of water evaporates within a second or two when added to the pan. Swirl in 2 teaspoons of the oil by adding it to the sides of the pan and swirling the pan. Make sure that the bottom of the wok or pan is coated with oil and add the eggs, swirling the pan so that the eggs form a thin pancake. Cook until set, 30 seconds to 1 minute. Using a spatula, turn the pancake over and cook until thoroughly set, 5 to 10 more seconds. Transfer to a plate or cutting board and allow to cool. Roll up or fold in half and cut into $\frac{1}{4}$-inch-wide by 2-inch-long strips. Note: You can also beat each egg separately and cook two pancakes, which will yield more strips of beaten egg.

3. Swirl the remaining 2 tablespoons oil into the wok or pan and add the garlic and ginger. Stir-fry no more than 10 seconds and add the carrots and/or bell pepper. Stir-fry for 1 minute and add the rice and scallions (white and light green parts only). Stir-fry, scooping up the rice with your spatula then pressing it into the hot wok and scooping it up again, for about 2 minutes. Add the soy sauce, peas or edamame, dark green parts of the scallions, egg strips, white pepper, and cilantro, stir for about 30 seconds and remove from the heat. Serve hot.

NOTE: If you want to make vegan versions of any of the stir-fried rice recipes, omit the eggs and Steps 1 and 2. You can sear tofu (about 6 ounces, cut into cubes) if you want to substitute another protein.

ADVANCE PREPARATION: Cooked rice will keep for up to 3 days in the refrigerator.

Stir-Fried Rice with Kale or Frizzy Mustard Greens

VEGAN WITHOUT THE EGGS /// **MAKES 2 TO 3 SERVINGS**

I came across frizzy mustard greens at my farmers' market. They look like a cross between frisée and curly kale and have a sharp, mustardy kick. They would be my first choice for this stir-fry, but curly kale and turnip greens also work very well. The kale has a similar texture, while turnip greens have more of a bite. I like this with any type of rice—brown, white, red, purple, Wehani, whatever you want to use.

Make the *Chinese-Style Stir-Fried Brown Rice* template (page 175) with the following additional ingredients and specifications:

¾ to 1 pound curly kale, turnip greens or frizzy mustard greens, or a mix

1. If using kale or turnip greens, stem, wash, and coarsely chop. If using frizzy mustard greens, cut away about 1 inch of the stem ends, wash, and coarsely chop. Set aside near your wok.

2. Proceed with Steps 1 and 2 of the template recipe.

3. In Step 3, omit the carrot and bell pepper, adding the prepared greens instead. Turn the heat to high and stir-fry for 1 minute to wilt the greens. Finish the stir-fry, omitting the peas or edamame, if you wish.

ADVANCE PREPARATION: Cooked rice will keep for up to 3 days in the refrigerator.

Stir-Fried Brown Rice with Tofu, Cabbage, Carrot, and Red Pepper

VEGAN WITHOUT THE EGGS /// **MAKES 2 TO 3 SERVINGS**

Stir-fried rice is a dish you can always pull out of a hat when you have just a few simple vegetables on hand. Say you've used half of a big cabbage for another dish and the remainder is lingering in the refrigerator along with that hairy carrot . . . .

Make the *Chinese-Style Stir-Fried Brown Rice* template (page 175) with the following additional ingredients and specifications:

½ pound firm tofu, drained, and cut into 2 x ¾ x ¼-inch dominoes

Additional 1 tablespoon peanut, sunflower, or grapeseed oil

1 pound green or napa cabbage, cored and shredded

1. Place the tofu dominoes on paper towels. Place another paper towel on top and let sit while you prepare the remaining ingredients.

2. Instead of dicing the carrot and bell pepper, cut them into ¼- × 2-inch matchsticks; you should have 1 cup julienne of each vegetable.

3. Proceed with Steps 1 and 2 of the template recipe.

4. After cooking the eggs, swirl the 1 tablespoon oil into the wok by adding it to the sides of the pan and swirling the pan, then add the tofu. Sear without stirring for 30 seconds, then stir-fry until lightly colored, 1 to 2 minutes. Season with a little soy sauce and remove to a plate.

5. Continue with Step 3, adding the cabbage with the carrots and/or bell peppers. Finish the stir-fry, adding the tofu with the soy sauce, egg strips, and other ingredients.

ADVANCE PREPARATION: Cooked rice will keep for up to 3 days in the refrigerator.

Stir-Fried Rice Noodles

VEGAN WITHOUT THE EGGS /// **MAKES 4 SERVINGS**

Rice noodles are delicate and light, and especially welcome to those who are gluten intolerant. They are usually packed in bunches in 14-ounce packages, and removing the amount you need from the package can result in a mess of broken noodles on your floor and counter. Take advice from my stir-fry guru, Grace Young, and hold the noodles above a paper shopping bag when you do this.

The noodle stir-fry template isn't very different from the stir-fried rice template. The step that corresponds to cooking rice ahead is a 20-minute soak for the noodles. I use eggs, vegetables, and very often tofu in my noodle stir-fries, just as I do with stir-fried rice.

You really need a wok for this, and tongs are the tool to use to toss the noodles; either that or two spoons or spatulas.

7 ounces thin rice stick noodles (½ of a 14-ounce package)

½ cup Simple Vegetable Stock (page 149)

1 tablespoon soy sauce

1 tablespoon Shao-hsing rice wine or dry sherry

1 tablespoon minced garlic

1 tablespoon minced fresh ginger

¼ to ½ teaspoon red pepper flakes; 1 to 2 teaspoons minced fresh green chile; or 1 to 2 teaspoons hot chile paste, such as sambal oelek

2 eggs, beaten

Salt

½ teaspoon sugar

2 teaspoons plus 2 tablespoons peanut oil, sunflower oil, or grapeseed oil

Prepared vegetable(s) of your choice (see variation recipes, pages 180–183)

½ to 1 cup coarsely chopped cilantro (can include stems); plus optional additional sprigs for garnish

1. Place the noodles in a large bowl and cover with warm water. Soak for at least 20 minutes, until soft. Drain in a colander and, using kitchen scissors, cut into 6-inch lengths (it's easier to stir-fry the noodles if they're cut). Set aside within reach of your wok.

2. Combine the stock, soy sauce, and rice wine or sherry in a small bowl. Combine the garlic, ginger, and pepper flakes or minced chile in another bowl. (If using chile paste, add it to the stock mixture.) Beat the eggs in a bowl and season with a pinch of salt. Combine ¼ to ½ teaspoon salt and the sugar in another bowl. Prepare the other ingredients and place in separate bowls within arm's reach of your wok.

3. Heat a 14-inch flat-bottomed wok over high heat until a drop of water evaporates within a second or two when added to the wok. Swirl in 2 teaspoons of the oil by adding it to the sides of the wok and swirling the wok. Make sure that the bottom of the wok is coated with oil and add the eggs, swirling the pan so that the eggs form a thin pancake. Cook until set, 30 seconds to 1 minute. Using a spatula, turn the pancake over and cook until thoroughly set, 5 to 10 more seconds. Transfer to a plate or cutting board and allow to cool. Roll up or fold in half and cut into $\frac{1}{4}$-inch-wide by 2-inch-long strips. Set aside. (You can also beat each egg separately and cook two pancakes, which will yield more strips of beaten egg.)

4. Swirl the remaining 2 tablespoons oil into the wok and add the garlic mixture. Stir-fry no more than 10 seconds and add the vegetables. Stir-fry for 1 to 2 minutes (depending on the vegetables). Add the noodles and the stock mixture. Reduce the heat to medium and stir-fry until the noodles are just tender, 1 to 2 minutes. Add the egg strips, salt and sugar, and chopped cilantro and stir-fry until well combined, another 30 seconds to 1 minute. Serve, garnished with cilantro sprigs if desired.

NOTE: If you want to make vegan versions of any of the stir-fried rice noodle recipes, omit the eggs. You can sear tofu (about 6 ounces, cut into cubes) if you want to substitute another protein.

ADVANCE PREPARATION: The softened noodles will keep for 2 or 3 days in the refrigerator. After soaking, drain and toss with a couple of teaspoons of sesame oil or the oil you're using for the stir-fry and refrigerate in a covered bowl.

SUBSTITUTIONS AND ADDITIONS: This is neither Chinese nor Southeast Asian, but I love soba noodles and often use them in my stir-fries. Substitute 8 ounces soba noodles for the rice noodles. See the directions for cooking soba on page 48. Toss the cooked noodles with a couple of teaspoons of sesame oil and set aside. Proceed with the recipe.

Stir-Fried Noodles with Tofu, Okra, and Cherry Tomatoes

VEGAN WITHOUT THE EGGS /// **MAKES 4 SERVINGS**

A stir-fry is a good home for okra because you cook it so quickly that there's no time for slime to emerge. It's nice and crunchy and complements the cherry tomatoes beautifully. But seek out the smallest okra you can find, as large okra need more time than they'll get in the wok.

Make the *Stir-Fried Rice Noodles* template (page 178) with the following additional ingredients and specifications:

1 pound small okra

Salt

½ cup cider vinegar

½ pound firm tofu, drained, and cut 2 x ¾ x ¼-inch dominoes

Additional 2 teaspoons peanut, sunflower, or grapeseed oil

Additional 1½ teaspoons soy sauce

¾ pound cherry tomatoes (about 1 pint)

1. Trim the stems off the okra, making sure not to expose the seeds, and place in a large bowl. Salt generously, douse with the vinegar, and let sit for 15 to 30 minutes. Drain the okra and rinse thoroughly. Dry on paper towels. Place the tofu on paper towels and place paper towels on top to blot.

2. Meanwhile, proceed with Steps 1 through 3 of the template recipe.

3. After cooking the eggs, swirl in the 2 teaspoons oil by adding it to the sides of the wok and swirling the wok. Add the tofu, let sear in the wok for 30 seconds, then stir-fry until lightly browned, 1 to 2 minutes. Add the $1^1/_2$ teaspoons soy sauce, toss for another few seconds, and remove to a plate.

4. In Step 4, after stir-frying the garlic mixture, add the okra and stir-fry for 2 minutes. Add the tomatoes and stir-fry for another minute, until the tomatoes begin to collapse. Continue with the stir-fry, adding the tofu with the egg strips and cilantro and stir-frying another 30 seconds to a minute, until well combined.

ADVANCE PREPARATION: You can prepare the okra through Step 1 several hours ahead. See the Stir-Fried Rice Noodles template (page 178) for advance preparation notes.

VARIATION:

You can omit either the tofu or the eggs. You will need less oil and soy sauce if you omit the tofu.

Stir-Fried Rice Noodles with Greens and Red Pepper

VEGAN WITHOUT THE EGGS /// **MAKES 4 SERVINGS**

You can use one type or a mix of greens for this stir-fry. Try some of the more unusual greens that you might find at the farmers' market, like amaranth or pea shoots. I often use beet greens, which bleed a pretty reddish pink into the noodles. I wouldn't say no to a lush bunch of spinach, or even to a couple of packages of baby spinach, either.

Make the *Stir-Fried Rice Noodles* template (page 178) with the following vegetables and specifications:

1 red bell pepper, cut into 2-inch julienne

¾ pound greens (usually one generous bunch beet greens, amaranth greens, chard, kale, spinach), stemmed, washed in 2 changes of water, and coarsely chopped; or 2 (6-ounce) bags baby spinach

1. Proceed with Steps 1 through 3 of the template recipe.

2. In Step 4, after stir-frying the garlic mixture, add the bell pepper and stir-fry for 1 minute. Add the greens and stir-fry for 1 minute, or until the greens collapse in the wok. Continue with the recipe.

ADVANCE PREPARATION: The softened noodles will keep for 2 or 3 days in the refrigerator. After soaking, drain and toss with a couple of teaspoons of sesame oil or the oil you're using for the stir-fry and refrigerate in a covered bowl.

SUBSTITUTIONS AND ADDITIONS: Substitute 1 pound broccoli, separated into florets and stems peeled and diced, for the greens. Blanch the broccoli for 1 minute in salted boiling water before you begin. Substitute 6 to 8 ounces tofu for the eggs (see photo). Cut them into 2 x 3-inch dominoes and sear them in Step 3.

CHAPTER TEN

Beans and Lentils

T HERE IS SOMETHING VERY REASSURING about having a fragrant pot of beans on the stove, plus they are certainly the most economical of foods. They're high in protein and fiber and packed with other phytonutrients. They're also filling, delicious, and versatile. It's no wonder that they are a peasant staple in so many cultures around the world.

I did not grow up in a bean-eating environment—Campbell's baked beans was the limit of my exposure to legumes. Then I ended up, in my late teens and early 20s, working for a few years with the United Farm Workers and living in South Texas, along the Rio Grande border. The families I lived with always had a bowl of pinto beans on the stove. They seasoned theirs with bacon, then refried them in lard. Later on, when I stopped eating meat, I developed my own way of making delicious simmered beans and *frijoles* without the bacon and lard.

When I was living in the Rio Grande Valley, every Saturday we'd go across the river to have dinner in Reynosa, often in a *cabrito* place where I didn't much enjoy the goat, but loved the pintos that came beforehand. They were generously seasoned with cilantro, another flavor that was new to me, and they hooked me. I fell in love with Mexico at that time and after 2 years in South Texas I headed farther south, to Cuernavaca and eventually to Oaxaca, where I settled in for a few months. There I lived on inky black beans seasoned with avocado leaves. Heaven. This coincided with the period of my life when I was really getting into cooking, and black beans became a very important part of my repertoire, especially when I became a vegetarian. The first recipe I claimed as my own was my black bean enchiladas, published in my first book, *The Vegetarian Feast.*

When I moved from Texas to France in the '80s (believe me, that wasn't as big a cultural change as moving from Connecticut and Boston to Texas in the late '60s) and began to experience and cook the cuisines of the Mediterranean, I learned more ways with beans. I ate slow-baked beans seasoned with mint and honey in Greece, savory borlotti beans with tomato sauce and pasta in Italy, winter squash and white beans seasoned with sage in Provence, and spicy vegetable and chickpea tagines in Tunisia. I learned and then unlearned many wives' tales about the right and wrong ways to work with beans (such as never salting until the end of cooking; always soaking, no matter what kind of bean)—all of which I discuss with you in this chapter.

Flavoring Beans

The herbs used to season beans in the recipe variations will vary with the type of beans and the cuisine at the origin of the recipe. Black beans and pintos, beans that I learned to cook in Mexico and South Texas, are seasoned with cilantro, fresh epazote (which has a very earthy flavor), or avocado leaves (which are anise-y)—if I can get those ingredients. For white beans, borlottis, and all types of limas and haricots, I use a classic Mediterranean bouquet garni with a bay leaf and a few sprigs each of thyme and parsley, sometimes sage. Usually I also include a Parmesan rind in the bouquet garni; I always have Parmesan rinds in the refrigerator or freezer, and they contribute a deep umami flavor that salt pork contributes to a nonvegetarian pot of beans. Other herbs and spices that I use when I'm making Mediterranean bean dishes include mint, dill, and cilantro.

Chickpeas are the exception to all the bean rules as far as flavoring is concerned. They are so distinctive that I don't feel that they need anything to bring them along if you're cooking them to use in another dish. If you're making a Mediterranean stew, that's another matter. But when I cook them on their own all I add is salt.

Simmered Beans

VEGAN /// **MAKES 6 SERVINGS**

All you really *need* to make a delicious, savory pot of beans is sufficient salt, onion, and garlic, which are the only aromatics called for in this template. I've cooked my beans using the first method in the template forever. But recently I began wondering if I really had to chop and cook the onion first to get the flavor I wanted. It depends, I concluded, on the nature of the bean dish. If I'm going to be introducing a host of other flavors into the beans, I now use Method 2, where the onion is simply halved and simmered with the beans. If I'm cooking the beans to have a great, simple pot of beans to enjoy throughout the week, with no other embellishment, then I stick to my time-honored formula, Method 1.

1 pound beans, rinsed and picked over for stones

2 quarts water

1 medium onion

1 tablespoon sunflower, grapeseed, or olive oil

2 to 4 large garlic cloves (to taste), minced

Herbs and other seasonings (see variation recipes, pages 189–191)

About 1 tablespoon salt (beans need a lot of salt, at least 1 teaspoon per quart of water)

1. Soak the beans in the water for at least 4 hours, or do the quick soak (page 188). If they will be soaking for a long time in warm weather, put them in the refrigerator. Keep the beans in the soaking water if cooking black beans, pintos, or borlottis. Otherwise, drain the beans.

2. **METHOD 1:** Chop the onion. Heat the oil over medium heat in a large, heavy soup pot or Dutch oven. Add the chopped onion and cook, stirring, until tender, about 5 minutes. Add half the garlic and cook, stirring, until fragrant, 30 seconds to 1 minute. Add the beans and soaking water; or, if drained, add fresh water to cover by 2 inches. Proceed with Step 3.

2. **METHOD 2:** Cut the onion in half. Omit the oil. Transfer the beans and soaking water to a pot; or, if drained, add fresh water to cover by 1 to 2 inches. Add the halved onion and half of the garlic. Proceed with Step 3. (When the beans are done, use tongs to remove the very soft onion pieces from the pot.)

3. Bring to a boil. The beans need to come to a full boil, but try to avoid a hard, rolling boil because that will loosen the skins; a gentle boil results in the best texture. Add any other seasonings if the variation recipe instructs you to add them now. Reduce the heat to low and skim off any foam that rises. Cover and simmer 30 minutes.

(continued)

4. Add the salt and remaining garlic. Continue to simmer until the beans are very soft and the broth is thick and fragrant, another 1 to 1½ hours. Taste for salt and garlic. The beans should be very tasty. Add more salt or garlic if one spoonful doesn't make you want to take another. Refrigerate overnight for the best flavor.

ADVANCE PREPARATION: The cooked beans will keep for 3 to 4 days in the refrigerator and freeze well.

To Soak or Not to Soak—No Simple Answers

There's so much conflicting information out there about soaking beans. Chefs I really respect insist that soaking isn't necessary. But in my experience soaking gives you the best result for most beans if you want even cooking and a really nice, soft, velvety texture. They don't need more than 4 hours; or use the quick soak in which you bring them to a boil, boil 1 minute, then cover and let stand for 1 hour. It works well.

I'm more confident about the outcome if I soak. The exception is black-eyed peas, which cook up in 45 minutes with no soaking required; and lima beans and large white beans, whose skins float away when you soak them so that the beans fall apart when they simmer. If you're cooking the beans for a puree this isn't a problem, but if you don't want them to fall apart, it is.

Don't drain the soaking water when you're making black or brown beans. You'll lose a lot in the way of nutrients and flavor if you do. The one exception, when you must throw away the soaking water, is red kidney beans, because there are toxins in this variety, which are rendered harmless after 20 to 30 minutes of cooking, but it also helps to throw out the soaking water. This does make me regretful though, because those red pigments carry with them lots of phytonutrients called anthocyanins, that are bound to do good things.

In some recipes I drain beans after soaking because I'm using them for baked beans and in most cases I need to be precise about the amount of liquid needed in the recipe. I tend to drain white beans generally, because I'm not crazy about the flavor of the soaking water; but it's not a requirement. There may, after all, be some as yet undiscovered nutrients that have leached into the soaking water.

Quick Soak for Beans

Rinse the beans and pick over for small stones. Combine with the water called for in the recipe in a large pot, which might be the pot you are going to cook the beans in. Bring to a gentle boil and boil for 1 full minute. Cover, turn off the heat, and let stand for 1 hour. Proceed with the recipe.

Mexican-Style Black or Pinto Beans

VEGAN /// **MAKES 6 SERVINGS**

We enjoy this great pot of black beans, with corn tortillas and rice or cornbread, as much as any fancy schmancy meal.

Make the *Simmered Beans* template (page 187) with the following additional ingredients and specifications:

1 sprig epazote, or 2 dried avocado leaves if available (optional)

¼ to ½ cup chopped cilantro (to taste), plus additional for garnish if desired

1. Use black or pinto beans, 4 cloves of garlic, and, if using Method 1, sunflower or grapeseed oil to cook the onion.

2. Follow either Method 1 or Method 2. Add the epazote or dried avocado leaves in Step 3, right after the beans come to a boil.

3. In Step 4, add half the cilantro when you add the salt, and the remaining cilantro at the end of cooking. Refrigerate overnight for the best flavor. When you reheat, add another tablespoon or two of cilantro if desired.

ADVANCE PREPARATION: The beans will keep for 3 or 4 days in the refrigerator and freeze well.

Black Beans with Greens

VEGAN WITHOUT THE CHEESE /// **MAKES 6 SERVINGS**

Black beans make a terrific vehicle for any number of greens. In Mexico, a family of greens related to lamb's lettuce, generically known as *quelites*, are combined with black beans in a wonderful soup. I like to use the beautiful red-tinged amaranth greens that many of the Asian vendors sell at our local farmers' markets, and that is also popular in Mexico. Spinach is good too, as is Swiss chard.

Make the *Simmered Beans* template (page 187) with the following additional ingredients and specifications:

1 generous bunch amaranth greens, spinach, or chard, stemmed, leaves washed in 2 changes of water, and roughly chopped (6 cups)

Chopped cilantro and crumbled queso blanco or feta cheese, for garnish (optional)

Follow Method 1 and use black beans. Use sunflower oil or grapeseed oil to cook the onion. Shortly before serving, bring the beans back to a simmer and stir in the greens. Simmer until the leaves are tender, 5 to 10 minutes (less for spinach). Taste and adjust seasonings. Serve with cilantro and a little crumbled white cheese sprinkled over the top if desired.

ADVANCE PREPARATION: The beans will keep for 3 or 4 days in the refrigerator and freeze well.

Mediterranean Simmered Beans

VEGAN WITHOUT THE PARMESAN RIND /// **MAKES 6 SERVINGS**

In addition to onions, garlic, and herbs, I include tomatoes in this recipe. To add rich, almost meaty flavor, I also include one or two Parmesan rinds in the bouquet garni.

Make the *Simmered Beans* template (page 187) with the following additional ingredients and specifications:

1 (14-ounce) can chopped tomatoes with juice

Salt and freshly ground pepper

A bouquet garni: a bay leaf, a couple sprigs each thyme and parsley, and if desired, a Parmesan rind (or two) wrapped in cheesecloth

About 2 tablespoons chopped fresh herbs, such as parsley or basil

1. Follow Method 1 and use white beans of any kind, borlottis, Christmas limas, other heirlooms, or chickpeas. Use olive oil to cook the onion. After softening the garlic, add the tomatoes and salt to taste. Cook, stirring often, until the tomatoes have reduced somewhat and smell fragrant, about 10 minutes.

2. In Step 2, add the bouquet garni with the beans and water. Bring to a gentle boil and proceed with the recipe. When the beans are done, stir in pepper to taste and chopped fresh herbs. Discard the bouquet garni. Refrigerate overnight for the best flavor.

ADVANCE PREPARATION: The cooked beans will keep for 3 to 4 days in the refrigerator and freeze well.

VARIATION: You can introduce a little heat to these beans by adding a dried red chile pepper to the bouquet garni.

Myths about Salting Beans

For years I believed what I was told about salting beans early in the cooking—that it would harden the skins and they would never cook properly if you did. This is apparently a wives' tale that really is a wives' tale. Habits die hard though, so I usually don't salt my beans until they've been simmering for about a half hour or so. It's really important to salt beans early enough so that they can absorb the salt; it's not just the broth that you're salting, after all.

Black-Eyed Peas with Collard Greens or Kale

VEGAN WITHOUT THE PARMESAN RIND AND FETA /// **MAKES 4 TO 6 SERVINGS**

If you like beans, I recommend always having a pound of black-eyed peas on hand in your pantry. They cook in 45 minutes and require no soaking, yet they have the rich, earthy depth of flavor of other beans that require more time. I've been berated by Southern cooks for not including ham hocks in my black-eyed peas, but I have never had a bowl and thought, "Gee, these would be really great if they just had some pork to flavor them." They have plenty going for them on their own.

Make the *Simmered Beans* template (page 187) with the following additional ingredients and specifications:

1 bay leaf

1 Parmesan rind (optional)

Salt and freshly ground pepper

1 bunch collard greens or kale, stemmed, washed in 2 changes of water, and chopped or cut into ribbons

Additional 1 tablespoon olive oil

¼ cup chopped fresh dill or parsley, or a mix (optional)

Crumbled feta cheese and/or fresh lemon juice for serving (optional)

1. Omit Step 1 of the template recipe. Use 1 pound black-eyed peas (about 2⅛ cups), rinsed and picked over for stones. Follow Method 1 and use olive oil. In Step 3, add the bay leaf and Parmesan rind (tied together if desired) to the pot before bringing to a boil and simmering 30 minutes.

2. In Step 4, add salt to taste (2 to 3 teaspoons) and the remaining garlic. A handful at a time, stir in the collard greens or kale. As the greens wilt, stir in another handful, until all the greens have been added. Bring back to a simmer, cover, and simmer over low heat for 15 to 30 minutes (kale will only need 15 minutes), until the greens and beans are tender.

3. Stir in the additional tablespoon of olive oil and the dill or dill and parsley (if using). Cover and continue to simmer for another 5 minutes. Add salt and pepper to taste. Serve warm or hot. If you wish, serve with crumbled feta and/or a squeeze of lemon.

ADVANCE PREPARATION: The beans will keep for 3 or 4 days in the refrigerator, with or without the greens added.

SUBSTITUTIONS AND ADDITIONS:

- *Substitute Swiss chard or beet greens for the collards or kale. Add them after the black-eyed peas have simmered 45 minutes and are tender; simmer for 5 to 10 minutes, until the greens are tender.*

- *Black-eyed peas are great on their own without the greens as well. For color, sauté a large diced red pepper with the onion.*

- *You can also cook black-eyed peas using Method 2. The beans will still have a lot of flavor.*

White Bean Stew with Winter Squash and Leeks

VEGAN WITHOUT THE CHEESE /// **MAKES 6 SERVINGS**

Winter squash makes a great partner for white beans—or most types of beans for that matter. It sweetens the broth as it simmers, as do the leeks. This is a perfect winter stew. The method is slightly different from the template, as I cook the beans separately for a while and then add the vegetables to them; I also use fewer beans. So I've presented this as a stand-alone recipe.

¾ pound white beans (such as navy, cannellini, or lima beans)

1 onion, cut in half lengthwise

1 garlic clove, crushed; plus 2 to 4 large garlic cloves (to taste), minced

1 bouquet garni: a couple sprigs each parsley and thyme, 1 bay leaf, 2 sage leaves, and a Parmesan rind wrapped in cheesecloth

7 to 8 cups water, as needed

2 tablespoons extra virgin olive oil

2 large or medium leeks, well cleaned and chopped

Salt and freshly ground pepper

1 pound winter squash, such as butternut, peeled and diced

1 tablespoon slivered sage

Freshly grated Parmesan or Pecorino for garnish (optional)

1. Unless you are using lima beans, soak the beans for 4 hours or longer in 2 quarts water.

2. Drain the beans and transfer to a heavy pot or Dutch oven. Add the halved onion, crushed garlic clove, bouquet garni, and 7 cups water. Bring to a gentle boil and cover. Reduce the heat and simmer for 1 hour. Remove and discard the onion and crushed garlic clove.

3. Heat the olive oil over medium heat in a heavy skillet. Add the leeks and a generous pinch of salt and cook, stirring, until the leeks soften, about 5 minutes. Do not brown. Add the minced garlic and cook, stirring, until fragrant, about 30 seconds.

4. Stir the leeks and garlic into the beans. Add the diced squash and bring back to a simmer. If the ingredients are not covered with liquid, add another ½ to 1 cup of water. Add salt to taste (about 2 teaspoons or more; beans need a lot of salt), cover, and simmer until the beans are thoroughly tender and the squash is so tender that it is beginning to fall apart, 30 minutes to 1 hour. Stir in the slivered sage and pepper to taste. Taste and adjust salt. Remove and discard the bouquet garni. Serve, garnishing each bowl with a sprinkle of freshly grated Parmesan or Pecorino if desired.

ADVANCE PREPARATION: The cooked beans will keep for 3 to 4 days in the refrigerator and freeze well.

Slow-Cooked Baked Beans

VEGAN /// **MAKES 4 TO 6 SERVINGS**

Baked beans should have a plush, pillowy texture, the result of slow cooking that allows the beans to stay intact while becoming very tender. I've found that I have the best success with baked beans if I bring the beans slowly to a boil on top of the stove, cook them partially at a low simmer, then transfer them to a moderately low oven—300° to 325°F (sometimes even lower). In most cases, baked beans call for less liquid than simmered beans; enough so that they're submerged, but they should end up being enrobed in a sauce rather than suspended in a broth.

1 pound beans, rinsed and picked over for stones

1 bay leaf

4 to 6 cups water

4 tablespoons extra virgin olive oil

1 large onion, finely chopped

Salt

2 to 4 garlic cloves, minced

1. Soak the beans for 4 hours or longer, or use the quick soak (see page 188). Do not soak lima beans. Drain the soaked beans and place in a flameproof casserole. Add the bay leaf and enough water to cover by an inch. Bring to a gentle boil over medium heat. Reduce the heat to low, cover, and simmer 1 hour. Check the beans at regular intervals to make sure they are submerged, and add water as necessary.

2. Meanwhile, heat the oven to 300°F. Heat 2 tablespoons of the oil over medium heat in a heavy skillet. Add the onion and cook, stirring, until tender, about 5 minutes. Add a generous pinch of salt and the garlic and cook, stirring, until the garlic is fragrant, 30 seconds to 1 minute.

3. Stir the onion and garlic into the beans, along with salt to taste (at least 1 teaspoon per $\frac{1}{2}$ pound of beans). Drizzle the beans with the remaining 2 tablespoons olive oil.

4. Cover the pot, place in the oven, and bake, stirring occasionally, until the beans are thoroughly soft, 1 to $1\frac{1}{2}$ hours. Check after 30 minutes to make sure that the beans are at a very slow simmer; if they are not simmering, turn the oven up to 325°F. Check also from time to time to make sure that the beans are submerged. Either add liquid or push the beans down into the simmering broth if necessary. Discard bay leaf. Taste and adjust seasonings. Serve hot or warm.

ADVANCE PREPARATION: Baked beans keep for 3 or 4 days in the refrigerator and can be reheated in a low oven or in the microwave. Baked beans don't freeze as well as simmered beans because there's not as much liquid, so they tend to dry out.

Greek Sweet-and-Sour Baked Beans with Tomatoes, Peppers, and Mint

MAKES 6 SERVINGS

One of my favorite baked bean dishes, this is inspired by a Greek recipe, and even though it's Mediterranean, for once in my bean-cooking life I'm not calling for garlic (add it if you wish). The sweet and sour flavors and the peppers and tomatoes should be prominent here. Like all baked bean dishes, the more time these beans have in the oven, the better the texture of the overall dish will be. The dish is prettiest when made with white beans. Serve with thick slices of country bread.

Make the *Slow-Cooked Baked Beans* template (page 193) with the following additional ingredients and specifications:

2 red bell peppers, diced

Salt and freshly ground black pepper

1 (28-ounce) can chopped tomatoes, pulsed with the liquid from the can to a coarse puree (or 3 cups of Pomì strained tomatoes or grated fresh tomatoes)

3 tablespoons mild honey, such as clover or acacia

2 tablespoons tomato paste

2 tablespoons red wine vinegar or sherry vinegar (or more to taste)

2 teaspoons sweet paprika

¼ cup chopped fresh mint

1. Follow Step 1 of the template recipe, using white, pinto, or borlotti beans.

2. In Step 2, after softening the onion (omit the garlic), add the bell peppers and a pinch of salt and continue to cook for 5 to 10 minutes, until the onion is soft and lightly colored.

3. In Step 3, stir the onion/pepper mixture and remaining 2 tablespoons oil into the beans, along with the pureed tomatoes, honey, tomato paste, vinegar, paprika, and salt to taste. Make sure the beans are just submerged in liquid (add water if necessary). Bring the mixture to a simmer.

4. Cover and bake as directed in Step 4, stirring every 20 minutes, until the beans are tender and the mixture is thick. Taste and adjust salt, add black pepper to taste, and stir in the mint. Cover, return to the oven, and bake another 15 minutes. Taste and adjust seasonings.

ADVANCE PREPARATION: This is even better if you make it a day ahead. It will keep for 3 or 4 days. Reheat on top of the stove or in a 325°F oven.

Baked Beans with Pomegranate Molasses and Walnuts

VEGAN /// **MAKES 6 SERVINGS**

This Iranian dish is another example of sweet-and-sour baked beans. Middle Eastern baked beans are sweetened with pomegranate molasses, which also has a sour tang to it. You can find the pomegranate molasses in Middle Eastern markets. The dish has a wonderful, complex mixture of textures and flavors.

Make the *Slow-Cooked Baked Beans* template (page 193) with the following additional ingredients and specifications:

2 large sweet red onions, finely chopped

Salt and freshly ground black pepper

⅓ cup pomegranate molasses

1 (28-ounce) can chopped tomatoes, pulsed with the liquid from the can to a coarse puree (or 3 cups of Pomì strained tomatoes or grated fresh tomatoes)

½ cup (2 ounces) finely chopped walnuts

1. Follow Step 1 of the template recipe, using white, red, or pink beans. Remove the bay leaf after the 1-hour simmer.

2. Meanwhile, continue with Step 2. Use 3 tablespoons olive oil and the 2 red onions (in place of the 1 onion) and cook the onions until tender and lightly caramelized, about 10 minutes. Turn down the heat to low and add 2 minced garlic cloves and a generous pinch of salt. Cover and continue to simmer, stirring often, until the onions have melted down to half their original volume, another 15 to 20 minutes.

3. In Step 3, stir the pomegranate molasses and tomatoes into the beans with the onions. Season with salt and pepper to taste. Cover and bake as in Step 4, baking the beans for 1 to 1½ hours.

4. Sprinkle the walnuts over the top and drizzle on the final tablespoon of oil. Return to the oven and bake uncovered for another 15 minutes. Taste and adjust seasonings. Serve hot or warm.

ADVANCE PREPARATION: You can make the dish through Step 3 up to 3 days ahead. You may want to add a small amount of water when you reheat. When the beans are bubbling, proceed with Step 4. You can make the entire dish ahead as well and reheat.

Stewed Lentils

VEGAN WITHOUT THE PARMESAN RIND /// **MAKES 6 GENEROUS SERVINGS**

I consider lentils a convenience food, so quickly do they cook. I use my simple bean cooking method, adding a halved onion to simmer with them and removing it at the end of cooking. If you're using lentils for a salad and want them a little bit on the al dente side, they will be done in 20 minutes. For stews and soups, 40 to 45 minutes will suffice. Lentils never need to be soaked, and for those of you whose digestion is sensitive to beans, you'll be happy to hear that they don't contain sulfur, the gas-creating compound present in most beans.

There are many ways to season stewed lentils. In Europe, in addition to bay leaf, thyme, parsley, onion, garlic, and sometimes a *mirepoix* of carrots and celery, they're traditionally simmered with some type of preserved pork. I find that a Parmesan rind, or, if you like heat, a canned chipotle chile pepper in adobo, provides plenty of smoky, "meaty" flavor. See other seasoning ideas in the variations following the template recipe.

As for the type of lentils to use in a given stew, I'd say that brown lentils are the most versatile—they work well with just about any type of seasonings you like. Chefs like the pricier small black "beluga" lentils (in their raw state they're small and glistening black like caviar, but the resemblance stops there), and the firm green Le Puy lentils from France, because they stay intact and maintain a firmer texture when cooked. Both green and black lentils are delicious. But the flavors of all three are similar enough to make brown, green, and black lentils interchangeable in most recipes, though I'd stick to brown lentils for Indian curries. Red lentils (they become more yellow than red-orange once cooked), available in Indian and Middle Eastern markets, have a different flavor, more akin to dried favas or split peas, and a very different texture when cooked, so do not substitute these.

1 pound brown, green, or black lentils, rinsed and picked over for stones

1 medium onion, cut in half

2 garlic cloves, crushed or minced

1 bay leaf, or a bouquet garni: a bay leaf, a couple of sprigs each thyme and parsley, and a Parmesan rind wrapped in cheesecloth

Salt and freshly ground pepper

Seasonings of your choice (see variation recipes, pages 198–201)

Place the lentils in a large saucepan or bean pot and add the onion, garlic, bay leaf or bouquet garni. Add enough water to cover by an inch or two and bring to a gentle boil. Add salt to taste (usually a teaspoon per ½ pound) and other seasonings called for. Cover and simmer until tender, about 45 minutes. Taste, adjust salt, and add pepper. Use tongs or a slotted spoon to remove the halved onion, bay leaf, or bouquet garni.

ADVANCE PREPARATION: Cooked lentils will keep for 3 days in the refrigerator and freeze well.

NOTE: For more ways to cook lentils, see the lentil minestrones on pages 45–46.

Eastern Mediterranean Lentils

VEGAN /// **MAKES 6 GENEROUS SERVINGS**

Make the *Stewed Lentils* template (page 197) with the following additional ingredients and specifications:

1 teaspoon cumin seeds, lightly toasted and ground

1 teaspoon coriander seeds, lightly toasted and ground

2 tablespoons extra virgin olive oil

1 medium or large onion, finely chopped

3 tablespoons chopped fresh cilantro, parsley, or dill; or a mix

1. Follow the template recipe, but omit the Parmesan rind and the halved onion. Add the ground cumin and coriander along with the salt when the lentils come to a boil.

2. While the lentils are simmering, heat the olive oil over medium heat in a medium skillet. Add the chopped onion and cook, stirring often, until golden brown, 10 to 15 minutes. If the onion begins to stick to the pan, add a pinch of salt.

3. When the lentils are tender, taste and adjust seasonings. Stir in the onion and chopped fresh herbs, heat through, and serve.

ADVANCE PREPARATION: Cooked lentils will keep for 3 days in the refrigerator and freeze well. Do not cook the final onion addition until ready to serve.

Toasting Spices

The purpose of toasting spices is to bring out and deepen their aromas. Heat a small, dry skillet over medium or medium-high heat. Add the spice—one spice at a time—and shake in the pan just until you begin to perceive the aroma and fragrance of the spice. Immediately remove from the pan and allow to cool before grinding (if that's the next step).

Indian Lentils

VEGAN //// **MAKES 6 GENEROUS SERVINGS**

Make the *Stewed Lentils* template (page 197) with the following additional ingredients and specifications:

1 teaspoon curry powder (optional)

1 teaspoon cumin seeds, lightly toasted and ground

1 teaspoon coriander seeds, lightly toasted and ground

½ teaspoon mustard seeds, lightly toasted and ground

¼ to ½ teaspoon cayenne (to taste)

¼ teaspoon turmeric

2 tablespoons sunflower oil or grapeseed oil

1 medium or large onion, finely chopped

3 tablespoons chopped fresh cilantro

1. Follow the template recipe, but omit the halved onion, the bouquet garni, and Parmesan rind. Add the spices along with the salt when the lentils come to a boil.

2. While the lentils are simmering, heat the oil over medium heat in a medium skillet. Add the chopped onion and cook, stirring often, until golden brown, 10 to 15 minutes. If the onion begins to stick to the pan, add a pinch of salt.

3. When the lentils are tender, taste and adjust seasonings. Stir in the onion and cilantro, heat through, and serve.

ADVANCE PREPARATION: Cooked lentils will keep for 3 days in the refrigerator and freeze well. Do not cook the final onion addition until ready to serve.

Veracruzana Lentils

VEGAN //// **MAKES 6 GENEROUS SERVINGS**

Make the *Stewed Lentils* template (page 197) with the following additional ingredients and specifications:

1 teaspoon cumin seeds, lightly toasted and ground

1 to 2 canned chipotle chiles in adobo (to taste), seeded and minced

Follow the template recipe, but omit the Parmesan rind. Add the cumin and chipotles along with the salt when the lentils come to a boil. Continue as directed.

ADVANCE PREPARATION: Cooked lentils will keep for 3 days in the refrigerator and freeze well. These will become more spicy as they sit.

Middle Eastern Lentils with Spinach and Dukkah

VEGAN WITHOUT THE YOGURT GARNISH /// **MAKES 4 TO 6 SERVINGS**

This is a thick pot of lentils seasoned with coriander seeds, cumin, and Aleppo pepper or chili. The lentils are cooked until just about softened, then lightly browned onions and spices are stirred in. In many ways it resembles an Indian dal; you can see how the cuisines of India and the Middle East have shared spices and techniques. The spinach will cook down when you add it to the lentils, so don't worry if it seems like this is a large quantity to be adding. The mixture is, however, thick like dal.

Make the *Stewed Lentils* template (page 197) with the following additional ingredients and specifications:

2 tablespoons extra virgin olive oil

1 large onion, finely chopped

Salt and freshly ground pepper

2 large garlic cloves, minced

2 teaspoons coriander seeds, lightly toasted and ground

2 teaspoons cumin seeds, lightly toasted and ground

Pinch of cayenne, or ½ teaspoon Aleppo pepper

1 bunch spinach, stemmed, leaves washed in 2 changes of water, and roughly chopped

GARNISH:

Plain yogurt, drained yogurt (see page 140), or garlic yogurt (see page 141)

Chopped cilantro or flat-leaf parsley

Dukkah (page 137)

1. Follow the template recipe, but omit the Parmesan rind and the halved onions.

2. While the lentils are simmering, heat the olive oil over medium heat in a large, heavy nonstick skillet. Add the chopped onion and cook, stirring, until tender, 5 to 8 minutes. Add a generous pinch of salt, the minced garlic, coriander, cumin, and cayenne or Aleppo pepper. Continue to cook, stirring, for a minute, until the garlic is fragrant.

3. Stir the onion mixture into the lentils. Add black pepper, taste, and adjust salt. Continue to simmer for another 15 minutes.

4. Add the spinach, which should still have some water on it from washing. Cover and let the spinach steam and collapse into the lentils for a couple of minutes. Uncover, stir the spinach into the lentils, and cover again. Simmer until the spinach is wilted but still bright, 3 to 5 minutes. Taste and adjust seasoning. Garnish each serving with a generous spoonful of yogurt, chopped cilantro or parsley, and dukkah.

ADVANCE PREPARATION: The lentils will keep in the refrigerator for 3 or 4 days. The mixture will thicken; thin out if desired with water.

CHAPTER ELEVEN

Tacos and Quesadillas

N LOS ANGELES, WHERE I live, taco trucks are a way of life and chefs too are quite creative with what goes into their tacos. Korean tacos are as popular as traditional Mexican tacos, which just goes to show you that you can wrap a warm tortilla around just about anything and call it a taco.

At home, vegetarian taco dinners can be easy and fun, and either simple or complex. The most comforting tacos are filled simply with beans, salsa, and a sprinkling of cheese; but in this chapter you'll find all sorts of vegetable fillings bathed in complex spicy salsas and set off with crumbled Mexican cheese or feta.

I use corn tortillas for both tacos and quesadillas. I love the flavor of corn tortillas, and they're nutritionally superior to those made with white flour. Plus they're a boon for friends who have trouble with gluten. I buy them in packs of 3 dozen, then divide them up so that I can freeze them by the dozen since I usually don't use 36 tortillas in a week.

TACO CONDIMENTS

YOU CAN FIND PLENTY OF GOOD bottled salsas, but nothing will match the salsas you make yourself.

Salsa Fresca

MAKES ABOUT 2 CUPS

Although Mexican restaurants serve fresh tomato salsa year-round, their tomatoes come from Mexico or Florida and off-season they have little flavor and a spongy texture. Those salsas are carried by the heat of the chiles and the pungency of the onions. I recommend using cooked salsas when tomatoes aren't in season, and reserving this classic for the height of summer. I soak the onion in cold water with a splash of vinegar to wash away some of the volatile compounds that otherwise remain with me for the rest of the day and detract from the overall flavor of the salsa.

¼ small white or red onion, minced

1 teaspoon red wine vinegar

1 pound fresh tomatoes, finely chopped

1 to 3 jalapeño or serrano chiles (to taste), minced (seeded for a milder salsa*)

¼ cup chopped fresh cilantro (or more to taste)

1 to 2 teaspoons fresh lime juice (optional)

Salt

*Chiles seem to be bred to be less hot these days, so I rarely seed them.

1. Place the minced onion in a bowl and cover with cold water. Add the vinegar and let sit for 5 minutes or longer. Drain and rinse with cold water.

2. In a medium bowl, combine all of the ingredients. If your tomatoes are full of flavor you won't need the lime juice. Ideally, allow to stand at room temperature for 15 to 30 minutes before serving so that the flavors will blend and ripen.

ADVANCE PREPARATION: The salsa is best served the day it's made, but you can make it a few hours ahead, or at least chop the ingredients. The problem with letting it sit very long is that the salt, so necessary for seasoning, draws out juice from the tomato so the salsa will become quite watery in time.

SUBSTITUTIONS AND ADDITIONS: Add one or more of the following:

- *1 Hass avocado, cut into very small dice*
- *Kernels from 1 ear of corn, steamed for 4 to 5 minutes*
- *1 (15-ounce) can black beans, drained and rinsed; or 1½ cups cooked black beans (see page 187)*
- *1 small cucumber, such as a Persian cucumber, peeled if waxy and cut into fine dice*

Salsa Ranchera

MAKES ABOUT 1½ CUPS

When you make this classic cooked tomato salsa with fresh tomatoes in season, roast the tomatoes on the grill or under the broiler. If you make it with canned tomatoes in winter, look for fire-roasted tomatoes. The grilled flavors of the vegetables mixed with the seared taste of the cooked salsa create the great depth of flavor that a good salsa ranchera should have.

1½ pounds fresh tomatoes; or 1 (14.5-ounce) can fire-roasted tomatoes, with juice

½ medium onion, peeled

2 garlic cloves, unpeeled

1 to 3 jalapeño or serrano chiles (to taste)

1 tablespoon grapeseed oil, sunflower oil, or canola oil

½ teaspoon salt (or more to taste)

1. To roast fresh tomatoes, heat the broiler or prepare a hot grill. If broiling, line a baking sheet with foil and place the tomatoes on it. Place under the broiler, close to the heat. Broil until charred on one side, usually 2 to 3 minutes. Using tongs, turn the tomatoes over. Broil until charred on the other side. If grilling, char the tomatoes on both sides, turning with tongs. Transfer the tomatoes to a bowl and allow to cool. Remove the skin and core using a paring knife.

2. Broil the onion on the baking sheet (or grill it), turning often, until charred. Allow to cool slightly.

3. Heat a dry, heavy skillet (or a Mexican griddle called a *comal*) over medium-high heat. Add the garlic cloves and toast, turning often, until soft and spotted brown in places. Allow to cool until you can handle them, then cut away the stem ends and remove the skins. Toast the chile peppers until charred in places in the same dry skillet. Cut away the stems. If your chiles are very hot (the ones I buy rarely are) and you want a milder salsa, seed the chiles; wear rubber gloves if you're doing this.

4. In a blender, combine the roasted tomatoes along with any juices that have accumulated in the bowl (or the canned tomatoes), the onion, peeled garlic, and stemmed chiles. Blend at high speed until the mixture is pureed but still has a bit of texture.

5. In a heavy saucepan, flameproof casserole, or straight-sided skillet, heat the oil over high heat until it ripples. It should be quite hot—when you add a drop of puree to it, the puree should hiss. Add the tomato puree and cook, stirring, until it thickens, darkens, and leaves a canal when you run a spatula or wooden spoon down the middle of the pan, 2 to 3 minutes. Reduce the heat to medium, season with salt, and simmer for a minute or

two longer. If you wish, before you remove it from the heat you can thin out the salsa with a little water. Taste and adjust salt.

ADVANCE PREPARATION: The salsa will keep for about 4 days in the refrigerator and freezes well. It will become more pungent.

VARIATION: CHIPOTLE SALSA RANCHERA

Substitute 1 or 2 adobo-packed chipotle chiles for the jalapeños or serranos.

VARIATION: CHILE GUAJILLO SALSA RANCHERA

Wearing rubber gloves, tear 4 guajillo or pasilla chiles into pieces and remove the seeds. Toast on both sides, pressing them down in a dry skillet or on a stovetop grill over medium-high heat, just until they blister, which will be in a matter of seconds. Remove from the heat. Substitute for the jalapeños or serranos.

VARIATION: BLACK BEAN SALSA RANCHERA

Stir $1\frac{1}{2}$ cups simmered black beans (see page 187) or 1 (15-ounce) can black beans, drained and rinsed, into the finished salsa.

Fresh Tomatillo Salsa

MAKES 2 CUPS

I love green tomatillos; I think I'm even a bigger fan of green salsa than red salsa. I love the tangy flavor of tomatillos against the heat of chiles. This salsa is one of my favorites, and so quick to throw together. The tomatillos require either a quick roast or a simmer, then everything is blended and it's done.

1 pound tomatillos, husked and rinsed

2 to 4 jalapeño or serrano chiles, coarsely chopped (to taste) seeded for a milder salsa

¼ cup chopped onion, soaked for 5 minutes in cold water, drained, and rinsed

¼ to ½ cup coarsely chopped cilantro (to taste)

¼ to ½ cup water, as needed

About ½ teaspoon salt

1. Place the tomatillos in a medium saucepan, add water to cover, and bring to a simmer. Simmer, flipping them over halfway through, until softened and olive green, about 10 minutes. Alternatively, roast under the broiler: Preheat the broiler, cover a baking sheet with foil, and place the tomatillos on top, stem side down. Place under the broiler close to the heat and broil until charred on one side, 2 to 5 minutes. Turn over and broil on the other side until charred on the other side, 2 to 5 minutes. You can also grill the tomatillos.

2. Transfer the tomatillos to a blender (tipping in any juice that may have accumulated on the foil if you roasted them). Add the chiles, onion, cilantro, and $\frac{1}{4}$ cup water to the blender and blend to a coarse puree. Transfer to a bowl, add the salt, and thin out as desired with water. Taste and adjust salt. Set aside for at least 30 minutes before serving, to allow the flavors to develop.

ADVANCE PREPARATION: This will hold for 3 or 4 days in the refrigerator, but the fresher it is, the more vivid the flavors will be. It will thicken as it sits and you will need to thin it out with water.

SUBSTITUTIONS AND ADDITIONS:

- *Add 1 or 2 garlic cloves—toasted if desired (as in the Salsa Ranchera recipe, page 206)—to the blender in Step 2.*

- *Substitute 1 or 2 chipotle peppers for the jalapeños or serranos.*

Pickled Red Onions

MAKES ABOUT 1 CUP

Pickled red onions, which turn a lovely pink color, are a favorite condiment with Mexican food of all kinds. They're also delicious with most of the Big Bowl combos in Chapter 7. Blanching the onion does away with the volatile flavors that would otherwise stay in your mouth for hours after eating these.

Salt and freshly ground pepper

1 small red onion, cut in half lengthwise and sliced very thin across the grain

1 to 2 garlic cloves (to taste), cut in half

⅓ cup cider vinegar

1. Bring a medium pot of water to a boil and add a generous amount of salt. Add the onion, blanch 45 seconds to 1 minute, and transfer to a bowl of cold water. Drain, rinse, and place in a medium bowl.

2. Add the remaining ingredients to the bowl along with about ¼ teaspoon salt and pepper to taste. Add enough water to cover the onion slices; they should be just barely submerged. Cover the bowl with plastic wrap and let stand several hours, then transfer to a jar and refrigerate.

ADVANCE PREPARATION: These will keep for several weeks in the refrigerator.

Soft Tacos

MAKES 8 TO 12 TACOS

The reason these are *soft* tacos is because the tortillas aren't fried. Unlike tacos made with crisp tortillas, some of these are most easily eaten with knife and fork. If you want to eat them with your hands, stack two tortillas, then fill. If you want to eat them away from the table, stack two and wrap the tacos in foil or wax paper (the way they do it at taco trucks) so they won't fall apart.

The easiest way to serve soft tacos for dinner is to place the warm tortillas on a plate or platter, top with the filling, then fold the tortilla over; or just leave them open and let the diner fold them over (or not). You can also let your guests assemble their own, with the filling and garnishes in serving dishes and the warm tortillas wrapped in a cloth in a basket.

Sometimes ingredients that go into a typical salsa are part of the filling for a taco, in which case no additional salsa is needed. In other taco dishes the salsa is an important condiment to complete the dish. As for cheese, you'll want a crumbling cheese (as opposed to a melting cheese), like queso fresco or feta. I like goat cheese as well. Queso fresco, a mild white cheese that I love for its texture, lightness, and mild flavor, is widely available in most supermarkets. I'm usually satisfied with two tacos but others will eat three or four (or more).

2 to 3½ cups filling of your choice (see suggestions opposite page and filling recipes, pages 212–217)

8 to 12 corn tortillas (double if stacking by twos)

1 to 1½ cups salsa (see pages 205–208), or more to taste

½ to 1 cup crumbled queso fresco, feta, or goat cheese (to taste)

OTHER GARNISHES

Shredded lettuce

Shredded cabbage

Other shredded vegetables of your choice

Sliced radishes

Chopped cilantro

Chopped epazote

Pickled Red Onions (page 209)

Lightly toasted pumpkin seeds or finely chopped toasted almonds

1. Prepare the filling as directed in the variation and taco filling recipes. Meanwhile, warm the tortillas (see opposite page).

2. Place one or two warm tortillas on each plate and top each one with a generous spoonful of the filling. Add salsa, cheese, or other garnishes. Fold the tortillas over (if desired) and serve. Alternatively, pass the hot tortillas and the filling(s), salsa, cheese, and other garnishes (or arrange on a buffet) and let diners assemble their own. Taco dinner parties are a lot of fun. If you want to be able to eat the tacos with your hands without them falling apart, stack 2 warm tortillas, top with the filling, place on a sheet of foil or wax paper, and fold over.

NOTE: See recipes on pages 212–217 for advance preparation notes on fillings. Tortillas should not be heated too far in advance because they will eventually stick together and tear.

GREAT TACO FILLINGS

- *Steamed or roasted potatoes and wilted greens (see page 3) tossed with Fresh Tomatillo Salsa (page 208)*
- *Scrambled eggs, with steamed or roasted potatoes stirred in*
- *Scrambled eggs, with roasted poblano peppers (see page 8) or Mediterranean Stewed Peppers (page 6, any version) stirred in*
- *Roasted vegetables (see page 15) with Chipotle Salsa Ranchera (page 207) or just tossed with a couple of minced chipotles and topped with queso fresco*
- *Simmered black beans (see page 187) and queso fresco*
- *Black Beans with Greens (page 189)*

Warming Tortillas

There are several ways to warm tortillas. If making tacos for a crowd, you can wrap up a big stack in foil and throw them in a 325°F oven for 15 to 20 minutes. Or you can quickly zap a few tortillas at a time in a microwave.

You can also steam or char them. My favorite method when I'm making a taco meal is steaming: Wrap the tortillas in a heavy dishtowel and steam for 1 minute above an inch of boiling water. Then turn off the heat and let them sit for 10 to 15 minutes without uncovering your steamer. They'll be warm, moist, and easy to fold over a filling. (This works as long as I don't have more than a dozen tortillas to deal with: If the stack gets too heavy, the tortillas tend to stick to one another.)

When I'm making tacos for just me, or for two at most, I warm and slightly char the tortillas directly over a gas burner on my stove. I love the smoky flavor of tortillas heated this way. If you're grilling, heat them directly on the grill.

Corn and Fava Bean Taco Filling with Fresh Tomatillo Salsa

VEGAN WITHOUT THE CHEESE /// **MAKES ENOUGH FOR 8 TO 10 TACOS**

I know, fava beans are Mediterranean, not Mexican (though there are some wonderful soups made with dried fava beans in the state of Veracruz). But they're so pretty and delicious with the corn, the texture soft and starchy against the juicy crunch of the corn kernels.

4 ears corn

1 tablespoon extra virgin olive oil

1 small red onion or spring onion, finely chopped

Salt

1½ pounds fava beans, shelled and skinned (see page 155; blanch the shelled favas long enough to cook them through, which could be 5 minutes or more if the beans are large)

¼ cup chopped cilantro

Fresh Tomatillo Salsa (page 208)

1. Cut the kernels off the corncobs. Heat the olive oil over medium heat in a large skillet and add the onion. Cook, stirring often, until tender, about 5 minutes. Add a generous pinch of salt and the corn kernels and continue to cook, stirring often, until the corn is tender, another 4 to 5 minutes. Stir in the fava beans and cilantro and about ½ cup of the salsa. Heat through and remove from the heat. Taste and adjust seasonings.

2. Use the filling to make 8 to 10 Soft Tacos (page 210), topping the tacos with the remaining salsa.

ADVANCE PREPARATION: You can make this filling a few hours before serving, but the fresher it is the better. Reheat gently in the pan.

SUBSTITUTIONS AND ADDITIONS:

- *Substitute cooked lima beans or other shell beans for the fava beans.*
- *Add 1 pound grated summer squash with the corn kernels and cook until wilted, about 5 minutes. Season generously with salt and pepper.*

The Well-Filled Taco

Generally, ¼ to ⅓ cup filling makes a well-filled taco. But some fillings, like scrambled eggs, are less bulky than others, so rather than give you precise measurements for the filling amounts, I've given a range. The right amount for a taco will allow you to fold the taco in half over the filling and pick it up without everything falling out.

Mushroom, Chipotle, and Chard Taco Filling

VEGAN WITHOUT THE CHEESE /// **MAKES ENOUGH FOR 10 TO 12 TACOS**

The best mushrooms for this taco filling are oyster mushrooms. They're nice and meaty, the closest you can find to wild mushrooms at an affordable price. The filling is a chipotle-spiked mushroom ragout, with Swiss chard thrown in. If your chard has thick stalks you can use them in this, or pickle them (see opposite page) and serve as a condiment.

1 tablespoon extra virgin olive oil

1 small onion, quartered lengthwise and thinly sliced across the grain

1 bunch Swiss chard, stemmed (stems diced if desired), wilted (see page 3), and coarsely chopped

1 pound oyster mushrooms or creminis, cleaned, stems trimmed, and sliced thick

Salt

1 to 2 garlic cloves (to taste), minced

1 to 2 canned chipotle chiles in adobo (to taste), seeded and chopped

1. Heat the olive oil over medium heat in a large heavy skillet. Add the onion and diced chard stems (if using) and cook, stirring often, until tender, about 5 minutes. Add the mushrooms and turn the heat up to medium-high. Cook, stirring, until the mushrooms begin to sweat and soften. Turn the heat back to medium and add about $\frac{1}{2}$ teaspoon salt, the garlic, and chipotles. Continue to cook until the mushroom liquid has just about evaporated from the pan but the mushrooms are nice and moist, 5 to 10 minutes. Add the chard and stir together for about a minute. Taste and adjust seasonings.

2. Use the filling (and queso fresco for the cheese) to make 10 to 12 Soft Tacos (page 210).

ADVANCE PREPARATION: The wilted chard and the cooked mushrooms, either before or after you put them together, will keep for about 3 days in the refrigerator. The pungency will increase.

Pickled Chard Stalks

MAKES 1 CUP

I hate throwing away chard stalks when they're thick and meaty. Here's a quick way to turn them into refrigerator pickles:

- ½ cup seasoned rice vinegar
- 1 tablespoon sherry vinegar
- ¼ cup sugar
- 1 cup water
- 2¼ teaspoons kosher salt
- 1 cup very thinly sliced chard stalks

In a large bowl, combine the rice vinegar, sherry vinegar, and sugar. Bring the water to a boil in a small pan, remove from the heat, and add to the vinegar and sugar mixture. Stir until the sugar is dissolved. Add the salt and stir well. Place the thinly sliced chard stalks in a jar or bowl and pour on the brine. Refrigerate for at least 2 days and for up to 2 weeks.

Roasted Tomato, Summer Squash, and Squash Blossom Taco Filling

VEGAN WITHOUT THE CHEESE /// **MAKES ENOUGH FOR 8 TO 10 TACOS**

If you can't get squash blossoms for these summer tacos, go ahead and make the filling without them. But if you have a garden and you're looking for ways to use squash flowers, they're welcome in a taco.

1 pound tomatoes

2 tablespoons extra virgin olive oil

½ medium onion, chopped

Salt and freshly ground pepper

2 large garlic cloves, minced

2 serrano chiles or 1 large jalapeño chile, minced

1½ pounds summer squash, cut into ½-inch dice

6 to 10 squash blossoms, sliced crosswise (optional)

1 cup cooked black beans (see page 187), rinsed if using canned

2 to 4 tablespoons chopped cilantro

1. Heat the broiler (or a grill, see Note). Line a baking sheet with foil and place the tomatoes on the foil. Place under the broiler, close to the heat, and broil until charred black. Turn over and broil on the other side until charred black. This usually takes 2 to 3 minutes. Remove from the heat and allow to cool.

2. Remove the skins from the tomatoes, core, and cut in half. Set a strainer over a bowl and, making sure the tomato is cool enough to handle, squeeze out the seeds, then rub the gelatinous pulp that surrounds the seeds through the strainer. Chop the tomato flesh and add to the bowl with the juice. Discard the seeds.

3. Heat the olive oil over medium heat in a large, heavy skillet. Add the onion and a pinch of salt and cook, stirring often, until tender, about 5 minutes. Add the garlic, chiles, summer squash, and more salt to taste. Turn the heat to medium-high and cook, stirring, until the squash is beginning to color, about 5 minutes. Add the chopped tomatoes and their juices and cook, stirring often, until the squash is just about tender and the tomatoes have cooked down slightly, about 5 minutes. Stir in the squash blossoms if using and continue to cook until the tomatoes have cooked down and the mixture is fragrant, about 5 more minutes. Stir in the beans and cilantro and add salt and pepper to taste.

4. Use the filling (and goat cheese as the cheese) to make 8 to 10 Soft Tacos (page 210).

NOTE: You can also grill the tomatoes (with the squash) on an outdoor grill. And while you're at it, grill the squash and onions too. Slice the onion (instead of chopping) and toss with the squash and a little olive oil. Grill in a grill pan over the coals.

ADVANCE PREPARATION: The filling will keep for 3 days in the refrigerator. The squash may throw off some juice in the refrigerator; just stir the dish well and use it, juice and all.

SUBSTITUTIONS AND ADDITIONS: Throw in a handful of chopped amaranth greens, quelites, or chopped spinach (or baby spinach) toward the end of Step 3 and cook, stirring, until they wilt.

Quesadillas

MAKES 1 SERVING

In Mexico, a number of filled corn tortilla preparations are called quesadillas, and sometimes I'm not sure why they're called quesadillas and not tacos; some don't even contain cheese! In most restaurants here in the States, and especially in chain restaurants, a quesadilla is a high-calorie, folded flour tortilla filled with lots of Monterey Jack or cheddar cheese. But in my house quesadillas are different. I make them with corn tortillas, which I stack under and over a filling that contains a melting cheese and a bean or vegetable preparation. As a quick after-school fix I'll make quesadillas with cheese only: I put a tortilla on a plate, top it with grated or sliced cheese, slap a tortilla on top of the cheese, and zap it for a minute and a half in the microwave. Then I quarter the quesadilla and serve it right away.

The cheese in my quesadillas is often secondary to the beans or vegetables; but even if the quantity is small, because it's a melting cheese (as opposed to the crumbly cheeses I use in tacos) it acts as a liaison, bringing everything together, deliciously. I like to use Monterey Jack, with a little Parmesan thrown in for flavor, or cheddar. Sometimes I'll add some goat cheese for an altogether different flavor, or mozzarella for a rich, stringy effect. Fillings vary; they can't be too chunky or the tortillas won't stack. If you have some leftover beans, not quite enough for a bowl of beans but too good to let go to waste, mash them up a bit and they'll be welcome in a quesadilla.

I don't always make quesadillas in the microwave; that's mostly reserved for the quick after-school fixes I need to make for a cranky adolescent who chooses to play basketball at lunch rather than eat. You can make stacked or folded quesadillas in a dry heavy skillet or on a griddle. They'll have a deeper, richer flavor and the tortillas don't get rubbery as they cool.

2 corn tortillas

About ⅓ cup quesadilla filling (see opposite page)

1 ounce either shredded Monterey Jack; a mix of Monterey Jack and Parmesan; cheddar cheese; or crumbled goat cheese

Salsa for serving (optional)

MICROWAVE METHOD

Place a tortilla on a plate. Top with the filling (if using simmered beans, lightly mash them with a fork or the back of a spoon). Sprinkle on the cheese, top with the remaining tortilla, and press down gently. Microwave for $1\frac{1}{2}$ minutes, until the cheese has melted. Cut into quarters and serve.

PAN METHOD

Place a tortilla in a heavy pan (cast iron is good). Top with the filling (if using simmered beans, lightly mash them with a fork or the back of a spoon). Sprinkle on the cheese. Turn the heat to medium-high and heat until the cheese begins to melt and the tortilla begins to brown lightly. Place another tortilla on top of the cheese and press down lightly. Flip the quesadilla over in the pan and heat until the cheese has melted, about 30 seconds. Flip back over and remove to a plate. Cut into quarters and serve.

VARIATION:

You can also make quesadillas in single tortillas, though in my experience they often break at the middle when you're heating them. Place the filling on one half of a tortilla and top with cheese. Fold the tortilla over. Heat in a heavy skillet, flipping the quesadilla over from time to time, until the cheese melts and the tortilla is browned in places.

QUESADILLA FILLINGS

- *Slow-Cooked Baked Beans (page 193) or Simmered Beans (page 187)*
- *Roasted Cauliflower (page 19) or Roasted Broccoli (page 18), or a mix*
- *Roasted Winter Squash (page 15)*
- *Wilted Greens (page 3), seasoned with olive oil, garlic, salt, and pepper (try this with goat cheese as well as with Monterey Jack)*
- *Pan-Cooked Mushrooms (page 11) or Mushroom Ragout (page 12)*
- *Melted Onions (page 10)*
- *Roasted Peppers (page 8)*

CHAPTER TWELVE

Savory Pies

S AVORY PIES CAN BE THE most impressive of vegetarian main dishes. They make a memorable centerpiece for a dinner party and are great for family dinners as well. Pies are more time-consuming than the recipes in some of the other chapters of this book because they require that you first make a crust, then the filling for the crust. But all of my recipes for dough yield two crusts, so you will always have a standby pastry in the freezer (unless you use the entire recipe for a torte or a galette). If you make Greek pies with phyllo dough, you don't need to make a crust at all; but you do need to remember to begin thawing the phyllo the night before.

With the exception of quiches, inspired by the wonderful quiches I've enjoyed in France, the pies in this chapter are Mediterranean. Sometimes I use a whole wheat, yeasted olive oil crust that's incredibly easy to work with and delicious; other times I use Greek phyllo dough for these pies.

Pizzas, the iconic Italian pie (though I've had wonderful savory tortas that aren't pizzas in Italy as well), also find their place in this chapter. They're easy to make at home and you can top homemade pizzas with any number of vegetables.

Working with Pastry Dough

This can be one of the most frustrating activities in cooking, but with my formula and the right technique it will cease to be something you dread, as I did for many years. If you happen to have a nifty piece of equipment called a Silpat baking mat, a silicone nonstick liner used in baking, your pastry dough life will change forever. If you don't have a Silpat, you'll do just fine with parchment paper.

1. Place a piece of parchment or a Silpat on your work surface and dust it with all-purpose flour. Place the dough on top. Tap the dough lightly with your rolling pin to soften it enough to roll it out. Dust the top very lightly with flour and roll the rolling pin from one end to the other, taking care not to press down too hard on the pin. Roll 3 times in one direction, from one end of the dough to the other. Gently lift the dough to make sure that it is not sticking to the Silpat. If it is, slide an offset spatula underneath and dust the work surface with flour. Give the dough a quarter-turn and roll again 3 times in one direction, then check to see that it isn't sticking. Continue to roll 3 times then turn, dusting as necessary, until the dough is about $1/4$ inch thick and the circle measures $1^1/2$ inches more than the circumference of your pan.

2. Very lightly dust the top of the dough. Place the rolling pin on one end of the dough. Wrap the end of the dough gently around it and roll the pin as you lift the dough and roll it over the pin. Then unroll the dough over a lightly buttered tart or cake pan. Gently ease the dough into the corners of the pan, where the sides hit the bottom, making sure that there is no gap between the dough and the pan. Don't press on the dough too much as that will make it thinner in places, and it will bake unevenly. Using a paring knife, cut away the overhang, or fold the overhang in and crimp the edge. Using a fork, poke rows of holes on the bottom of the pie shell. Refrigerate the dough uncovered for at least 2 hours but preferably overnight.

QUICHE

MY QUICHE ISN'T ALTOGETHER TRADITIONAL. I use whole wheat flour in the crust and I don't use cream in my custard—just milk, eggs, and Gruyère or a mix of Gruyère and Parmesan. Thanks to my work with French pastry chef Jacquy Pfeiffer, I have been able to perfect a delicious whole wheat *pâte brisée,* and my custard as well is based on Jacquy's formula. I've learned from him to combine egg yolks with whole egg for a custard with just the right flavor and texture. There isn't a lot of custard in my quiches; there's enough to hold the pie together, but the vegetables tend to take center stage. In most of my quiches, the filling, with the custard, does not reach the top of the pie shell.

Whole Wheat Pâte Brisée

MAKES TWO 9-INCH PIE CRUSTS

This is a classic, buttery French pastry dough based on a recipe by Chicago-based French pastry chef Jacquy Pfeiffer. Instead of using entirely all-purpose flour, I use half whole wheat flour, resulting in a rich pie crust with a nutty, complex flavor.

I worked with Jacquy on his book *The Art of French Pastry* and became a devoted convert to using metric weights as opposed to cup measures when I make pastry of all kinds. It's much easier and more accurate to weigh ingredients on a scale than to measure them in cups, with results that are always consistent. If you don't believe me, try weighing a cup of flour. Now weigh another cup, and you will see that the weight will be different. Do this 10 times if you really want to be convinced. That's the exercise Jacquy puts his students through when they begin at the school he founded in Chicago, the French Pastry School.

222 grams French-style butter such as Plugrá (8 ounces), at room temperature

175 grams whole wheat flour or whole wheat pastry flour (approximately 1½ cups less 1 tablespoon)

175 grams unbleached all-purpose flour (approximately 1½ cups less 1 tablespoon)

7 grams fine sea salt (1 teaspoon)

92 grams water (6 tablespoons)

1. Make sure that your butter is at room temperature. Place it in the bowl of a stand mixer. Sift together the flours and salt and add to the mixer. Mix at low speed just until well combined. Do not overbeat. Add the water and beat at low speed just until the mixture comes together. Do not overmix or you will activate the gluten in the flour too much and your pastry will be tough.

2. Weigh the dough and divide into two equal pieces. Place each half on a sheet of plastic and flatten into a square about ½ inch thick. Wrap well and refrigerate for at least 2 hours, preferably overnight.

3. Lightly brush two 9-inch tart pans with a *very* small amount of soft butter (if you can see the butter, you've used too much). Roll out the dough and line the tart pans. Using a fork, pierce rows of holes in the bottom, about an inch apart. This will allow steam to escape and aid in even baking. Refrigerate uncovered for several hours or preferably overnight.

4. To prebake, heat the oven to 325°F. Remove a tart shell from the refrigerator and place on a sheet pan. Line the tart shell with a sheet of parchment. Fill all the way with pie weights (which can be beans or rice used exclusively for prebaking pastry, or special pie weights). Place in the middle of the oven and bake for 15 minutes. Remove the pie weights and parchment and return to the oven. Bake for another 15 minutes, or until light golden brown and evenly colored. There should be no evidence of moisture in the dough. Remove from the oven and allow to cool.

(continued)

ADVANCE PREPARATION: The dough should be mixed up at least a day ahead and will keep in the refrigerator for 2 to 3 days. For best results, mix it up 2 days ahead, roll it out the next day, and leave it in the refrigerator overnight, uncovered, before pre-baking. It also freezes well. You can freeze it either before or after rolling out. Double wrap the dough you are freezing in plastic and then in foil. If you have lined the pan, you can transfer it directly from the freezer to the oven to prebake (remove all wrapping first); you will not need to use pie weights.

TEMPLATE

Quiche

MAKES 6 SERVINGS

In the heyday of 1960s and 1970s vegetarianism, the quiche ruled. It was the go-to vegetarian dish, and I logged hours making them when I had a vegetarian catering service. It was the first thing I taught when I started my career as a vegetarian cooking teacher.

Then the quiche seemed to go out of fashion. But it shouldn't have. A good quiche is a wonderful dish—how can you resist a savory cheese and custard tart? Vegetable quiches filled with spinach, mushrooms, onions, leeks, or asparagus may be nothing new, but so what? They are timeless, a dinner that we never get tired of.

2 egg yolks

2 whole eggs

1 (9-inch) Whole Wheat Pâte Brisée pie crust, fully baked (page 223) and cooled

½ teaspoon salt

Freshly ground pepper

⅔ cup milk

1 to 2 cups vegetable filling of your choice (see suggestions on the opposite page and filling recipes, pages 225–227)

3 ounces Gruyère cheese , shredded, or 1 ounce Parmesan and 2 ounces Gruyère (¾ cup total)

1. Heat the oven to 350°F.

2. Beat together the egg yolks and whole eggs in a medium bowl. Set the tart pan on a baking sheet to allow for easy handling. Using a pastry brush, lightly brush the bottom of the crust with some of the beaten egg and place in the oven for 5 minutes. Set aside. The egg seals the crust so that it won't become soggy when it comes into contact with the custard.

3. Add the salt, pepper, and milk to the remaining eggs and whisk together.

4. Spread the vegetable filling in an even layer in the crust. Sprinkle the cheese in an even layer on top of the filling. (You can also simply toss the vegetable filling with the cheese and spread in the bottom of the crust. And, if you are making a simple cheese quiche with no vegetables, just sprinkle the cheese over the bottom of the crust in an even layer.) Pour in the egg custard, making sure to scrape in every last bit with a rubber spatula. Bake the quiche

until set and just beginning to color on the top, about 30 minutes. Allow to sit for at least 15 minutes before serving.

ADVANCE PREPARATION: Most quiches will keep well for a day. They're good at room temperature or can be warmed in a low oven. Don't warm in the microwave as the crust will become soggy. Most fillings can be made a day ahead. If you do this, refrigerate uncovered so that moisture will evaporate. If you see that moisture has accumulated in the bowl with your filling, drain so that you don't introduce it into the custard.

QUICHE FILLING IDEAS

- *1¹⁄₂ to 2 cups leftover vegetables from another dish*
- *Mushroom Quiche: 1¹⁄₂ to 2 cups Mushroom Ragout (page 12) or Pan-Cooked Mushrooms (page 11)*
- *Onion Quiche: 1 cup Melted Onions (page 10). If you can start this the day before, make the melted onions and refrigerate uncovered overnight, so that some of the liquid evaporates.*
- *Tomato Quiche: Whisk 1 cup Marinara Sauce (made with fresh or canned tomatoes, pages 24 and 26) and the cheese into the custard.*

FILLING

Wilted Greens and Onion Quiche Filling

MAKES ENOUGH FOR ONE 9-INCH QUICHE, SERVING 6

You can use whatever greens you have on hand for this. Chard and spinach make a sweeter filling than the more robust greens like kale and broccoli raab. They all work for me.

1 tablespoon extra virgin olive oil

1 medium onion, chopped

Salt and freshly ground pepper

1 to 2 garlic cloves (to taste), minced (optional)

1 to 1½ cups wilted greens (spinach, chard, beet greens, kale, broccoli raab; see page 3), chopped medium-fine

1 teaspoon fresh thyme leaves (optional)

1. Heat the oil over medium heat in a medium skillet. Add the onion and cook, stirring often, until tender, about 5 minutes. Add a generous pinch of salt and the garlic and cook, stirring, until fragrant, about 30 seconds. Add the wilted greens and optional thyme, season with salt and pepper, and stir together for about a minute, until the greens are nicely infused with the oil. Allow to cool.

2. Use the filling in the quiche template recipe (opposite page).

Asparagus, Scallion, and Herb Quiche Filling

MAKES ENOUGH FOR ONE 9-INCH QUICHE, SERVING 6

This is my favorite springtime quiche.

1 tablespoon extra virgin olive oil or butter

½ cup chopped scallions or spring onions

Salt and freshly ground pepper

2 tablespoons minced chives or a mix of chives and fresh tarragon

1 pound asparagus

1. Heat the oil or butter over medium heat in a medium skillet. Add the scallions or spring onions and a generous pinch of salt. Cook, stirring often, until tender but not browned, about 5 minutes. Stir in the chives and tarragon. Transfer to a bowl.

2. Break off the tough bottoms of the asparagus and discard. Cut the stalks into ½- to 1-inch lengths. Steam over an inch of boiling water for 4 to 5 minutes (5 minutes if the asparagus is thick). Remove from the heat. Rinse with cold water and drain on paper towels or dishtowels. The asparagus should be dry. Toss with the scallion or onion mixture.

3. Use the filling in the quiche template recipe (page 224).

ADVANCE PREPARATION: The filling can be prepared a day ahead. Keep uncovered in the refrigerator.

Leek Quiche Filling

MAKES ENOUGH FILLING FOR ONE 9-INCH QUICHE, SERVING 6

I have a fondness for leek quiche, having lived for 12 years in France, where a richer version of this leek quiche, *flamiche*, is a classic.

3 large leeks (1½ to 1¾ pounds), white and light green parts only

2 tablespoons extra virgin olive oil or 1 tablespoon each olive oil and butter

Salt

1 garlic clove, minced (optional)

1. Cut away the root ends and dark green leaves from the leeks and cut in half lengthwise. Run under cold water to remove sand. If the leeks are very sandy, soak them for 15 minutes or so, then run under cold water again. Drain on paper towels. If the leeks are very fat, cut the halves in half again lengthwise. Cut the leeks crosswise into thin slices.

2. Heat the oil or oil and butter over medium heat in a lidded skillet or saucepan. Add the leeks and a generous pinch of salt. Cook gently, stirring, until they begin to soften. Turn the heat to medium-low, cover, and cook gently until the leeks are very soft but not browned, stirring often, 10 to 15 minutes. If they begin to stick or brown, add a little more salt and/or a spoonful of water or wine. Stir in the garlic (if using) and cook until fragrant, another 30 seconds to 1 minute. Transfer to a bowl. If you're working ahead, refrigerate uncovered for a few hours or overnight.

3. Use the filling in the quiche template recipe (page 224).

   ADVANCE PREPARATION: The filling can be prepared a day ahead. Keep uncovered in the refrigerator.

MEDITERRANEAN VEGETABLE PIES, TORTES, AND GALETTES

MEDITERRANEAN PIES, WHETHER SINGLE-CRUSTED PIES, double-crusted tortes or *tortas* (in Italian), or free-form galettes, are not as custardy as quiches, and the crust is more rustic, with olive oil standing in for butter. The fillings consist of larger proportions of vegetables, bound with egg, which can be beaten with a small amount of milk (though in most of my recipes they aren't). Many of the fillings here also make delicious gratins. (If I were to use the fillings in a gratin, I would use the Provençal Gratin template on page 87, adding a cup of cooked rice to the mix.) But there is something so beautiful and dramatic about a dinner in a crust. Consequently I often make these for dinner parties; galettes are the showiest. Once cooled, slices of these pies and galettes—particularly the galettes—are quite portable. They'd make a welcome lunch at work or school, at a picnic, or on an airplane.

Yeasted Whole Wheat Olive Oil Pastry

MAKES ENOUGH FOR ONE 9- OR 10-INCH DOUBLE-CRUSTED TORTE, ONE GALETTE, OR TWO 9- OR 10-INCH TARTS

This is hands-down my favorite savory pie crust. It's incredibly easy to make (one of the reasons I love it so much). Yeasted crusts are less rich and more rustic than French-style short crusts and they're easier to manipulate; they don't crack and tear. You don't need to bake fully before you fill them, as you do with quiche pastry. If you fully prebake the pastry it will burn when you bake the pie.

Remember to roll this thin so that it doesn't become too bready, and freeze it if you aren't using it right away.

7 grams active dry yeast (approximately 2 scant teaspoons)

110 grams lukewarm water (approximately ½ cup)

2 grams sugar (approximately ½ scant teaspoon)

55 grams egg, at room temperature, beaten (1 extra large egg)

50 grams extra virgin olive oil (approximately ¼ cup)

125 grams whole wheat flour (approximately 1 cup)

1. In the large bowl of a stand mixer (with the paddle attachment), dissolve the yeast in the water, add the sugar, and allow to sit until the mixture is creamy, about 5 minutes. Beat in the egg and olive oil. Combine the flours and salt, and stir into the yeast mixture. Work the dough until it comes together in a coherent mass, adding flour as necessary. Turn out onto a lightly floured surface and knead gently, adding flour as necessary, just until the dough is smooth; do not overwork the dough or it will be too tough. Shape into a ball. Place in a lightly oiled bowl, cover the bowl tightly with plastic wrap, and allow the dough to rise in a draft-free spot until doubled in size, about 1 hour.

125 grams unbleached all-purpose flour (approximately 1 cup), or more as needed; or use 250 grams (approximately 2 cups) whole wheat flour and omit all-purpose

5 grams fine sea salt (approximately rounded ¾ teaspoon)

2. If making single-crusted pies, lightly oil two 9- or 10-inch tart pans or cake pans with olive oil. If making a double-crusted torte, oil just 1 pan. If making a galette, line a backing sheet with parchment. Turn the dough out onto a lightly floured surface and gently knead a couple of times just to deflate. For pies, divide into 2 equal pieces; for a torte, separate out two-thirds for the bottom and one-third for the top; for a galette, keep as one piece. Shape each piece into a ball without kneading it. Cover the dough loosely with plastic wrap and let rest for 5 minutes.

3. Roll the dough out into thin round(s) and line pans as directed in the recipe. If not using right away, line pans or roll out flat, double wrap in plastic, and freeze to prevent the dough from rising and becoming too bready. The dough can be transferred directly from the freezer to the oven.

ADVANCE PREPARATION: Once rolled out, the dough will keep for a month in the freezer, well wrapped.

NOTE: If you don't have a stand mixer, you can work the ingredients by hand using a whisk and a wooden spoon.

Mediterranean Vegetable Pie

MAKES 1 SINGLE-CRUSTED PIE, SERVING 6 TO 8

½ recipe Yeasted Whole Wheat Olive Oil Pastry (page 228)

2 or 3 eggs (depending on the filling)

Salt and freshly ground pepper

Vegetable filling of your choice (see filling recipes, pages 233–235)

2 to 4 ounces cheese (shredded Gruyère, a mix of Gruyère and Parmesan, or crumbled feta)

1. Heat the oven to 350°F. Line a lightly oiled 9- or 10-inch tart or cake pan with the dough. Using a fork, pierce at regular intervals to allow for even baking. (Refrigerate until ready to prebake and fill. Freeze if holding the dough for longer than an hour, as it will continue to rise in the refrigerator and it can become too bready.)

2. Set the lined pan on a baking sheet to allow for easy handling. Beat the eggs in a medium bowl. Using a pastry brush, lightly brush the bottom of the crust with some of the egg. Place the crust in the oven to prebake for 10 minutes. Set aside.

3. Add salt (I usually use about ½ teaspoon) and pepper to the beaten eggs. Stir in the vegetable filling and cheese. Mix together well. Turn into the crust, scraping every last bit out of the bowl with a rubber spatula. Level the top with a spatula.

4. Bake until set and lightly browned, 35 to 45 minutes.

ADVANCE PREPARATION: Mediterranean pies will keep for a few days in the refrigerator. You can warm them in a medium oven or serve them at room temperature. They freeze well. Double-wrap with plastic before freezing. When ready to use, unwrap and thaw overnight in the refrigerator, at room temperature for a couple of hours, or in a 350°F oven for about 30 minutes. Once thawed, reheat in a 300°F oven for 15 to 20 minutes.

Mediterranean Vegetable Torte

MAKES 1 DOUBLE-CRUSTED PIE, SERVING 8

For a torte with a top and bottom crust you'll use all of the dough. The bottom crust doesn't get prebaked before you fill it because you need to crimp the top and bottom edges together, so the torte is baked at a higher temperature.

Yeasted Whole Wheat Olive Oil Pastry (page 228)

2 or 3 eggs (depending on the filling)

Salt and freshly ground pepper

Vegetable filling of your choice (see filling recipes, pages 233–235),

2 to 4 ounces cheese (shredded Gruyère, a mix of Gruyère and Parmesan, or crumbled feta)

1 egg beaten with 1 tablespoon milk or water for egg wash

1. Divide the pastry into 2 unequal portions, one-third and two-thirds of the pastry.

2. Heat the oven to 375°F. Beat the eggs in a large bowl and add salt and pepper to taste. Stir in the vegetable filling and cheese.

3. Oil a 9- or 10-inch tart pan, cake pan, or springform pan. Roll out the large ball of dough and use to line the pan, with the edges of the dough overhanging. Add the filling.

4. Roll out the remaining dough ball and set it over the filling. Crimp the edges of the top and bottom together. Cut 4 small slits in the top crust with a sharp knife and brush with the egg wash.

5. Bake until golden brown, 45 to 50 minutes. Allow to rest for at least 10 minutes before serving. This can also be served at room temperature.

ADVANCE PREPARATION: Mediterranean tortes will keep for a few days in the refrigerator. You can warm them in a medium oven or serve at room temperature. They freeze well, before or after baking, for up to a month. Double-wrap in plastic before freezing. When ready to use: If frozen before baking, unwrap and transfer directly from the freezer to the preheated oven; increase baking time by 15 minutes. If baked before freezing, unwrap and thaw overnight in the refrigerator, at room temperature for a couple of hours, or in a 350°F oven for about 30 minutes. Once thawed, reheat in a 300°F oven for 15 to 20 minutes.

Mediterranean Vegetable Galette

MAKES ONE 9- OR 10-INCH GALETTE, SERVING 8 GENEROUSLY

Galettes are beautiful free-form pies. I use the entire dough recipe for the crust and roll it out to one big round, 16 to 18 inches in diameter. The filling should not be runny, so it usually contains no milk, though it does usually contain a couple of eggs.

2 eggs

Salt and freshly ground pepper

Vegetable filling of your choice (see filling recipes, pages 233–237)

2 to 4 ounces cheese (shredded Gruyère, a mix of Gruyère and Parmesan, or crumbled feta)

Yeasted Whole Wheat Olive Oil Pastry (page 228), in one large piece

1 egg beaten with 1 tablespoon milk or water for egg wash

1. Beat the eggs in a large bowl and add salt and pepper to taste. Stir in the vegetable filling and cheese.

2. Dust a large work surface with flour and turn out the dough. Shape into a ball and let rest for 5 minutes. Then roll out into a thin round, 16 to 18 inches in diameter. If the dough springs back, give it a 5-minute rest, then continue. Line a baking sheet pan with parchment and place the round in the middle, with the dough edges overlapping the pan edges.

3. Place the filling in the middle of the pastry and spread it to a circle, leaving a 3- or 4-inch margin all the way around. Fold the pastry edges in over the filling, pleating them to cover the filling and drawing them up to the middle of the galette, so that the filling is enclosed. The finished galette should be 9 or 10 inches in diameter. There can be a small circle of exposed filling in the middle but it shouldn't be more than an inch in diameter. Cover with plastic wrap and place in the freezer for 45 minutes to 1 hour. This helps the galette retain its shape when you bake it.

4. Meanwhile, heat the oven to 375°F. Remove the galette from the freezer and brush the pastry with egg wash. Bake until golden brown, 45 to 50 minutes. Let sit for at least 15 minutes before serving.

ADVANCE PREPARATION: The galette keeps for a couple of days and is good cold or reheated. They freeze well, before or after baking, for up to a month. Double-wrap in plastic before freezing. When ready to use: If frozen before baking, unwrap and transfer directly from the freezer to the preheated oven; increase baking time by 15 minutes. If baked before freezing, unwrap and thaw overnight in the refrigerator, at room temperature for a couple of hours, or in a 350°F oven for about 30 minutes. Once thawed, reheat in a 300°F oven for 15 to 20 minutes.

Cabbage, Onion, and Red Pepper Filling (for Galette, Torte, or Pie)

MAKES ENOUGH FOR 1 GALETTE, TORTE, OR PIE, SERVING 6 TO 8

If you want to make something elegant with the humblest of vegetables, this is the thing to make. You can use green or savoy cabbage. The onions and red peppers contribute sweetness, along with some color. You can prepare the filling while your dough is rising.

2 tablespoons extra virgin olive oil

1 medium onion, finely chopped

Salt and freshly ground black pepper

1 large red bell pepper, finely chopped

2 large garlic cloves, minced

1½ to 1¾ pounds cabbage (1 small), cored and finely chopped

3 to 4 tablespoons chopped fresh dill, parsley, chives, or a mix

1. Heat the olive oil over medium heat in a large, wide heavy skillet. Add the onion and cook, stirring often, until tender, about 5 minutes. Add a generous pinch of salt and the bell pepper and continue to cook, stirring often, until the pepper is tender and the onion is very soft and beginning to color, about 5 more minutes. Add the garlic and cook, stirring, until fragrant, 30 seconds to 1 minute. Stir in the cabbage and cook, stirring often, adding more salt to taste about halfway through, for 10 to 15 minutes, until the cabbage is cooked down and fragrant but still has some color. Stir in the fresh herbs and black pepper to taste. Taste and adjust seasonings.

2. Use the filling in the pie template (page 230), torte template (page 231), or galette template (opposite page), using 3 ounces Gruyère or feta cheese. Use 3 eggs for a pie or torte, 2 eggs for a galette.

   ADVANCE PREPARATION: The vegetable mixture can be made 1 or 2 days ahead through Step 1 and kept in a bowl, uncovered, in the refrigerator.

Winter Squash and Sage Filling (for Galette, Torte, or Pie)

MAKES ENOUGH FOR 1 GALETTE, TORTE, OR PIE, SERVING 6 TO 8

You will find the delicious marriage of sage and winter squash in the cuisines of both Provence and Italy. I cut the squash into chunks and roast them until very tender, then cut away the peels and mash the squash with a fork.

2½ pounds winter squash (such as 1 large or 2 smaller butternut squash)

3 tablespoons extra virgin olive oil

1 large onion, chopped

Salt and freshly ground pepper

2 to 3 large garlic cloves (to taste), minced

2 tablespoons chopped fresh sage

1 cup cooked medium-grain rice (optional)

1. Scrape away the seeds and membranes from the squash and cut into large pieces. (If using butternut, cut in half crosswise, just above the bulbous bottom part, then cut these halves into lengthwise quarters and scrape away the seeds and membranes.) Using 1 tablespoon of the oil, roast the squash in a 425°F oven following the directions on page 15. Allow to cool. Peel, place in a bowl, and mash with a fork, large wooden spoon, potato masher, or pestle. Turn the oven down to 375°F to bake a torte or galette, or 350°F to bake a pie.

2. Heat the remaining 2 tablespoons olive oil over medium heat in a large, heavy skillet. Add the onion and a pinch of salt and cook, stirring often, until very soft and lightly colored, about 8 minutes. Stir in the garlic and continue to cook until the garlic is fragrant, 30 seconds to 1 minute. Stir in the squash, sage, and cooked rice (if using). Remove from the heat and season to taste with salt and pepper.

3. Use the filling in the pie template (page 230), torte template (page 231), or galette template (page 232), using 3 ounces Gruyère and 1 ounce of Parmesan. Use 3 eggs for a pie or torte, 2 eggs for a galette.

   ADVANCE PREPARATION: The squash mixture can be made through Step 2 a day or two ahead and kept in a bowl, uncovered, in the refrigerator.

Summer Squash Filling (for Galette, Torte, or Pie)

MAKES ENOUGH FOR 1 GALETTE, TORTE, OR PIE, SERVING 6 TO 8

You can use any type of summer squash for this. I like to use the firmer, meatier varieties like rond de Nice and pattypan.

2 tablespoons extra virgin olive oil

1 large onion, chopped

Salt freshly ground pepper

2 to 3 large garlic cloves (to taste), minced

2¼ pounds summer squash, cut into very small dice

2 teaspoons fresh thyme leaves, coarsely chopped; or ¾ teaspoon dried

3 tablespoons chopped fresh flat-leaf parsley

1 cup cooked medium-grain rice (optional)

1. Heat the olive oil over medium heat in a large, heavy skillet. Add the onion and a pinch of salt and cook, stirring often, until tender, about 5 minutes. Stir in the garlic and continue to cook until the garlic is fragrant, 30 seconds to 1 minute. Stir in the squash, thyme, and salt to taste. Cook, stirring often, until the squash is tender, about 10 minutes. Add the parsley and rice, stir together, and remove from the heat. Season to taste with salt and pepper.

2. Use the filling in the pie template (page 230), torte template (page 231), or galette template (page 232), using 2 eggs and 3 ounces Gruyère.

ADVANCE PREPARATION: The squash mixture can be made through Step 2 a day or two ahead and kept in a bowl, uncovered, in the refrigerator. Drain any liquid in the bowl before using the filling in Step 2.

Greens and Chickpea Filling (for Galette)

MAKES ENOUGH FILLING FOR ONE 9- TO 10-INCH GALETTE, SERVING 8 GENEROUSLY

Use robust greens for this large galette—kale, collards, or mustard greens. You can even use the bagged Southern greens mix that they sell at supermarkets, which are already stemmed and washed. The filling has Middle Eastern overtones, with lots of well-cooked onion and the Middle Eastern blend of thyme, sesame, and ground sumac called za'atar. You can prepare the filling while the pastry dough is rising.

2 tablespoons extra virgin olive oil

1 large onion, quartered lengthwise and cut into thin slices across the grain

Salt and freshly ground pepper

2 large garlic cloves, minced

2 pounds sturdy greens, stemmed and washed (or a 1-pound bag of Southern greens mix), wilted (see page 3) and coarsely chopped

2 tablespoons chopped fresh mint, dill, or parsley

2 teaspoons za'atar (see Note)

1 (15-ounce) can chickpeas, drained and rinsed; or 1½ cups cooked chickpeas

1. Heat the olive oil over medium heat in a large, heavy skillet. Add the onion and cook, stirring often, until soft and golden, about 10 minutes. After the first couple of minutes of cooking, add a generous pinch of salt so they don't brown too quickly or stick to the pan. When the onions are nicely colored and soft, add the garlic and continue to cook until fragrant, another 30 seconds to 1 minute. Stir in the greens and combine well with the onions. Add the chopped fresh herbs and za'atar, and season to taste with salt and pepper. Stir in the chickpeas and taste and adjust seasonings.

2. Use the filling in the galette template (page 232), using 3 to 4 ounces crumbled feta cheese.

NOTE: To make your own za'atar, mix together 2 tablespoons dried thyme, $1\frac{1}{2}$ teaspoons sesame seeds, $1\frac{1}{2}$ teaspoons sumac, and $\frac{1}{8}$ teaspoon salt. Keep in a jar.

ADVANCE PREPARATION: The filling can be made up to 4 days ahead and kept in the refrigerator. The assembled galette can be frozen for up to a month. Double wrap with plastic wrap before freezing. Transfer directly from the freezer to the oven for baking; increase baking time by 10 to 15 minutes.

GREEK PIE (PITTA)

ALTHOUGH THE GREEKS DON'T ALWAYS USE layered phyllo for their pies, when I use phyllo dough the filling always has Greek or Balkan origins and flavorings, defined by a liberal use of fresh herbs (like parsley, mint, and dill) and feta cheese. If you've remembered to thaw your phyllo dough overnight in the refrigerator—rarely can you buy it unfrozen—then a pie can be quickly assembled once you've made your filling, much more quickly than a pie made with homemade pastry.

TEMPLATE

Greek Phyllo Pie (Pitta)

MAKES ONE 10-INCH PIE, SERVING 6 GENEROUSLY

Greek phyllo pies are packed with vegetables bound with eggs, but don't contain milk as it would make them so moist that the phyllo wouldn't crisp. Mine almost always contain feta cheese, or a combination of feta and other Greek or Balkan cheeses like kefalotyri (which is sort of like Romano) or graviera (which is sort of like Gruyère). The Greeks use more cheese (as well as olive oil) than I do, and so can you if you want to.

2 tablespoons each melted unsalted butter and extra virgin olive oil; or ¼ cup melted butter; or ¼ cup olive oil (for brushing the phyllo)

12 sheets phyllo dough

Vegetable filling of your choice (see recipes, pages 240–241)

1. Heat the oven to 375°F. Combine the melted butter and olive oil. Brush a 10-inch tart pan or cake pan, either ceramic or metal, with some of the butter and/or oil.

2. Lay a sheet of phyllo in the pan, tucking it into the corners of the pan, with the edges overhanging the rim. Brush it lightly with butter/oil and rotate the pan slightly, then place another sheet on top, positioning it so that the edges overlap another section of the pan's rim. Continue to layer in 5 more sheets of phyllo, brushing each one with butter/oil and staggering them so that the overhang on the rim is evenly distributed and covers the entire pan.

3. Fill the lined pan with the filling. Fold the overhanging edges in over the filling, brushing each one lightly with the butter/oil.

4. Layer the remaining 5 sheets of dough over the filling, brushing each sheet with butter/oil and rotating the pan slightly after each addition. Crimp the edges into the sides of the pan; just push them into the sides of the pan and let them bunch; those bits will be delicious when they crisp up. Brush the top with the butter/oil. Pierce the top of the pie in several places with a sharp knife.

5. Bake until the top is golden brown, 40 to 50 minutes. Serve warm or at room temperature. Re-crisp the crust if necessary in a low oven for 10 to 20 minutes.

ADVANCE PREPARATION: You can assemble the pie several hours or days before baking and then freeze. Transfer directly from the freezer to the preheated oven, and increase the baking time by about 10 minutes. Most finished *pittas* keep for a few days in the refrigerator, but you must keep re-crisping the phyllo. This is easily done, either in a low oven (300°F) for 10 to 20 minutes, or in a hot oven that has just been turned off, for 5 to 10 minutes.

Working with Phyllo

Because phyllo dough is so thin, it can dry out quickly once it's exposed to air. Once it gets dry it becomes brittle and difficult to work with, as it breaks apart when you manipulate it. The way to prevent this from happening is to cover the sheets you aren't placing in the pan with two clean dishtowels.

Most phyllo comes frozen in long 1-pound packages. Do not buy the smaller sheets that are sold in smaller boxes, as they're not quite large enough for these recipes. Thaw the phyllo overnight in the refrigerator, not at room temperature. If the dough thaws too quickly it will sweat and the sheets will stick together.

Open up the package of phyllo and unfold the sheets of dough. Remove the number of sheets your recipe calls for (maybe two or three extra in case some of the sheets stick and shred), and fold the remaining dough back up. Double wrap tightly in plastic, then in foil. Return to the box if you wish, and either refrigerate or freeze.

Lay your phyllo dough out on a work surface and cover completely with a dishtowel. Moisten another dishtowel, and place on top of the dry towel. Remove one phyllo sheet at a time, following the recipe.

Herb and Greens Pitta Filling

MAKES ENOUGH FOR ONE 10-INCH PIE, SERVING 6 GENEROUSLY

I prefer this to the more common Greek spinach pie, spanakopita. Spinach becomes disappointing when it's baked for a long time in the phyllo, whereas chard and beet greens stand up to the amount of time the pie requires in the oven. If you use chard you can also include the chopped stems, which contribute a nice element of texture to the dish. If you don't feel like spending the time it takes to pick parsley off the stems to get the amount of parsley that the Greeks would use, use less, or forgo the parsley and season the pie with dill alone, or with dill and thyme.

2 tablespoons extra virgin olive oil

1 large onion, finely chopped

Salt and freshly ground pepper

2 to 4 large garlic cloves (to taste), minced

2 to 2½ pounds (2 to 3 generous bunches) Swiss chard or beet greens, wilted (see page 3) and chopped

¼ to ½ cup chopped fresh dill

¼ cup chopped fresh flat-leaf parsley

2 teaspoons fresh thyme leaves

3 eggs

6 ounces feta cheese, crumbled (about 1½ cups); or 4 ounces feta plus 2 ounces kefalotyri

1. Heat the olive oil over medium heat in a large skillet and add the onion and chard stems if using. Cook, stirring often, until very tender but not browned, about 8 minutes. Add a generous pinch of salt if the onion begins to brown. Add the garlic and cook, stirring, until the garlic is fragrant, another 30 seconds to 1 minute. Stir in the chopped greens and herbs, season to taste with salt and pepper, and stir the mixture for a minute, until the greens are coated with oil. Remove from the heat.

2. Beat the eggs in a large bowl. Crumble in the cheese and stir in the greens. Season to taste with more salt and pepper if necessary, bearing in mind that the cheese is salty.

3. Use the filling in the Greek phyllo pie template recipe (page 238).

ADVANCE PREPARATION: The blanched greens will keep in the refrigerator in a covered bowl for 3 days. You can assemble the pie several hours or days before baking and freeze. Transfer directly from the freezer to the preheated oven, and increase the baking time by about 10 minutes. The finished tart keeps for a few days, but you must keep re-crisping the phyllo

Greek Winter Squash and Leek Pitta Filling

MAKES ENOUGH FOR ONE 10-INCH PIE, SERVING 6 TO 8

Walnuts contribute wonderful texture to one of my favorite vegetable combos, leeks and winter squash. Mint is a favorite seasoning for these vegetables; they're all very compatible. In Greece, and in Turkey, dried mint is used. I love the flavor, but I'm more likely to run out to my garden and grab some fresh leaves.

2½ pounds winter squash, such as kabocha or butternut

3 tablespoons extra virgin olive oil

2 large leeks, white and light green parts only, well cleaned and chopped

Salt and freshly ground pepper

¼ cup chopped fresh mint or 1 to 2 tablespoons dried (to taste)

¼ teaspoon freshly grated nutmeg

½ cup walnuts, lightly toasted if desired, chopped medium-fine

3 ounces feta cheese, crumbled (about ¾ cup)

2 eggs, beaten

1. Scrape away the seeds and membranes from the squash and cut into large pieces. (If using butternut, cut in half crosswise, just above the bulbous bottom part, then cut these halves into lengthwise quarters and scrape away the seeds and membranes.) Using 1 tablespoon of the oil, roast the squash in a 425°F oven following the directions on page 15. Allow to cool. Peel, place in a bowl, and mash with a fork, large wooden spoon, potato masher, or pestle. Turn the oven down to 375°F to bake the pie.

2. Heat the remaining 2 tablespoons olive oil over medium heat in a large, heavy skillet. Add the leeks and a pinch of salt and cook, stirring, until tender and just beginning to color, about 5 minutes. Add to the squash. Add the mint, nutmeg, walnuts, and feta. Season to taste with salt and pepper. Stir in the eggs.

3. Use the filling in the Greek phyllo pie template recipe (page 239).

ADVANCE PREPARATION: The squash can be cooked and mashed 3 or 4 days ahead, and kept in the refrigerator in a covered bowl. The filling, without the eggs, will keep for 2 or 3 days in the refrigerator. The pie can be assembled, double wrapped and frozen for up to a month. Transfer directly from the freezer to the oven and add 15 minutes to the baking time. You can bake this a few hours ahead but you will have to re-crisp in a low (300° to 325°F) oven for about 15 minutes before serving.

SUBSTITUTIONS AND ADDITIONS: Some versions of this pie also include ¼ to ½ cup currants. Add to the squash mixture if desired.

PIZZA

PIZZA IS AMERICA'S FAVORITE SAVORY PIE and an easy one to make at home. At its simplest, pizza is a vehicle for tomatoes, but you can adorn these pies with any number of vegetables. Take your pick.

I use whole wheat flour in my pizza crust and like to keep one at the ready in my freezer at all times. Then a pizza dinner becomes as easy to throw together as a pasta dinner.

Pizza Dough

MAKES ENOUGH FOR TWO 12- TO 14-INCH PIZZAS, EACH SERVING 2 OR 3

This is a very easy, no-hassle dough. I use a little more than half whole wheat flour for it; you can vary the proportions and see what you like. It's an easy dough to work with, just a little bit sticky but easy to press out, and very forgiving. You can mix it up, put it in a storage bag, and refrigerate it, then forget about it for up to 2 days. Bring it back to room temperature, knead it a little bit, and proceed. I always make this in a stand mixer now, though I used to use a food processor and have also mixed the dough by hand. All methods are included.

8 grams active dry yeast (2 teaspoons)

225 grams warm water (approximately 1 cup)

5 grams sugar (1 teaspoon)

12.5 grams extra virgin olive oil (1 tablespoon), plus additional for brushing the pizza crusts

185 grams whole wheat flour (approximately 1½ cups)

125 to 185 grams unbleached all-purpose flour (approximately 1 to 1½ cups)

10 grams (1½ teaspoons) salt

In the bowl of a stand mixer, in a large bread bowl (if you're mixing by hand), or in a measuring cup (if you're mixing in a food processor), dissolve the yeast in the water. Add the sugar and stir together. Let sit 2 or 3 minutes, until the water is cloudy. Stir in the olive oil. Whisk together the flours.

STAND MIXER METHOD

1. Add 310 grams (2½ cups) of the flour mixture and the salt to the yeast mixture all at once. Mix together using the paddle attachment, then change to the dough hook. Knead at low speed for 2 minutes, then turn up to medium speed and knead until the dough comes cleanly away from the sides of the bowl, clusters around the dough hook, and slaps against the sides of the bowl, 8 to 10 minutes. Add flour as needed and hold on to the machine if it bounces around. Turn out onto a lightly dusted work surface and shape into a ball. The dough should be a little sticky but firm. Continue with Step 2.

HAND METHOD

1. Fold 310 grams of the flour mixture and the salt into the yeast mixture a cup at a time, using a large wooden spoon. As soon as you can scrape the dough out in one piece, scrape out onto a lightly floured work surface and knead for 10 minutes, adding flour as necessary, until the dough is firm. Continue with Step 2.

FOOD PROCESSOR METHOD

1. Place 310 grams (2½ cups) of the flour mixture and the salt in a food processor fitted with the steel blade. Pulse once or twice. With the machine running, pour in the yeast mixture. Process until the dough forms a ball on the blades. Remove from the processor and knead on a lightly floured surface for a couple of minutes, adding flour as necessary for a firm, slightly tacky dough. Continue with Step 2.

ALL METHODS

2. Transfer the dough to a clean, lightly oiled bowl, rounded side down, then turn rounded side up. Cover the bowl tightly with plastic wrap and leave in a warm spot to rise for 1 hour. When it is ready, the dough will stretch as it is gently pulled.

3. Weigh the dough and divide into 2 equal balls. Shape each ball by cupping between your hands, with the sides of your hands touching your work surface, and moving the dough in a clockwise circle between your hands, working the dough round and round until it becomes a ball. Put the balls on a lightly oiled baking sheet, cover with lightly oiled plastic wrap or a damp dishtowel, and leave them to rest for 15 to 20 minutes before rolling or pressing out.

ADVANCE PREPARATION: You can keep the dough in the refrigerator, before rolling out, for a couple of days. To refrigerate, press out the gasses from the dough and place in a resealable bag or a lightly oiled bowl covered with plastic wrap. Allow the dough to come to room temperature, deflate, then press or roll out. The rolled-out dough also freezes well for 6 weeks: Roll out, line pans, double wrap airtight, and freeze. Top the frozen dough and bake as directed. It will take a minute or two longer.

Pizza

MAKES ONE 12- TO 14-INCH PIZZA, SERVING 2 OR 3

½ recipe Pizza Dough (page 242)

Extra virgin olive oil

Semolina or flour

Topping of your choice
(see variation recipes, pages
245–246)

1. An hour before you wish to bake your pizza, position a rack at the lowest setting, place a pizza stone on the rack, and heat the oven to 450°F.

2. Roll or press out the dough: Place a ball of dough on a lightly floured surface. I find that it's easiest to press it out. Lightly flour the dough if it is sticky. While turning the dough, press down on its center with the heel of your hand, gradually spreading it out to a round 12 to 14 inches in diameter. Alternatively, use a rolling pin, turning the dough or switching the direction of the pin to get an even round. The dough should be slightly thicker around the edges. If the dough continuously springs back, let it rest for 5 minutes, then continue rolling.

3. Lightly oil a pizza pan and dust with semolina, or dust a paddle with semolina or flour. Place the dough on the pizza pan or paddle. If the edges aren't already a little thicker than the rest of the dough, use your fingers to form a slightly thicker raised rim around edge of the round. Let rest for 10 minutes.

4. Brush the rim of the pizza round with a little olive oil, then top the pizza with the topping of your choice. Place on the stone or slide from the paddle onto the stone. Bake until the rim of the pizza is crisp and lightly browned, 12 to 14 minutes.

ADVANCE PREPARATION: See advance preparation notes for pizza dough on page 243.

Pizza with Broccoli Raab and Mozzarella

MAKES ONE 12- TO 14-INCH PIZZA, SERVING 2 OR 3

There's a generous amount of broccoli raab—seasoned the classic Southern Italian way with garlic, olive oil, and red pepper flakes—topping this pizza. I don't think pizza needs tomato sauce to be pizza, but if you're partial to tomato sauce, spread ¼ to ½ cup on the crust before topping it with the broccoli raab and mozzarella.

Make the *Pizza* template (opposite page) with the following topping ingredients and specifications:

Additional 3 tablespoons extra virgin olive oil

1 to 2 garlic cloves (to taste), minced

¼ teaspoon red pepper flakes (or more to taste)

1 bunch broccoli raab, blanched (see page 5) and finely chopped

1 teaspoon fresh thyme leaves

1 teaspoon finely chopped fresh rosemary

Salt

5 ounces mozzarella, shredded

2 tablespoons toasted pine nuts

1. Heat the oven and pizza stone, roll out the pizza dough, and form the dough round as directed in the template (Steps 1 through 3).

2. Heat 1 tablespoon of the olive oil over medium heat in a large, heavy skillet. Add the garlic and red pepper flakes and cook, stirring, until fragrant, 30 seconds to 1 minute. Add the chopped and blanched broccoli raab, herbs, and salt to taste. Cook, stirring, for another minute. Taste and adjust seasoning.

3. In Step 4, after brushing the rim of the crust with olive oil, top with the broccoli raab, distributing it evenly over the dough. Place clumps of mozzarella in the places where the dough is most exposed. Drizzle on the remaining 2 tablespoons olive oil. Bake as directed. Sprinkle the baked pizza with pine nuts and serve.

ADVANCE PREPARATION: Blanched broccoli raab will keep in the refrigerator for 3 days and can be frozen.

Pizza with Tomato Sauce, Arugula, Parmesan, and Fava Beans

MAKES ONE 12- TO 14-INCH PIZZA, SERVING 2 OR 3

Throw a generous handful of arugula onto this pizza when you pull it from the oven, and you've added a sort of salad topping. I like to add the Parmesan shavings before I add the arugula and favas—the heat of the pizza is all it needs to begin to melt.

Make the *Pizza* template (page 242) with the following topping ingredients and specifications:

½ cup marinara sauce (pages 24–27)

1 to 2 ounces Parmesan shavings

½ cup skinned fava beans (page 155), optional

Generous handful of chopped arugula or baby arugula

1. Heat the oven and pizza stone, roll out the pizza dough, and form the dough round as directed in the template (Steps 1 through 3).

2. In Step 4, after brushing the rim of the crust with olive oil, spread the marinara sauce over the surface in a thin layer. Bake as directed, then immediately distribute pieces of shaved Parmesan over the entire pizza. The heat of the pizza will melt it. Arrange fava beans on top, sprinkle on the arugula, and serve.

ADVANCE PREPARATION: The marinara sauce will keep for about 3 days in the refrigerator.

CHAPTER THIRTEEN

Couscous and the Stews That Go with It

THE RECIPES IN THIS CHAPTER, along with many of the stir-fries in Chapter 9, are the most naturally vegan meals in my repertoire and I always recommend them when people ask me for a vegan menu for a dinner party. It's not that way in Tunisia and Algeria, the source of these adapted recipes, where couscous is served with a stew that, even when vegetables and beans are the main event, usually includes meat of some kind for flavoring—a lamb, veal, or mutton shank or shoulder, or a shin bone, or some dried mutton. Called tagines after the earthenware vessel with the conical lid that they're cooked in, the Tunisian and Algerian dishes are spicy, seasoned with a chile paste called harissa and a spice mix made with coriander seeds, cumin seeds, caraway seeds, paprika, and cayenne called *tabil*. Moroccan tagines are more meat-centric, and the spices used are sweet rather than hot. The palate is different, closer to Persia or the Middle East (which is interesting as it's farther away from those countries than Tunisia or Algeria).

When I was invited on a gastronomic tour of Tunisia by Oldways Preservation Trust in 1993, I had no idea that I'd discover a cuisine that would influence just about every couscous dish I'd make thereafter. I'd been living in Paris for 12 years, where going out for couscous is the equivalent of going out for Mexican food in Texas or California. But in Paris I didn't experience the array of vegetable tagines that I tasted in Tunisia. It was the robust, gutsy spicing and the high regard for produce that won my palate. Tunisian tagines are easy to convert to filling, satisfying vegetarian meals that have great depth of flavor.

I use beans in virtually all of my vegetarian couscous dishes. They produce a savory broth and contribute lots of high-quality protein. Chickpeas are the beans you'll most often find in Tunisian and Algerian stews, but you can experiment with other varieties—white beans or limas, Christmas limas or scarlet runner beans. Black-eyed peas are another popular bean in North Africa.

Tunisian cooks don't begin their tagines by sweating the vegetables. They just throw them all in the pot. This practice was fascinating to the many chefs on my Tunisian tour. But I sometimes like to coax a little more flavor out of the aromatics by first sweating them in a little oil, since there's no added taste provided by a meat bone.

In Tunisia, cooks will use spices that are already mixed, and if you make these dishes often I urge you to make up your own jar of *tabil* (page 255) and substitute it for the individual spices listed in the recipes. Also, homemade harissa is easy to make (page 254) and tastes a lot better than the harissa that comes in a tube; but I do admit, I keep a tube on hand at all times and use it whenever I run out of the homemade stuff or don't have time to make my own.

ABOUT COUSCOUS, AND HOW TO RECONSTITUTE IT

COUSCOUS IS NOT A WHOLE GRAIN, it's a semolina product. It's made by rubbing together large grains of semolina with smaller, finer grains sprayed with salted water. The grains affix to each other, forming the larger granules of semolina we know as couscous.

Commercial couscous has been steamed and dried, and it must be reconstituted and steamed (*never* boiled) again before it can be eaten. Ideally, some of the broth from the stew you are serving with it will be used for reconstituting, and the grains will also steam above the simmering broth, absorbing more flavor.

When it comes to preparing couscous I've been back and forth with colleagues, friends, experts in North African cooking, and experts in French cooking who learned to prepare couscous from North Africans. Purists insist that you have to begin by making the couscous from scratch, with semolina. That's not going to happen in my house and most probably it won't in yours either. Close-to-purists will insist that you have to go through a process of dousing the couscous with water and steaming it for a certain amount of time, then spreading it on a surface and rubbing apart the grains, dousing, then steaming again, and repeating this process again until the grains are fluffy. Others insist that you must steam it for at least 45 minutes above your tagine in a hermetically sealed steaming basket or the top part of a *couscousier* (a special two-piece couscous pot with a big vessel for the stew on the bottom and a perforated steamer on the top). I was told by one specialist that if I didn't do it this way the couscous would continue to expand in my stomach and would give me a terrible bellyache. That's never happened.

I've duly followed every different set of directions that I've read or been given. It is true that when you take what amounts to over an hour of steaming, resting, and drying; steaming, resting, and drying; and steaming one more time, you will get a particularly appealing, fluffy couscous. But the ends don't justify the means unless you have a *lot* of time on your hands. With the packaged couscous we get in the states (and elsewhere—it's all I worked with when I lived in Paris), I get perfectly good results reconstituting it in warm water, then steaming it above my tagine for 20 minutes—or even more efficient, in a couple of 2-minute blasts in the microwave. This is, effectively, steaming, and I think the results are excellent and fluffy, and allow you to make couscous as often as you want to without it being a production.

Reconstituting and Steaming Couscous in the Microwave

IN A LARGE BOWL (microwave-safe if steaming in the microwave), combine the couscous with salt to taste (I usually use 1/2 to 3/4 teaspoon per cup of couscous). Count on 1/3 cup of uncooked couscous per generous serving (in North Africa this is not a generous serving; traditional recipes call for more than 1/2 cup per person, but I always have a lot left over when I make that much). Drizzle 1 tablespoon of olive oil per cup of couscous over the couscous and if the recipe has instructed you to remove a cup of broth from the stew you're making, sprinkle the cup of broth over the couscous. Stir well, or moisten your fingers and rub the couscous with them to evenly distribute the oil and broth. Add enough warm water to cover by 1/2 inch and let sit for

20 minutes, or until all of the liquid is absorbed. Stir every 5 minutes with a wooden spoon or rub the couscous between your moistened thumbs and fingers (moistening your hands will prevent the couscous from sticking to them) so that the couscous doesn't lump. The couscous will now be fairly soft; fluff it with a fork or with your hands.

The traditional way to finish reconstituting the couscous is to place it above the simmering stew for 45 minutes. However I don't find that it needs this long if it's been properly reconstituted, and I usually don't want to simmer my stew for that long at the point at which I need to heat my couscous. I've found that steaming it in a microwave results in perfectly fluffy couscous.

Steaming Couscous in the Microwave

IF YOU CHOOSE TO STEAM IN THE MICROWAVE, first cover the bowl with a plate that fits snugly, then place the bowl in the microwave. Heat at 100 percent power for 3 minutes. Remove from the microwave *carefully* and allow it to sit for 1 minute. Carefully remove the plate and fluff the couscous with forks or a spoon. Cover again and microwave 2 to 3 more minutes. Be very careful when you remove the plate as it will be hot, as will the bowl, and the couscous will be steamy. You can reconstitute the couscous a day ahead and reheat in the microwave shortly before serving.

Steaming Couscous Above the Stew

IF YOU FINISH THE COUSCOUS BY steaming above your tagine, place it in a steaming basket, colander, or strainer lined with cheesecloth (or the top part of a couscousier) and make sure that it is not touching the liquid in the pot. If there is a space exposed between the steaming basket and the edge of the pot, fill it with a rolled up dishtowel. Cover and steam for 20 to 30 minutes. If you have the time, fluff the couscous and steam for another 10 to 20 minutes.

IF YOU ARE MAKING COUSCOUS FOR a big crowd and want to get ahead, transfer it to a lightly oiled baking dish, douse with a little more broth from the stew, and cover tightly with foil. The couscous can sit out for a couple of hours. Warm in a 300°F oven for 15 to 30 minutes. You can refrigerate it if you wish; increase the reheating time in the oven by 10 to 15 minutes.

Couscous with Vegetables and Beans

VEGAN /// **MAKES 6 GENEROUS SERVINGS**

If you want a spicier couscous, use more harissa. I prefer to make a mildly seasoned stew and let guests add more harissa to taste. I use chickpeas most often for my couscous stews.

1½ cups dried chickpeas, white beans, or other beans of your choice, soaked in 2 quarts water for at least 4 hours (or do the quick soak, page 188); or 1½ cups black-eyed peas (no need to soak)

1 to 2 tablespoons extra virgin olive oil (to taste)

1 large onion, chopped

Salt

2 to 4 large garlic cloves (to taste), minced

2 teaspoons coriander seeds, lightly toasted and ground

¾ teaspoon caraway seeds, lightly toasted and ground

½ teaspoon cumin seeds, lightly toasted and ground

1½ teaspoons sweet paprika

½ teaspoon cayenne (or more to taste)

A bouquet garni: a few sprigs each parsley and cilantro

Vegetables of your choice (see variation recipes, pages 255–259)

2 tablespoons tomato paste (optional)

1 tablespoon harissa (page 254), or more to taste; plus additional for serving

2 cups uncooked couscous

1. Drain the soaked beans and place in a large saucepan with 2 quarts water. Bring to a gentle boil, reduce the heat, and simmer 1 hour.

2. Heat the olive oil over medium heat in a large heavy soup pot or Dutch oven. Add the onion and a pinch of salt and cook, stirring, until tender, about 5 minutes. Add the garlic, ½ teaspoon salt, and the spices and stir together until fragrant, 30 seconds to 1 minute. Add the beans and their broth, the bouquet garni, and the vegetables. Bring to a gentle boil and add the tomato paste, harissa, and salt to taste—at least 2 teaspoons. Reduce the heat, cover, and simmer until the beans are very tender and the broth aromatic, 30 minutes to 1 hour. Taste and adjust salt. Remove a cup of the broth to mix with the couscous when you reconstitute it.

3. Reconstitute and steam the couscous (see page 251). Serve the couscous in wide bowls or mound onto plates and top with the stew. Pass more harissa at the table.

ADVANCE PREPARATION: Most tagines benefit from being made a day ahead and will keep for 3 or 4 days in the refrigerator. See specific recipes.

SUBSTITUTIONS AND ADDITIONS: If you are gluten intolerant and can't eat couscous, which is a semolina product, you can still enjoy the stews in this chapter. Add 1 to 1½ pounds potatoes, sliced or diced, to the stews. Serve in wide bowls, without the couscous. Or serve the stews as they are, with cooked millet or quinoa.

Harissa

MAKES 1 CUP

Harissa is the spice paste that is stirred into couscous stews throughout Tunisia and Algeria. You can buy it in a tube or jar, but I've never had a commercial harissa that tasted authentic, like the harissa I remember from couscous restaurants in Paris and the many wonderful couscous meals I was treated to in Tunisia. Keep this in a jar in the refrigerator and top it up with olive oil whenever you use it. That way it will keep for a long time.

2 ounces dried guajillo chiles, or a combination of guajillos and other hot dried chiles such as Japanese chiles or chiles de árbol

2 ounces dried Anaheim or pasilla chiles

4 garlic cloves, halved, green shoots removed

½ teaspoon caraway seeds, lightly toasted and ground

¼ teaspoon coriander seeds, lightly toasted and ground

1½ teaspoons salt

2 tablespoons water

3 tablespoons olive oil, plus additional for topping

1 Wear rubber gloves to seed the dried chiles: Take the stems off and remove the seeds. Place in a bowl and cover with hot or boiling water. Place a small plate or a lid over the chiles to keep them submerged in the water and soak for 1 hour. Drain.

2. Turn on a food processor and drop in the garlic. When it is all chopped and adhering to the sides of the bowl, stop the machine and scrape down. Add the drained chiles, the spices, and salt. Process until everything is chopped. Stop the machine and scrape down the sides. Turn on again and, with the machine running, add the water and olive oil. Process until the mixture is smooth, stopping to scrape down the sides if necessary.

3. Transfer the sauce to a jar. Wipe the inside edges of the jar with a paper towel, then pour on a film of olive oil to cover the harissa. Top with a lid and refrigerate. The harissa will keep for 6 weeks in the refrigerator if you top it up with olive oil after each use.

Winter Vegetable Couscous

VEGAN /// **MAKES 6 GENEROUS SERVINGS**

This humble vegetable stew with big flavors is an easy recipe to include in your weekly repertoire, and it's also always been a hit when I serve it for a dinner party. Chickpeas are my first choice for the beans.

Make the *Couscous with Vegetables and Beans* template (page 253), with the following additional ingredients and specifications:

2 leeks, white and light green parts only, well cleaned and cut into thick slices

2 large carrots, peeled and cut into thick slices

1 parsnip, peeled, cored, and cut into thick chunks (optional)

1 pound winter squash, peeled, seeded, and cut into large dice

2 medium turnips or 1 kohlrabi, peeled and cut into wedges

½ cup chopped fresh parsley or cilantro, or a mix

1. Use chickpeas and boil as directed in Step 1.

2. In Step 2, add the leeks, carrots, parsnip (if using), winter squash, and turnips or kohlrabi when you add the partially cooked beans and bouquet garni. Continue with the recipe, but simmer only 30 to 45 minutes, until the squash is beginning to fall apart and the beans are tender. Then stir in the parsley and/or cilantro and simmer another 10 minutes. Remove a cup of the broth to mix with the couscous when you reconstitute it. Continue with the recipe.

ADVANCE PREPARATION: The stew can be made a day ahead and reheated. Leftovers will keep for 3 or 4 days in the refrigerator. The couscous can be reconstituted up to a day ahead, then steamed before serving.

Tunisian Spice Mix (Tabil)

MAKES ABOUT ⅔ CUP

Make your own *tabil* so that you don't have to measure out spices every time you make couscous. To figure out how much to use, add up the number of teaspoons of the different spices called for in the recipe.

¼ cup coriander seeds, lightly toasted (page 198)

1½ tablespoons caraway seeds, lightly toasted (page 198)

1 tablespoon cumin seeds, lightly toasted

3 tablespoons sweet paprika

1 tablespoon cayenne

Grind all the spices in a spice mill and blend together. Keep in a jar and use in couscous recipes.

Spring Vegetable Couscous

VEGAN /// **MAKES 6 GENEROUS SERVINGS**

Because there are fresh fava beans in this beautiful, light spring couscous, I only use 1 cup of dried beans. The harissa is optional because I don't like to overpower the sweetness of the spring vegetables. Use it if you want the heat.

Make the *Couscous with Vegetables and Beans* template (page 253) with the following additional ingredients and specifications:

¾ pound spring onions, chopped (optional)

2 large carrots or 4 to 6 smaller young spring carrots, peeled and sliced

2 large, 4 medium, or 12 baby artichokes, trimmed and cut into wedges (sixths for large artichokes, quarters for medium, and halves for baby (see opposite page)

1 bunch baby turnips, peeled and quartered (omit if baby turnips aren't available)

1 generous bunch cilantro, chopped

2 pounds fava beans, shelled and skinned (see page 155)

1 tablespoon chopped Preserved Lemon (page 260), or more to taste

1. Use just 1 cup (instead of 1½ cups) of chickpeas or white beans, cooking them in the 2 quarts of water as directed in Step 1.

2. In Step 2, if spring onions are available, use them instead of the large onion; if not available, use the chopped onion. Add the carrots, artichokes, turnips (if using), and half the cilantro when you add the partially cooked beans and bouquet garni. Continue with the recipe, but omit the tomato paste. If you do not want the spice of the harissa, omit the harissa as well. Simmer the stew until the beans are very tender and the broth aromatic, about 30 minutes.

3. Shortly before serving, add the fava beans, remaining cilantro, and chopped preserved lemon to the vegetables and simmer for 10 minutes.

4. Reconstitute and steam the couscous as directed.

   ADVANCE PREPARATION: The stew can be prepared through Step 2 a day ahead. Reheat to a simmer and proceed with the recipe.

How to Trim Artichokes

Whether you're working with baby artichokes, globe artichokes, or something in between, the method for trimming them down to the meaty hearts is the same.

1. Fill a bowl with water and add the juice of ½ lemon. Lay the artichoke on your cutting board and, with a sharp knife, slice off the top quarter: about ½ inch away from the tip for baby artichokes, 1 inch away for large globe artichokes. Slice off the stem. Rub the cut parts with the other half of the lemon.

2. Break off the tough outer leaves at the base of the artichoke, until you get to the lighter green leaves near the middle. (If you're paring down large or medium globe artichokes, break off as many leaves as you can at the base of the leaves, so that you can steam them separately to enjoy with a dipping sauce, such as a vinaigrette or a vinaigrette mixed with a little mayonnaise and plain yogurt, my favorite). Using a paring knife, trim away the woody "shoulders" that remain at the bottom of the artichokes, above the stem, exposing the smooth, pale base of the artichoke (also known as the heart).

3. **FOR BABY ARTICHOKES:** These have tender inner leaves, so you can get away with leaving them there and simply cut the artichokes in half or quarters and cut away the chokes, if they have developed, using a paring knife. Place the trimmed artichokes in the bowl of acidulated water right away as you work with them.

   FOR LARGER ARTICHOKES: You'll want to remove all of the leaves until you get to the lighter, papery ones with the sharp tips that cover the choke. Take your paring knife and cut away this papery crown of leaves and the fibrous chokes underneath them. Then with your paring knife, trim the sides of the base smooth. Place in the bowl of acidulated water right away as you work with them.

Couscous with Fennel, Collard Greens, and Black-Eyed Peas

VEGAN /// **MAKES 6 GENEROUS SERVINGS**

Black-eyed peas turn up surprisingly often in the Mediterranean, especially in Greece but also in Tunisia. They take to North African seasonings. In the spring, fennel appears in farmers' markets and CSA boxes, the same time of year that collard greens are at their most tender.

Make the *Couscous with Vegetables and Beans* template (page 253) with the following additional ingredients and specifications:

1 large or 2 small fennel bulbs (about ¾ pound), trimmed, quartered, cored, and finely chopped

1 generous bunch collard greens, stemmed, washed in 2 changes of water, and chopped or cut into ribbons

½ cup chopped fresh parsley or cilantro, or a mix

1. Use black-eyed peas, but no need to soak them; just rinse under cold running water. Omit Step 1.

2. In Step 2, add the fennel when you add the garlic (use 4 cloves) and a generous pinch of salt and cook, stirring until the fennel has softened, about 5 minutes. Then add the ground spices and stir until fragrant about a minute, followed by the black-eyed peas and 2 quarts water. Bring to a boil, reduce the heat, and add salt to taste. Cover and simmer 30 minutes.

3. Continue with the recipe, adding the collard greens with the harissa and tomato paste. Simmer for just 15 to 30 minutes, until the beans and collards are tender and fragrant. Remove 1 cup of the broth to mix with the couscous when you reconstitute it. Stir in the parsley and/or cilantro and simmer another 5 minutes. Taste and adjust seasonings, adding salt, garlic, or harissa as desired. Continue the recipe at Step 3.

ADVANCE PREPARATION: The stew can be made a day or two ahead. You may want to add more liquid when you reheat.

Preserved Lemons

Lemons preserved in a salt brine are a staple ingredient in North African cooking. They are used as both a condiment and a flavoring ingredient in tagines (stews) and salads. In this collection I call for them in the Spring Vegetable Couscous (page 256), but you can also use them as a condiment for other couscous stews. They also make a nice condiment for salads, grains, and vegetables and are a great addition to the Big Bowl recipes in Chapter 7. They're very salty and meant to be used as a seasoning rather than a stand-alone pickle.

Thin-skinned lemons are best for preserving; Meyer lemons, the sweet-tasting light orange–hued lemons from California, are particularly well suited. Because a little preserved lemon goes a long way, you needn't pickle too many at a time, but you need enough to tightly pack the jar you are using. I've seen many different recipes for preserved lemons and tried several of them. They all seem to work. This is how I do it.

6 to 12 organic lemons or (preferably) organic Meyer lemons, or enough to fill a wide-mouth 1-pint or 1-quart jar

⅓ to ⅔ cup sea salt

Fresh lemon juice as needed

Extra virgin olive oil for topping off the jar

1. Sterilize your jar by submerging it in boiling water for a minute. Very carefully lift the jar out of the water using tongs. Tip the water in the jar into the pot as you remove it, so that you don't get scalded. Set the jar on a clean dishtowel, open side down, to drain.

2. Quarter each lemon lengthwise from the pointed (bud) end down to within about ½ inch of the stem end, making sure to keep the lemon intact. Pack the cut lemons with salt. Place the lemons in the jar, packing as many salted lemons as will fit. Add additional lemon juice to completely cover the lemons. Sprinkle 2 tablespoons salt over the top and cover tightly. Set in a cool place or in the refrigerator (that's where I keep mine) for at least 3 weeks. The lemons are ready when they have softened. To use, simply remove from the jar, rinse, and slice or chop as directed. If any lemons are exposed to air in the jar, top up with extra virgin olive oil.

ADVANCE PREPARATION: These will keep for at least 6 months; I usually keep them around for a year. Store them in the refrigerator and cover the surface with olive oil after you remove any lemons from the jar.

Acknowledgments

A COUPLE OF YEARS AGO I sent a one-sentence email to my agent, Angela Miller, with the idea for this book and a working title. She sent a one-sentence email back saying "Love it." "So, should I write a proposal?" my next email asked. The rest is history. Thanks, Angela, for loving the template concept and moving it along.

And thanks to Rodale editor Elissa Altman, writer and editor extraordinaire, for also loving the concept and bringing the book to fruition. Thanks to designers Amy King, Jeff Batzli, and Laura Palese and to photographers Tom MacDonald and Mitch Mandel, for making the book so beautiful.

I am as always grateful to those who follow my Recipes for Health column on nytimes.com and to all of my followers on Facebook. You inspire me to make cooking make sense and to strive to make everything I cook delicious. Thanks as well, as always, to my son Liam, for loving what I cook and sometimes putting up with night after night of recipe tests from the same chapters.

Index

Boldface page numbers indicate photographs. <u>Underscored</u> references indicate boxed text or charts.